BODY

AND

IMAGE

BODY AND IMAGE

EXPLORATIONS IN LANDSCAPE

PHENOMENOLOGY 2

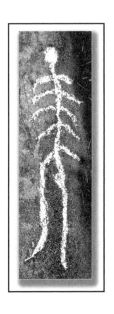

Christopher Tilley

With assistance of Wayne Bennett

Left Coast
Press Inc.

Walnut Creek, California

Left Coast
Press Inc.

Left Coast Press is committed to preserving ancient forests and natural resources. We elected to print this title on 30% post consumer recycled paper, processed chlorine free. As a result, for this printing, we have saved:

4 Trees (40' tall and 6-8" diameter)
1,297 Gallons of Wastewater
2 million BTU's of Total Energy
167 Pounds of Solid Waste
312 Pounds of Greenhouse Gases

Left Coast Press made this paper choice because our printer, Thomson-Shore, Inc., is a member of Green Press Initiative, a nonprofit program dedicated to supporting authors, publishers, and suppliers in their efforts to reduce their use of fiber obtained from endangered forests.

For more information, visit www.greenpressinitiative.org

Environmental impact estimates were made using the Environmental Defense Paper Calculator. For more information visit: www.papercalculator.org.

LEFT COAST PRESS, INC.
1630 North Main Street, #400
Walnut Creek, CA 94596
http://www.LCoastPress.com

Copyright © 2008 by Left Coast Press, Inc.

ISBN 978–1–59874–313–5 hardcover
ISBN 978–1–59874–314–2 paperback

Library of Congress Cataloguing-in-Publication Data
Tilley, Christopher Y.
  Body and image : explorations in landscape phenomenology 2 / Christopher Tilley ; with assistance of Wayne Bennett.
    p. cm.
  Includes bibliographical references and index.
  ISBN 978-1-59874-313-5 (hardback : alk. paper) —
  ISBN 978-1-59874-314-2 (pbk. : alk. paper)
  1. Megalithic monuments. 2. Architecture, Prehistoric. 3. Petroglyphs. 4. Land settlement patterns, Prehistoric. I. Bennett, Wayne, 1954– II. Title.
  GN790.T54 2008
  930.1'4—dc22

                    200804089

Printed in the United States of America

♾ The paper used in this publication meets the minimum requirements of American National Standard for Information Sciences—Permanence of Paper for Printed Library Materials, ANSI/NISO Z39.48–1992.

08 09 10 11 12 5 4 3 2 1

CONTENTS

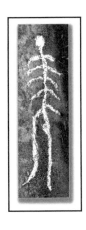

ILLUSTRATIONS

TABLES

PREFACE

This is the second book in a trilogy of volumes on landscape phenomenology following on from the first volume, *The Materiality of Stone* (Tilley 2004). In this volume I attempt to explore the relationship between images and bodily experience, developing a kinaesthetic approach to the interpretation of images on rocks in landscapes. The general theoretical and conceptual approach is outlined in Chapter 1. Chapters 2–4 consist of three extended case studies chosen because they represent contrasting periods, societies, economies, and landscapes in prehistoric Europe. Chapter 2 considers Mesolithic imagery from Vingen, western Norway, imagery dominated by the depiction of animals in a foraging society. Chapter 3 discusses the relationship between megalithic architecture and imagery in the context of the middle Neolithic landscape of eastern Ireland. Chapter 4 examines Bronze Age rock imagery from the Norrköping area of eastern middle Sweden (see p. 12 and Figure 3.1 for the location of the study areas in Scandinavia and Ireland). In the concluding chapter some comparative observations are made in relation to the different case studies, together with a series of reflections on what it means to interpret the landscape through phenomenologically walking in it.

This book, like any other, has its own particular biography and trajectory. My interest in Vingen was first stimulated by reading Hallström's (1938) account during the preparation of my book on the Nämforsen rock art locality in Northern Sweden (Tilley 1991). I had to wait for fifteen years before I had the opportunity to visit it and experience the drama of the place. About the same time, an interest in Irish megalithic art was stimulated by taking a field trip of students to Loughcrew and the bend of the Boyne, together with Julian Thomas. The idea of conducting fieldwork in the Norrköping area of middle eastern Sweden was by comparison recent, an interest generated by visiting some of the localities during the summer of 2001 when I was conducting ethnographic research on domestic gardens in Sweden. The study of the Norrköping landscape was the first to be undertaken, during the summer of 2003. This was subsequently written up as a draft chapter in the winter of 2003–04. Fieldwork in Ireland was conducted during the spring of 2004 following exploratory visits during the summer of 2003, but only finally written up

The location of the Norrköping and Vingen rock carving localities in Scandinavia. The Irish localities studied are shown on Figure 3.1.

during the summer of 2006. Fieldwork was undertaken at Vingen during June 2005 and subsequently written up that summer. The final versions of Chapters 1 and 5 were written during the summer and autumn of 2006 and the spring of 2007 while at the same time revising the drafts of Chapters 2–4.

A small part of Chapter 1 was initially presented at a conference on 'cognition and signification in northern landscapes' organized by Lars Forsberg and Eva

Walderhaug, held at the University of Bergen in November 2004. Chapter 4 was first presented as part of a series of lectures on the topic of phenomenology and landscape held at the University of Kalmar, Sweden, in March 2005. A few of the observations made at Newgrange in Chapter 3 were presented at a conference, 'Cult in Context', held at Magdalen College, Cambridge, organized by David Barrowclough, Caroline Malone, and Simon Stoddart in December 2006. Part of the concluding Chapter 5 was presented at a research seminar in the College de France, Paris, 'The ecology of perception and the aesthetics of landscape', organized by Nicolas Ellison in March 2007. I am grateful for the comments I received on all these occasions.

All the periods of fieldwork were extremely intensive. The summer light at Vingen was such that it was even possible to work long after midnight. Time not dedicated to studying the images themselves in the field was often spent reflecting on, writing down, and analysing fieldwork experiences, providing new ideas and further impetus for the next day's work. A book inevitably changes and develops in focus as it goes along. The idea for a comparative analysis of visual imagery in the landscape developed out of the fieldwork conducted during 2001 in the Simrishamn area of southeast Sweden, published in *The Materiality of Stone*, as discussed in Chapter 1; but it was only during the last period of fieldwork on which the book is based, at Vingen, that I 'discovered' (it rather forced itself on me!) the significance of the weather—hence the absence of much substantive discussions of this in relation to the Swedish and Irish images. The experience of the Vingen rock carving area was particularly powerful, not only because of the drama of the place, but as a result of actually living and sleeping among the carvings, completely cut off from the outside world. As usual, I am indebted to Wayne Bennett, who provided enormous help, support, enthusiasm, critical, and interpretive comment throughout the fieldwork periods and then also prepared all the illustrations.

I am most grateful to Gro Mandt and Trond Lødøen for inviting us to Vingen and sharing their knowledge of it. On the visit to study the rock carvings, Trond and Sigrid Gunderson provided much needed shelter and hospitality. They introduced us to the different parts of the rock carving area over a period of several days. They also helped locate individual panels on Vingeneset, Urane, and Bak Vehammaren which would otherwise have proved quite impossible to find. Gro and Trond have also kindly provided me with copies of the unpublished documentation, to appear in their forthcoming book, of the rocks at Hardbakken, Teigen, and Leitet, which has been of great help in writing this account. They also generously provided useful comments on a draft of Chapter 2 for which I am most grateful. Clare Tuffy, manager of the Newgrange Visitor Centre, was kind enough to facilitate unrestricted access to the interiors of Newgrange, Dowth, and Knowth. Mike Rowlands provided useful criticism of a draft of Chapter 1, and Muiris O'Sullivan was kind enough to read through and comment on a draft of Chapter 3. I also want to acknowledge the useful comments of two referees who chose not to remain anonymous: Cornelius Holtorf and Andrew Jones. I have not followed all their advice, but I am most most grateful for it. The inadequacies, of course, remain my own. I also want to thank the publisher, Mitch Allen, for his enthusiastic support for the book and the wider project of which it forms a part.

Christopher Tilley
London, 2008

CHAPTER ONE

BODY AND IMAGE

A PHENOMENOLOGICAL PERSPECTIVE

'Our perception being a part of things, things participate in the nature of our perception' (*Bergson* 1991: 182).

'The first drawing on a cave wall founded a tradition only because it was the recipient of another: that of perception' (*Merleau-Ponty* 1973: 83).

"What do pictures *really* want?' (*J. Mitchell* 1996).

INTRODUCTION

A few years ago I undertook a study of the rock carvings in the Simrishamn area of southeast Sweden. One of the major places with rock carvings, Simris 19 is today a sadly marooned block, quarried away on two sides and cut off from the beach by a modern road. Opposite the carved rock one finds a small car park and a picnic area. A large 'hällristning' sign points toward the rock with the carvings. Because of its accessibility there were a fair number of visitors to the site, and because I had a clipboard, scrolls of documentation, and must have looked as if I knew something about the carvings, people would ask me how old they were and what they meant. The first question was easy, the latter much more difficult, since this was precisely what I was attempting to find out! Couples would arrive, or family groups, stay for about ten or fifteen minutes, and then drive off. After a morning I became a little irritated by the constant interruptions to my work and by my new status as unofficial guide who, quite remarkably, spoke broken Swedish with an amusingly thick English accent. Better, I thought, to leave the rock when people came and wait until they went away. This might save a good deal of time.

But my study of the Simrishamn carvings was only partly concerned with what the images might mean. I wanted to experiment with a phenomenologically informed kinaesthetic approach to the rock art. In other words, I was interested in what effects the carvings themselves had on my body as someone looking at them: What did I have to do to see the carvings? How did I have to move? How did the qualities of the stone itself (colour, smoothness, presence or absence of cracks, surface morphology, size, and the like) affect my perception and relate to the positioning of the carvings? How might the location of the rock in the landscape affect my perception of it in relation to its surroundings? These questions were not in any direct way related to the meaning of the images at all. They were concerned with what the rock and its carvings were doing to me: their bodily or kinaesthetic influence on the way I moved and what I perceived.

In relation to Simris 19, I rapidly realized that it was not possible to see the carvings in any way that I might wish, or decide. If I wanted to see them closely, I was forced to move about the rock in a particular manner and in a particular sequence. The carvings were exerting their own power and influence in relation to what I saw and from where I saw it, and how I saw it. I was no longer a free agent who could simply move about and see whatever images I liked from wherever I liked. There was a dialectic at work between the rock itself, and its landscape location, and the positioning of the images carved on it. Even if one had no clue at all about what the images meant, it was still possible to describe bodily movement in relation to them. Furthermore, might not these patterns of bodily movement, dictated by the images themselves, be a fundamental part of the significance of the rock art? Might it not just be an arbitrary intellectual presupposition that meaning is somehow primary in the study of rock art?

Moving off the Simris 19 rock when people arrived, I decided to learn something from watching them observing the carvings. What did they do? What did they look at? How did they move? Where did they go? Were my own bodily movements simply a fickle personal engagement no doubt encouraged and helped by the fact that I had detailed plans of the carvings whereas they did not? People would approach from across the road. They would then stand below the rock and look across at the images on it. Although the total carved area is small enough for most of the images to be seen at once and from off the rock, those farther away are indistinct and difficult to make out. Furthermore, from any particular perspective many of the iconic images—the boats and the axes, and the human figures—appear upside down, while others are right side up. In relation to the perceiving body, this is a bit like displaying a painting upside down on the wall, or even hanging it at an angle—intensely irritating!

In order to see the images more clearly, people would climb onto the rock and walk *within* the image fields. In so doing, their feet were keeping the rock glassy and shiny. Other rocks with carvings in the area, not now visited, are covered with lichen and vegetation and browned by soil stains. They have lost some of their important experiential qualities. People would typically move around the groups of images in a circular fashion: clockwise or counterclockwise from bottom to top. They would also move around the sides of different groups of images in order to see them from different perspectives. Images that were the wrong way up from one angle righted themselves from another. What I had experienced, they were experiencing. The images themselves were orchestrating a spatial dance: bodies were moving in relation to them. People rarely stood still for any length of time but were moving and twirling and adopting different positions: generally looking down, but sometimes crouching or with their heads to one side, and sometimes it was obviously necessary to touch the carvings as well as to look at them. So these images had a direct influence, agency, and power in themselves: they set people in choreographed motion around them. And this force of the image was quite independent of verbal exegesis—of talking about meaning—although the movement often promoted talk of a rather different kind: 'Oh, look! There's a man holding a huge axe. I didn't see him from over there!' The main difference between my experience of the carvings and those of other visitors was a matter of knowledge. Having a plan, I knew what I was supposed to be seeing (for anyone unfamiliar with the study of prehistoric rock art, it has to be pointed out that at the wrong time of day and in the wrong kind of light it is often impossible to see anything on a rock that is known to be covered with images, such are the effects of weathering over thousands of years) and where it was, and therefore could see more on different areas of the rock. As a result, my movements were more complexly choreographed, or influenced by the images, and their relationships to each other. But the essentials were the same. The images on the Simris 19 rock prompted a 'placial' (I prefer to use this word to the much more abstract and distanced term 'spatial') dance around distinct groups of carvings within the overall image field occupied by all the carvings. By means of this extended anecdote I hope to have introduced the reader to some of the essential elements and important differences between iconographic and kinaesthetic approaches to rock art. I now want to discuss this in a more formal way.

THE ICONOGRAPHIC VERSUS THE KINAESTHETIC

I use the term 'iconographic' as a shorthand term to refer to the entire tradition of interpreting prehistoric rock art from its nineteenth-century origins to the present day. This approach to rock art has, of course, radically altered over the years, in tandem with wider intellectual trends within archaeological research. In the context of Scandinavian rock art research addressed in Chapters 2 and 4 (for a discussion of research on Irish megalithic art, see Chapter 3), the manner in which the images have been interpreted has altered in relation to the differing perspectives and intellectual agendas of 'traditional', 'new' or functionalist, and 'post-processual' or interpretive archaeology (Mandt 1995). Early work on the southern Scandinavian material attempted to find in it an entire pantheon of Nordic gods and related the carvings to the Nordic sagas. For Almgren (1927) the southern Scandinavian carvings were to be related to fertility cults and sun symbolism in the context of an agricultural economy. The material from northern Scandinavia, mainly depicting game animals, was alternatively understood in terms of hunting magic (Gjessing 1932; Hallström 1938), functionalist ideas that continued to be employed and refined during the 1960s and 1970s in broad comparative analyses (e.g., Hagen 1976; Malmer 1981). 'Post-processual' approaches have, alternatively, rigorously pursued a linguistic analogy in which the carvings can be read as texts and as sign systems (e.g., Nordbladh 1980; Tilley 1991). Gender differences and relations and transformative human states have been read into the carvings (e.g., Yates 1993; Tilley 1999; Mandt 2001; Hauptman Wahlgren 2002), and they have been related to totemic systems of social classification and structures of social and political power (Tilley 1991), shamanism (e.g., Helskog 1987; Devlet 2001; Viste 2003), social geographies (e.g., Bertilsson 1987; Mandt 1991), symbolic and experiential qualities of the landscape (e.g., Helskog 1999; Bradley 2000; Goldhahn 2002; Hauptman Wahlgren 2002), or various combinations of all of these. Such a list could go on and on. Despite all these changes, and the recent blossoming of different alternative approaches in a healthy theoretical pluralism (Mandt 1995; Hauptman Wahlgren 2000), there has remained a core concern subscribed to implicitly, and more usually explicitly, by all rock art researchers. The fundamental question and the foundation for all this research has always been: What does it mean? This, whatever the particular answers given or types of analyses undertaken, has been the primary motivation for rock art research, providing both the driving force and the intellectual motivation. Even if the question of meaning has been frequently sidestepped, in favour of an obsession with chronology in older traditional and functionalist studies, it still provided, and provides, the principal justification for empirical documentation: unless and until we have documented this art as precisely and comprehensively as possible, we cannot begin to understand what it means.

The hoped-for outcome of an iconographic approach is to lead us to a better understanding of the images as bearers of meaning, images that necessarily require decoding and interpretation. The potential outcome of a kinaesthetic approach is to tell us something different: about the manner in which the bodily postures and motions of people changed or remained the same in relation to the imagery and the manner in which it was encountered on different rocks.

Iconographic approaches are usually primarily cognitive in nature. They grant primacy to the human mind as a producer of the meaning of the images through sensory perception. It is the mind that responds to that which is seen in a disembodied way. Structuralist studies and, in particular, most semiotic perspectives have nothing to tell us about the role of the body in perception. Of course, they do underscore the structuring and structured qualities of the human mind which produces, or decodes, and thinks through the images. Kinaesthetic approaches, by contrast, stress the role of the carnal human body: perception is regarded as being both afforded and constrained by the sensuous human body. The general claim is that the manner in which we perceive, and therefore relate to visual imagery, is fundamentally related to the kinds of bodies we have. The body both limits and constrains, and enables us to perceive and react to imagery in specific embodied ways.

In iconographic approaches the rock art itself becomes ultimately superficial because it always represents something else, something more fundamental than itself. So, in studying images, we might perhaps hope to reclaim the intentions of the artist. It is these that are primary, and the task is to recover these from their material manifestations. Or the art may be held to be a visual representation of underlying structuring principles generating social practices. These are fundamental, and the aim of analysis is to go beyond the superficiality of the visual image to recover the underlying system. Alternatively, various styles of rock art may be held to objectify or represent particular cosmologies or mythological systems or rites. Again these are primary. The images themselves are simply manifestations of something deeper and more fundamental, something that might also be expressed in words or actions, or in structured systems of ceremonial beliefs and practices. What is common to all iconographic approaches is that they require us to go beyond and beneath the image to explain its meaning. The image itself is never enough. It is a material manifestation of something believed to be much deeper and more fundamental. What is curious about this approach, from a kinaesthetic perspective, is that the power of visual imagery ultimately becomes *dematerialised* because it is simply an opaque representation of something else: individual intentions, societal culture and values, history, myths and cosmologies, gender relations, or politics and power.

The intellectual background to the traditional iconographic approach to rock art is mainly derived from art historical analysis and developments in that field, and more widely, the analysis of visual culture heavily influenced since the 1970s by linguistics and a textual model, together with limited use of ethnographic analogies. As mentioned earlier, it has been transferred by archaeologists to the study of rock art in one form or another in terms of discussions of genres and styles, traditions and historical horizons, or more recently in the form of various structuralist and semiotic and post-structuralist approaches. It might be suggested that this is the wrong starting point to consider rock art because it ignores the very materiality of the medium, pretending that stone is just another form of canvas or page to be written on.

In the history of rock art research, the heavy influence of the art historical tradition in which we attempt to decode meaning, a language of pictorial representation, has had two striking and deleterious effects. First, the landscape context of rock carvings has hardly been discussed, or analyzed at all, in relation to the art. It has been peculiarly treated like a backdrop, in many ways equivalent in significance to the whitewashed walls of an art gallery in which paintings are displayed. Second, the material medium of the rock has been reduced in publications documenting the carvings to a white, two-dimensional space. Rock, being regarded as 'natural' rather than 'cultural', has been effectively eliminated from the documentation. Only the images themselves are regarded as significant. The rock itself is only an interpretive worry: Might the cupmark be simply a hollow caused by erosion? Is this line a crack? Have carvings differentially eroded away? With all the emphasis put on the images themselves, the rock carvings become decontextualised, both from their own landscapes and even from the rocks on which they are found. They become pure images. Because rock carvings have been represented as images on a two-dimensional surface, they become understood and thought of simply as surreal, disembodied images, rather than a physical form and presence on a rock at a particular place and in a particular landscape. It is then perhaps not so surprising that rock art has proved so difficult to understand: half the information has usually been stripped away in the process of documentation before the analysis of that which is left on paper even begins. From a kinaesthetic approach, the material medium—that is, the rock and its landscape context—is as fundamental in understanding the art as the imagery itself. Indeed, the claim is that one cannot be understood except in relation to the other. Thus, rock art is a relational nexus of images, material qualities of rocks, and landscapes.

This chapter attempts to develop such a kinaesthetic perspective on visual imagery. It suggests that a truly phenomenological study of imagery is grounded in the kinaesthetics of bodily movement. It explores the manner in which imagery impacts on and through the body and is understood through the medium of the relationship of the body to the phenomenal world within which it is enveloped. It suggests that an inappropriate 'gallery view' of imagery, the dominant perspective of the art historian until very recently, has led us astray in the study of prehistoric rock art (and, indeed, of other non-mobiliary forms of 'classical' art such as the paintings in the Sistine Chapel or contemporary earthworks, environmental art, and performance and body art, which have a fundamental carnal as opposed to purely cognitive significance). I argue that imagery works first and foremost through the flesh to influence the embodied mind. In this process cognition is secondary rather than primary. When the question of meaning arises, it works its way through and is distributed in relation to the plural kinaesthetic motions of the sensing and sensed body. What the body does in relation to imagery, its motions, its postures, how that imagery is sensed through the fingers or the ear or the nose, as much as through the organ of the eye, actively constitutes the mute significance of imagery which to have its kinaesthetic impact does not automatically require translation into either thoughts or meanings. The kinaesthetic significance of imagery is thus visceral. It works through the muscles and ligaments, through physical actions and postures which provide affordances for the perceptual apparatus of the body in relation to which meaning may be grafted on, or attached. Meaning is derived from and through the flesh, not a cognitive precipitate of the mind without a body, or a body without organs. However, to pretend that a kinaesthetic approach on its own is all that is required to study rock art would be little more than an exercise in empty rhetoric. There needs to be something more, and this, I argue, is a rejuvenated form of 'phenomenological semiotics' approached through the prism of a theory of metaphor and linked to sensory perception in the broadest sense.

The text attempts to develop this general argument for a kinaesthetics of rock art through a series of critical reflections on the work of key thinkers in phenomenological philosophy and anthropological approaches to art, material, and visual culture. I realise that for some readers, especially those with a pragmatic and empirical disposition, much, if not all, of this discussion will appear useless and irrelevant. I, on the other hand, feel it to be both necessary and relevant to develop the position I am advocating within a wider historical, philosophical, theoretical, and conceptual context. The argument begins with a brief discussion of ideas first outlined in Bergson's *Matter and Memory* (Bergson [1896] 1991), in which some key aspects of a phenomenological and kinaesthetic approach to images can be found. This serves as an introduction to a more detailed consideration of Merleau-Ponty's studies of art and aesthetics (collected together in Johnson 1993) and his final work, *The Visible and the Invisible* (Merleau-Ponty 1973). I then critically consider 'agency' theories of art currently fashionable in anthropology, principally through the work of Gell (1998; 1999). This leads to the development of a kinaesthetic, as opposed to a cognitive, understanding of the significance of imagery. Finally, the link between a kinaesthetic approach and a traditional 'iconographic' perspective concerned with meaning is explored through the notion of a phenomenological semiotics.

BODY, IMAGE, AND MEMORY IN BERGSON

Bergson's contemporary significance is that he helped to direct philosophical inquiry back to the body, rejecting the dualism of materialism on the one hand—stressing the physical realities of things (and the body as a thing)—and idealist approaches on the other—putting all the emphasis on the mind and, most crucially, on perception as being a product of the operation of that mind which has no bodily basis. The outcome of such dualistic thought is to oppose an inert and objective 'outside' world inhabited by the body and a living heterogeneous and subjective 'inside' world of the mind, inevitably leading to discussions of the reality or ideality of the sensory perception and recognition of images in the external world. Do we see the 'real thing' or only a 'cognised image of that thing'? Do the things that we perceive exist in themselves or only in our minds?

For Bergson, the carnal body mediates these dualities; it provides the ground for all perception. The problem with standard views of perception, either materialist or idealist, is that perception is regarded as entirely a cognitive act which either reflects the way things really appear in the world or produces a representation of them. The most significant point about Bergson's conceptualisation of the body is that it is a body in action, a moving body rather than the frozen or static body of the materialist (or empiricist), or idealist, gazing at the world. The moving body experiences a flux of sensations in time, linking matter to memory. That which we perceive is intimately linked to the manner in which we encounter and remember the world through ambient movement in it, and as part of it. The body in motion is always betwixt and between, transitional. Following a path means not being present in a position, but always passing through. Movement relates to a reality that is very different from a divisible and measurable empiricist 'space' and an abstracted spatialised and measurable time in which past and present become a dynamic unity and perception is inhabited by temporality. This means that the body itself has to be put at the centre of analysis:

> As my body moves in space, all the other images vary, while that image, my body, remains invariable. I must, therefore, make it a centre, to which I refer all the other images. My belief in an external world does not come from, cannot come, from the fact that I project outside myself sensations that are unextended. . . . *My body* is that which stands out at the centre of these perceptions; *my personality* is the being to which these actions must be referred. (Bergson 1991: 46–47, hereafter *MM*)

The moving body is not for Bergson distinct from 'personality'—it is that person. It provides perceptions that are also recollections. Memories consist of images that may either be recalled in the mind (voluntary memories) or are a product of an inscribed corporeality, habits that accumulate in the movement of that body (involuntary memories) (*MM*: 81–82). The former are like pictures in the mind; the latter require no visualisation. Bodily memory, made up of the 'sensori-motor systems organized by habit, is then a quasi-instantaneous memory to which the true memory of the past serves as base' (*MM*: 152). Voluntary or bodily memories are thus not just visual but corporeal, involving the full human range of sensory perception from sight to sound to taste to touch to smell. There is a 'mental ear' as much as a 'mental sight', an auditory 'image' as much as a visual 'image' registered in the body (*MM*: 129). The general tendency is for corporeal memory to take over from voluntary memory in familiar surroundings. In a town unknown to me, I halt at different street corners, deciding where to go. Movement is broken and discontinuous. Later, after a 'prolonged sojourn in the town, I shall go about it mechanically, without having any distinct perception of the objects which I am passing' (*MM*: 93). Perception is an action of the body, and pure perception is a recording of sensations brought about by objects that are external to the mind. But perception is never a mere contact of the mind with an object in the present; it is replete with memory images 'which complete it as they interpret it' (*MM*: 133) so, and as a consequence of this, 'to *picture* is not to *remember*' (*MM*: 135). The 'present' of the self always has one foot in the past and another in the future, because the present conjoins sensations or perceptions and movements:

> My actual sensations occupy definite portions of the surface of my body; pure memory, on the other hand, interests no part of my body. No doubt, it will beget sensations as it materializes, but at that very moment it will cease to be a memory and pass into the state of a present thing, something actually lived. (*MM*: 139)

So, through the perceiving and moving body, past and present interpenetrate each other. Perception draws the past into the present and reworks it; sense and significance form part of each other through their embodied mediation. Memory may consist of sensory 'images' produced in the mind or worked through habitually in the movements of the body which remembers itself without sensory images. The self is a combination of perception and memory, always reworking embodied perception in a creative and generative process, creating at any particular moment a new self in relation to the old selves that preceded it. Merleau-Ponty comments:

> He does not at all say that things are, in the restrictive sense, images, mental or otherwise—he says that their fullness under my regard is such that it is as if my vision took place *in them* rather than in myself. . . . Never before had anyone established this circuit between being and myself, which has the result that being is 'for me,' the spectator, but that in return the spectator is 'for being'. (Merleau-Ponty 1962a: 138)

In other words, perception involves immersion in a world of duration and simultaneity, which constitutes the self. Our perceptive being is brought about through our involvement in a world of things that participate in the character of our perception. Merleau-Ponty's phenomenology expands and develops aspects of Bergson's conceptualisation of the body in relation to matter and memory, and it is perhaps no coincidence that he was appointed to the same chair of philosophy that Bergson occupied in Paris.

THE FLESHY IMAGE: MERLEAU-PONTY

Merleau-Ponty specifically attempted to develop a genuinely phenomenological perspective on imagery through a consideration of the art of painting. In so doing, he regarded painting as philosophy in action. By thinking through what painters actually do in their practice, one could develop a theory of the embodied significance of imagery. Thus, he did not apply a ready-made theory of imagery in order to understand paintings, but rather built up that theory from a study of the relationship between painters and that which they actually produced. In other words, Merleau-Ponty attempted to construct a thoroughly materialist rather than idealist perspective, and this is the enormous virtue of his effort. His dual interest was both in the images themselves and the processes by means of which those images emerged in paint on canvas through the technique of the painter. What is at stake here is the relationship between the image and reality, that which is beyond and outside the picture itself.

In 'Cézanne's Doubt'(Merleau-Ponty 1993a; hereafter CD) this is explored in relation to Cézanne's attempt to paint what he actually saw rather than follow the Renaissance rules of linear perspective which could only provide a mathematically inspired illusion of reality. While the Renaissance artists created pictures according to rules of outline, composition, and the distribution of light, Cézanne wanted to capture 'nature', the world outside on the canvas: 'It took him one hundred working sessions for a still life, one-hundred fifty sittings for a portrait' (CD: 59), and he still was not satisfied with the result. The 'suicidal' attempt, according to one contemporary critic, to represent reality while abandoning the very means for doing so (linear perspective, attention to composition, outline, light, and shadow) virtually destroyed him and his faith in what he was able to produce. What others saw in his paintings was not 'nature' but distortion. Cézanne's incessant attempt to capture the reality of the distant mountain in his paintings always finally failed. In the end, and as he grew old, he wondered whether he had trouble with his eyes.

Empiricist perspectives on perception, never failing to imply that they represented a truth, had long distinguished between primary and secondary aspects. For Locke the primary aspects of perception were visual, mathematical, and spatial— things that could be measured. Point, line, plane, and ratio were therefore of primary significance in painting. Secondary aspects of perception were 'subjective' and therefore insignificant (colour, sound, odour, touch, taste). But to Cézanne's 'innocent' painterly eye, colour was absolutely fundamental to both the world he tried to paint and visual sensation. The significance of things resided as much in the colours they possessed as in their forms. One could not be understood or represented apart from the other. Cézanne did not want to separate thought from feeling, the apparent stability of things seen from the shifting manner in which they appear (CD: 63). He understood that what we actually perceive is neither geometric nor photographic. Objects that are close to us appear smaller, those farther away, bigger than in a photograph. The contour of an object bounded by a line has nothing to do with the visible world (lines do not bound mountains) and everything to do with a geometric perspective: 'to trace just a single outline sacrifices depth—that is, the dimension in which the thing is presented not as spread out before us but as an inexhaustible reality full of reserves. . . . The outline should be a result of colours if the world is to be given its true density' (CD: 65). This is precisely why Cézanne paid so much attention to colour: the colours on the palette, a material medium, could be articulated so as to provide an echo of the world. Cézanne's concern with colour was far more than a concern with the visual. He was also trying to portray the depth, smoothness, softness, and hardness of objects and even claimed one could see their odour (CD: 65). He wanted to capture the manner in which the world emerged through colour. In his landscape paintings he was as much interested in their geological foundations and the manner in which they emerged on the surface. The landscape 'thinks itself in me' . . . and 'I am its consciousness', he would say (CD: 67).

From a phenomenological perspective, what we witness here is Cézanne's immersion in that which he was painting. It was part of him, and he was part of it. In other words, subject and object are mutually constitutive. There is a clear bracketing of prejudicial assumptions with regard to what is primary versus secondary in human experience, and a rejection of rules for 'correct' representation and perspective based on such assumptions. Renaissance perspective painting is the visible manifestation of scientism and technological reductionism. Cézanne reverses the terms of the debate, and colour becomes primary as a means of depicting the density and textures of things and revealing them in their emotional intensity. Perception arises not from a disembodied mind but from a lived relation and bodily presence in the world. Both the painter and the philosopher share the same problem: how to interpret and express through the medium of paint, or words, the observation of lived experience. Cézanne fuses himself with 'nature' to reconstruct a view of the world from a lived perspective, a pre-scientific perception of the visible, which is neither a mimetic duplication of the form in which that world actually exists (what he sees) nor solely the product of his subjective imaginative expression (what he thinks). These are all fundamental aspects of a phenomenological approach to visual imagery.

Merleau-Ponty develops these perspectives further in 'Eye and Mind' (Merleau-Ponty 1993b; hereafter EM), his last published work prior to his sudden death. In this, and in his unfinished text *The Visible and the Invisible* (Merleau-Ponty 1973), he develops a new ontology of experience articulated in relation to the union of the visible and invisible in human experience. Again painting provides a key to a new understanding, but here Merleau-Ponty is less concerned with the 'worldly' landscapes of Cézanne than in the abstractions of Klee and the lapidary remark that became his credo: 'Art does not represent the visible; rather it makes visible' (Foster et al. 2004: 141). Basic colour terms such as 'red' are merely abstractions in comparison with the *precise* red of the woollen garment or the metallic surface. The precise red of the thing concretises a field of visibility; it summons up a hidden depth of the thing uniting the visible with the invisible; the sensible thing captures the invisible in the visible (Merleau-Ponty 1973: 132). The invisible provides a depth and richness to the visible world. Imagery brings forth the invisible depth of the world and, however 'realistic', is always a translation, simply because a grape on canvas, even in the most figurative style of painting, is not like the grape itself. In this respect, differences between figurative imagery and nonfigurative imagery, 'classical' or 'modern' art, is undermined. Neither captures reality, but both are similarly mediated through the body of the subject; they involve a relationship between his or her being and the sensible world (EM: 127). The eye of the painter is a 'thinking eye', an embodied eye. Painting is a celebration of the enigma of visibility. It gives visible existence to what profane or ordinary thought believes to be invisible. A mind cannot paint, or sculpt—the body does (EM: 123). The body intertwines vision and movement, sight and touch, and sight is like touch:

> My body simultaneously sees and is seen. That which looks at all things can also look at itself and recognize, in what it sees, the "other side" of its power of looking. It sees itself seeing; it touches itself touching; it is visible and sensitive for itself. (EM: 124).

The body in the world, with its bilateral symmetry, vertical axis, back and front, is simultaneously an object and a subject, a thing among things, and a subject immersed in relation to things, sensing and sensed. While painters look at the world, the world looks at them; the relations are reversible. Merleau-Ponty reports the comments of Klee: 'In a forest, I have felt many times over that it was not I who looked at the forest. Some days I felt the trees were looking at me' (EM: 129). Herein resides Merleau-Ponty's philosophy of vision in this thesis of perceptual interchange or reversibility. The painter looks and he is in turn looked at, and this external gaze has a profound effect on the manner in which that vision is made visible within the imagery. In other words, the painter's vision is indebted to the mute powers or visibility of the sensible. It does not take place in isolation. There is an important relation of reciprocity at work between the flesh of the painter and the flesh of the world in which he or she is immersed (Merleau-Ponty 1973: Chapter 4):

> Essence and existence, imaginary and real, visible and invisible—painting scrambles all our categories, spreading out before us its oneiric universe of carnal essences, actualized resemblances, mute meanings. (EM: 130)

Through depth, space, and colour, the painter represents the visible, and this does not necessarily require any form of iconic or figurative resemblance. One analogy Merleau-Ponty gives is looking at the tiled bottom of a swimming pool. We do not see it *despite* the ripples of the water and the reflections. We see it through them, through the 'distortions' and ripples of sunlight, the 'aqueous power, the syrupy and shimmering element' (EM: 142) which are fundamental to the visual experience. It is both specific and placial, related to space and time, materialised, a depth experience of embodied vision, a mixture of the visible and the invisible and the inherent visibility of the invisible in all things. In attempting to describe visual experience through material media, the artist's vision is touched by the world just as his or her vision touches it. A line on a painting does not represent that which is visible in the world; it rather renders its visibility. Klee wanted to 'let a line muse': 'the beginning of the line's path establishes or installs a certain level or mode of the linear, a certain manner for the line to be and to make itself a line, "to go line"' (EM: 143).

Merleau-Ponty, despite emphasizing the synaesthetic nature of human experience throughout his work, involving an intertwining of all the body senses, gives a particular power and importance to vision. An overriding concern and privileging of the visual is manifested in the attention he pays to the visual arts, and vision in general, while ignoring music or cooking and paying rather little attention to odour and sound. In his later work, visual perception provides a new way of thinking through and understanding embodied and fleshy carnal perception in general. It is interesting in this respect to note that in his analysis, the sensation of touch provides the key metaphor for understanding vision, and vision is itself understood through employing the metaphor of flesh. The reversibility thesis is first introduced by considering touch (Merleau-Ponty 1962b: 123; cf. Merleau-Ponty 1973: 133), the manner in which my right hand touches my left hand and is simultaneously touched by it, and then extended to objects: I touch a thing and it touches me back. This provides the model for visual 'touch' or the manner in which the world touches us even when it is beyond the reach of the body. Touch provides three distinct kinds of experiences: encountering the sleek or the smooth versus the rough; touching a thing and being touched by it; and touching one's own body where subjective and objective experiences cannot be disentangled, as the body is both subject and object (Merleau-Ponty 1973: 133–34). In an analogous way, vision occurs in the movement of the eyes in relation to the visible world, being seen by that world, and the eyes seeing themselves seeing in the mirror. So touch and vision involve the same sets of embodied relations between the subject and the world—but what of odour, sound, and taste? The general reversibility thesis can easily be extended in relation to auditory experience: we can speak and hear the vibrations of ourselves speaking in our throats in a relation of interiority; we can hear the world outside and it can hear us; we can smell and be smelled, smell ourselves smelling. Beyond this we can see ourselves smelling and touching and anticipate the taste of things before they enter our mouths. Taste is dependent, in part, on touch. All aspects of carnal experience are thoroughly intertwined, inseparable from one another. Sensory experience is a totality.

For Merleau-Ponty, painting is grounded in a visual metaphysics and in an ontological understanding of the human subject as seeing and being seen. In so doing, he raises the invisible to the same ontological status as the visible. An anonymous visual 'flesh' of the world grounds subject and object, seer and seen, body and mind:

> We have to reject the age-old assumptions that put the body in the world and the seer in the body. . . . Where are we to put the limit between the body and the world, since the world is flesh? . . . The world seen is not 'in' my body, and my body is not 'in' the visible world ultimately: as flesh applied to a flesh, the world neither surrounds it nor is surrounded by it. A participation in and kinship with the visible, the vision neither envelops it nor is enveloped by it indefinitely. The superficial pellicle of the visible is only for my vision and for my body. But the depth beneath this surface contains my body and hence contains my vision. My body as a visual thing is contained within the full spectacle. (Merleau-Ponty 1973: 138)

This passage says it all: the body as seer and seen is embraced within a field of vision beyond and outside the self, anonymous, all encompassing, in which everything is constituted, a field of worldly visuality that can see the subject from every point of view while he or she has a single, if shifting, visual field within the generalised visuality of the world. The binding visual 'flesh' of the world is neither opaque nor transparent; it resides in plays of light and shadow, being and becoming. My vision is an exemplar of a universal visuality existing prior to my being. This visuality is mediational, and it completely explodes any binary opposition between 'subject' and 'object'. Painting (understood as an expression of phenomenological observational principles) does not seek to represent things as things but rather seeks to express their carnal essences or the properties (invisible depths) that make them things in the first place. It is not about mimetic imitation, an attempt to produce an exact copy of the world. Vision is presence in absence: we look at things in the world and become fused with them. We become part of them and they become part of us. The painter's expression of this world, his or her particular interpretive style, is an operation of his or her body, a worldly event. However, in comparison with language, it only produces a 'voice of silence', a radically different mode of signification (Merleau-Ponty 1993c). Cézanne performed phenomenological analysis of the world through the medium of paint, while Merleau-Ponty himself uses 'another less heavy more transparent body'—namely, language (Merleau-Ponty 1973: 153). One is not superior or inferior to the other. They remain incommensurable domains, alternative expressive mediums for thinking through perceptual experience of that world. For Merleau-Ponty, vision was clearly the 'noblest of the senses'. It is a fleshy, all-encompassing medium within which the subject observer is immersed. None of the other senses are considered in this way, although to do so would fully embrace their synaesthetic entanglement. Jay's (1993) argument that Merleau-Ponty's perspective is part of a general trend towards a suspicion or 'denigration of vision' in twentieth-century French thought seems to be entirely unfounded. Vision for Merleau-Ponty was co-present with the lived world. Merleau-Ponty provides for us a foundational perspective for the phenomenological understanding of the visual, which will now be explored in relation to Gell.

GELL: IMAGES AS PERSONS

Gell (1992; 1998) argues that much of the anthropological tradition of thinking about art fails to engage with what is really important, the specificity and efficacy of art as a material medium that does something as opposed to being simply considered a bearer of meaning. Gell's book *Art and Agency,* subtitled, 'An Anthropological Theory' (Gell 1998), could equally well be understood as 'a phenomenological theory' of the significance of visual forms. It is somewhat surprising, therefore, that there is only one passing mention of the work of Merleau-Ponty in a discussion of Malekulan sand drawings (Gell 1998: 95), and his name does not even appear in the book's references. Yet he informs us that Merleau-Ponty's (1962b) *The Phenomenology of Perception* was one of a few books he took with him to provide inspiration during his fieldwork in Papua New Guinea (Gell 1999: 6), and he cites from it elsewhere in a discussion of language (Gell 1995). He probably knew the major themes of this book inside out, and his work is perhaps best understood as phenomenology under another name, that name being anthropology.

The general approach taken in *Art and Agency* elaborates on ideas first published in a paper on the 'enchantment of technology' (Gell 1992), in which he sets out a captivating thesis with characteristic wit and humour. Why, he asks, does art put us under a spell? What is its magic, its power? Why is it thought to be a 'good thing'? Why do we persist in having an 'art cult' in our own society? In short, wherein resides the *value* in art? His answer is that an anthropology of art must first challenge that category in order to understand it in the first place. As far as Gell is concerned, and as becomes clear in a passage in which he refers to a matchstick model of Salisbury cathedral, for the term 'art' we could easily substitute another—'material culture' or 'visual culture'—although he avoids doing so himself. Studies of art have always been dominated by a concern with aesthetics, providing a kind of 'theology' for the subject, and anyone interested in art almost has to ascribe it some kind of aesthetic value. This is what makes an artwork more than a mere variety of thing and makes it valuable to study. Gell's first manoeuvre, then, is to make a complete break with aesthetics, asserting a 'methodological philistinism' (ibid.: 42). Rather than assume that artworks do have some inherent aesthetic value ('truth' within them), we have to bracket off these considerations and think about what art *does* within any particular social context. This is not an art historical concern with symbolic meaning, nor does it concern itself with the manner in which art can be a vehicle of power, marking out social distinctions. The focus of attention is on the artwork, or thing itself, with 'the fascination which all well-made art objects exert on the mind attuned to their aesthetic properties' (ibid.: 43).

Art objects have power and significance because of the way they are made; art is an 'enchantment of technology'. The power that art objects possess stems from the technological processes they embody—in short, the sheer skill and dexterity required to make them. This technological enchantment of the thing puts people under a spell, so that the art object has an inherent power, or aura. Socially it produces the technology of enchantment. Art produces the technological means for persuading people of the necessity and desirability of the social order (ibid.: 44). In other words, its significance is ideological, a means of thought control. The intricately decorated Trobriand prow-boards of the canoes used in *kula* exchange in the Massim region, Papua New Guinea, function as weapons in psychological warfare. The *kula* exchange partner, seeing one of these canoes arriving, will be dazzled and give up his shells. The technical difficulty in carving these prow-boards and the magical spells that are bound up with the production process make this an enchanted technology, and the artist is therefore an 'occult technician': 'It is the way an art object is construed as having come into the world which is the source of power such objects have over us—their becoming rather than their being' (ibid.: 46). Similarly, the power of portraiture or of a landscape painting is derived from the sheer skill required to produce, with pigment, the likeness of a person or a landscape, something beyond the capability of a normal mortal. So this is a processual view of the significance of the aesthetics of the thing. Technological virtuosity is intrinsic to the efficacy of artworks in their particular social contexts. In small-scale societies, the two principal social contexts in which art objects work their technological magic are in political ritual and ceremonial or commercial exchange.

This general argument with reference to the work that art objects do, rather than what they might mean, or symbolise, is greatly expanded in *Art and Agency* (Gell 1998; hereafter *AA*). In the opening chapter he argues against trying to develop a specific theory for 'primitive' art in colonial and post-colonial societies that anthropologists typically study; nor does he find the notion of anthropology being concerned with developing a cross-cultural aesthetics particularly useful. Many artworks in non-Western societies simply do not generate an aesthetic response in a conventional sense. A warrior on a battlefield is unlikely to find the design on the warshield of his opponent aesthetically interesting! It is designed to induce fear. Gell also rejects structuralist and semiotic approaches which have dominated the anthropology of art since the 1970s. They assume that art is primarily about non-verbal communication and meaning, but in Gell's position the true significance of art is the work it performs, and this is couched in the emphasis put on agency, intention, causation, result, and transformation (*AA*: 6). Art is a system of action, and an anthropological theory of art does not try to define its objects in advance: 'Anything whatsoever could, conceivably, be an art object from an anthropological point of view' (*AA*: 7). In other words, by 'art' Gell means material culture. These material forms, or art objects, need to be understood in terms of social relations over the time-frames, or biographies, of individuals, which Gell takes to be a distinctively anthropological perspective. Moreover, these things need to be considered from a Maussian or anthropological perspective as being like persons, subjects rather than objects. Simply put, because things are like 'persons', they, like persons, can possess agency (*AA*: 9). This is the central 'phenomenological' thesis. The essential differ-ence between Merleau-Ponty's discussions of the fleshy nature of a field of visuali-ty, discussed earlier, and the notion that the painter is seen by the trees that he is painting, and Gell's approach is essentially the use of the term 'agency', together with Gell's more restricted range of reference to material forms. For Merleau-Ponty, we can argue, it is not just artefacts that might be said to possess a certain kind of agency, but the entire material world, 'cultural' and fabricated or 'natural' and unal-tered. If Merleau-Ponty provides us with a phenomenological approach to the land-scape, then Gell offers one in relation to the artefact.

The crucial part of Gell's approach is obviously what he means by the agency of things and how this relates to, or differs from, the agency of persons. Agency is a process involving indexes and effects. Things are material indexes producing a cog-nitive operation, which Gell refers to as the 'abduction of agency' (*AA*: 13). By this term he means drawing inferences from the thing in an analogous manner to the way in which we might think that someone who smiles is friendly. The gesture is indexical of the state of that person. Agency is attributable to both persons and things 'who/which are seen as initiating causal sequences of a particular type, that is, events caused by acts of mind or will or intention. . . . An agent is one "who caus-es events to happen" in their vicinity' (*AA*: 16). Agency is a culturally prescribed way of thinking about causality. The 'intention' may be lodged either in the mind of a person or in a thing. The agency of things is of a second order from the agency of persons (because they do not have minds), but things acquire agency through becoming enmeshed in human social relationships. This is partly because persons typically form *animistic* social relationships with things and tend to anthropomor-phise or personify them (*AA*: 18 ff.). More generally, it is because material forms intervene in the world; they have specific *effects* on persons. While not having a mind, they have palpable influence. Persons, or things, act relationally as agents with regard to other persons or things that are acted on: In Gell's terminology the agent has agency in relation to a 'patient' (recipient), and this, in effect, is his version of Merleau-Ponty's reversibility thesis. Objects may be 'caused' by their makers in an indexical manner, just as smoke implies fire. The technology of their production draws the agency of the maker inside these things. Similarly, the maker or a recipi-ent of the thing may be 'caused' (effected, influenced) by that object in either an active or passive manner. The nature of that 'causation' or agency of the thing may be crucially related to the process of representation: the thing may look like what it represents—that is, it may be iconic—or it may not, as in aniconic representation (e.g., the stone represents a god, but the god does not 'look like' or bear a resemblance to a god; *AA*: 26). Gell uses the term 'prototype' to identify what the index (material form) represents visually or nonvisually. So an anthropology of art is about persons in the vicinity of things and involves the entanglement of indexes, artists, recipients, and prototypes, which Gell sets out in a table of logical possibilities (Table 1.1). While artists may make 'indexes', they may themselves be vehicles of the agency of others. In other words, they are not to be considered as the self-sufficient and 'free' agents of much Western art theory.

Gell's usage of the terms 'icon' and 'index' is drawn more or less directly from the semiotics of Pierce, who distinguished among iconic signs that look like what they represent (a painting of a rose looks like a rose), indexical signs where the relationship is causal or inferential (smoke is a result of fire, footprints in the sand index the movement of a person), and symbols which have a purely arbitrary, conventional, or

Table 1.1. Gell's 'art nexus'

| | | AGENT | | | |
		Artist	Index	Prototype	Recipient
PATIENT	Artist	Artist as source of creative act. Artist as witness to act of creation.	Materiality inherently dictates to artist the form it assumes.	Prototype controls artist's action. Appearance of prototype imitated by artist. Realistic art.	Recipient cause of artist's action (as patron).
	Index	Material stuff shaped by artist's agency and intention.	Index as cause of itself: 'self-made'. Index as a 'made thing'.	Prototype dictates the form taken by index.	Recipient the cause of the origination and form taken by the index.
	Prototype	Appearance of prototype dictated by artist. Imaginative art.	Image or actions of prototype controlled by means of index, a locus of power over prototype.	Prototype as cause of index. Prototype affected by index.	Recipient has power over the prototype. Volt sorcery.
	Recipient	Recipient's response dictated by artist's skill, wit, magical powers, etc. Recipient captivated.	Index source of power over recipient. Recipient as 'spectator' submits to index.	Prototype has power over the recipient. Image of prototype used to control actions of recipient. Idolatry.	Recipient as patron. Recipient as spectator.

agreed upon meaning such as the cross as a symbol of Christ (Pierce 1955). He only ascribes the agency of things to iconic or indexical effects and effectively subsumes the former in relation to the latter (i.e., icons are types of indexical signs). He eliminates symbolic signs from his account. This is firstly because he is keen to deny any interpretive role for an anthropological semiotics, regarding objects as visual signifiers, and secondly because the index and the icon have an intrinsic connection with the objects they denote, whereas symbols do not.

Gell's approach to the agency that things possess in relation to people is entirely cognitive. Abduction is a cognitive operation. Things affect people's ('patients') minds in various ways. The Asmat shield produces terror in the opposing warrior: 'These designs seem to have been *composed* in a mood of terror, and we are terrified by them . . . because submitting to their fascination, we are obliged to share in the emotion which they objectify' (*AA*: 31). The captivation or fascination produced by the Trobriand prow-boards 'ensues from the spectator becoming trapped within the index because the index embodies agency that is essentially indecipherable. Partly this comes from the spectator's inability mentally to rehearse the origination of the index' (*AA*: 71). In relation to pattern, 'geometric' or decorative art, Gell suggests that decorative patterns applied to artefacts attach people to things. This is part of the technology of enchantment: 'The world is filled with decorative objects because decoration is often essential to the *psychological* functionality of artefacts (*AA*: 74; my emphasis). A common way of discussing decorated surfaces is to refer to their 'animation'. Our eyes become lost in their 'mazy dance' (*AA*: 76). Decoration makes objects come alive in a nonrepresentational way. Complex patterns may enthrall the viewer, acting as 'mind traps' (*AA*: 80). This cognitive 'stickiness' of patterns is attributed by Gell to a blockage in the 'cognitive process of reconstructing the intentionality embodied in artefacts' (*AA*: 86). How could this have originated? Patterns have an agency that may be agonistic or defensive as well as beneficial. Patterns may be protective devices, trapping evil spirits, defensive screens, or obstacles impeding passage (*AA*: 83). Mazes present 'cognitive obstacles': one knows there is a way through, but the only way to do this is to trace its winding course. In the most general sense the circulation of things, or indexes, transform the conscious experience of agents, so that stylistic traditions chart and manipulate social relationships. Here Gell refers to a 'structural isomorphy between something "internal" (mind or consciousness) and something "external"— aggregates of artworks' (*AA*: 222). Gell conceives the agency of persons as being relational on account of their position within a social network, and 'mind' also becomes manifested in style: in the things produced over a lifetime, distributed in the world, by an artist or within a particular culture.

While Gell has a great deal to say about the cognitive agency of 'art', he has virtually nothing to say about the manner in which things affect the body of the agent in which the mind is merely a part. Gell's agents (in the sense of Gell's people) have minds (individual and personal or mobile and 'distributed' through things), but they do not seem to have bodies (*AA*: Chapter 8). The closest he gets to considering the relationship between art and the body is in his discussion of Malekulan sand drawings. What was important about these sand drawings (executed on the beach and washed away by the sea) was the performative aspect of their execution. Layard (1936) had discussed similarities between the maze-like style of Malekulan graphic art and the complex choreography of their dance. Gell remarks, 'it is surely useful to consider the act of drawing as akin to dancing, and the design as a kind of frozen residue left by this manual ballet' (*AA*: 95). What is fundamental here is the impression of the finger running through the sand, creating a continuous, incredibly involuted line that becomes or emerges as ephemeral figure against the ground of sand, the trace of the body in the medium. But Gell does not consider the implications of this more fully; for him, that which links together Malekulan dancing, drawing, and music is a 'certain cognitive indecipherability' manifested in the performance. That indeed may be the case, but the kinaesthetics of the body in movement is surely fundamental to all these cultural forms.

The Reductive Contemplation of the Visible in Art

What links together both Merleau-Ponty's and Gell's discussion of art is the almost exclusive attention they pay to vision (tempered in Merleau-Ponty by some consideration of touch). Things are considered to be simply subjects and objects of vision. Their acoustic, olfactory, and tactile qualities are rarely even mentioned. Vision is effectively ennobled and subtracted out of the human sensorium. I want to suggest here that the attention paid to vision detracts from a fuller and more truly phenomenological approach to art. Such a position arises as a direct result of the *kinds* of artworks that both Merleau-Ponty and Gell were 'thinking through' in order to arrive at their own particular perspectives. In 'Cézanne;s Doubt', in the illustrations accompanying 'Eye and Mind', and in the more general discussions in *The Visible and the Invisible,* Merleau-Ponty exclusively considers paintings (apart from two sculptures), while making passing references to the work of artists such as Duchamp. The photographs and line drawings of artefacts illustrating Gell's *Art and Agency* are almost exclusively of paintings or small portable sculptures, or of objects found in ethnographic museums. The only exceptions are a photograph of part of a Trobriand canoe, a line drawing of a tattooed Marquesan man, drawings of arm, hand, and leg tattoos, and photographs of the exterior and part of the interior of a Maori meeting house. The latter is the only nonportable 'art' object that Gell considers in his own art canon.

Precisely because Merleau-Ponty and Gell have a 'gallery' notion or view of what art is (both were keen visitors to museums of modern art) and primarily conceive of artworks exclusively in terms of paintings and small-scale sculptural forms that can be placed in a gallery, they reduce the significance of art to vision, and as a result the agency of things is considered almost entirely in terms of a visual consciousness. The title of Merleau-Ponty's paper 'Eye and Mind' says it all—a phenomenological theory becomes reduced to the art and philosophy of looking and the way in which that looking affects the mind. Of course, a fundamental part of Merleau-Ponty's phenomenological philosophy is precisely to attack any notion of mind being separate from the body. The mind is in the body and cannot be understood apart from that body. It is because of the kind of bodies we have that we think in a distinctively human way.

But in considering art, Merleau-Ponty effectively reduces the body to the eye. This is the only sensory organ that is really significant in his analysis, with some mentions of the contact of the hands. But what of the body that smells and tastes and hears and moves, that has different postures and bilateral symmetry? This body provides only a kind of vaguely patterned ground against the dominant figure of the gaze of a penetrating eye. The point is that contemplating a painting or a sculpture, in the Louvre in Paris or the National Gallery in London, is, on the whole, a singularly disembodied experience. The work is separate from the body that created it and is separate from the viewer or 'recipient' who receives it. The dictum of the officialdom of the art establishment is that one may not touch. All these works of art are rather small-scale. Even the largest of paintings can be seen, or encompassed, all at once, at a suitable distance in relation to the movements of the eye. Even worse than this is the miniaturisation and contemplation of the art object in the form of photographs and line drawings in texts, which no doubt contribute to their analyses. I strongly suspect that if Merleau-Ponty or Gell had thought through either classical or contemporary art by visiting the Sistine Chapel or through experiencing firsthand 'earthwork' or 'land' or 'environmental' art, they might have had a rather different perspective.

Going beyond the All-Encompassing Eye:
The Touch in Seeing

In relation to the eye that sees and the mind that thinks, can we posit a more embodied (or bodily) relation? In relation to a discussion of the agency of iconic as opposed to geometric images, Gell discusses Hindu image worship (*AA*: 116–21). Worshipping images allows one to obtain *darshan* from the god, a blessing obtained through looking into the eyes of the image. The eye is the medium through which the blessing is transferred. To be in the presence of the image allows one to internalise the blessings and powers conferred by its divine gaze. Sight is conceived as being a kind of touch. Gell cites Kramrisch: 'Touch is the ultimate connection by which the visible yields to be grasped. While the eye touches the object the vitality that pulsates in it is communicated' (Kramrisch 1976: 136, cited in *AA*: 117). Here we have a form of synaesthetic experience, a blending together of the visual and the tactile, precisely the same kind of notion we also find in Merleau-Ponty's consideration of a visual flesh in general. Except here it is specific to the eyes of the idol and the eyes of the worshipper, between which there radiates a specific connection. Seeing, like touching, is a form of contact. The logic is one of looking and being seen. Sometimes the eyes of the images, as in Jain temples, are set with little mirrors so that the devotee can see himself or herself looking. The devotee looks and simultaneously sees the god looking. Eye contact gives access to a mind (*AA*: 120).

Consider this Indian calendar image from the 1980s (Figure 1.1). An interpretive understanding of the visual content of such an image is obviously dependent on a prior understanding of Hindu mythology and what such images of the gods mean in that cultural context. Decoding the meaning of the image relies on situating it within the context of the religious and mythological system. The work that the

Figure 1.1. A 1980s Indian calendar image of Ravidas who cuts open his chest to reveal his brahmanic sacred thread. *Source: Pinney 2004.*

image performs is as a partial representation of a wider underlying mythological system of belief. This particular image is of Ravidas, who cuts open his own chest to reveal his brahmanic sacred thread. If we had no knowledge of Hindu Indian mythology or its cultural context, the possibility of understanding such an image fully would seem remote, and this, of course, is precisely the problem archaeologists encounter in attempting to understand prehistoric imagery. The important point here is that in a traditional iconographic analysis, what such an image means is enough. We apparently know everything important about it.

Pinney explores this in relation to the contemporary use of inexpensive, mass-produced chromolithographs in a rural Indian village in Madhya Pradesh (Pinney 2004: 182 ff.). These visual forms are valued for the access they give to divine energy, and the villagers are not interested in what the image looks like but in what it can 'do' (ibid.: 190). They have absolutely no interest in their production or the artist who created them. The image's past is quite irrelevant. What is significant is what the image can do in the future, the divine power it might bestow. The image in a pile on the market stall is simply a bit of paper. Taking it into the home, seating or displaying it, transforms it into a divine presence. Pinney argues, in a similar vein to Gell, that such images are not just pale reflections of what really matters and what is more important, in this case, the prior Hindu mythological system. Visual culture is an important domain in its own right, and it works on and through the body. The image of Ravidas is typical of inexpensive, mass-produced chromolithographs popular among rural villagers in India, framed and displayed and worshipped in domestic shrines in their houses. The images provide access to divine energy, and this is mediated through the form of the image itself. Absolutely typical of these images is the gaze. The worshipper looks at the image and the image returns its gaze. One looks and is, in turn, looked upon. The eyes of the devotee, 'an organ of tactility', become conjoined with the god, allowing the flow of divine energy and the possibility of physical transformation and intervention in the world. Some of these images are even framed with mirrors so the observer can simultaneously see the image and see him- or herself in the act of seeing. Pinney comments:

> Like the vast majority of villagers Pannalal Nai, a retired factory worker, lights incense sticks in front of his images at sunrise and dusk. He asks for the protection of all that is valuable to him: 'give barkat [divine energy], food, water, children, small children, protect all this.' As Pannalal performs this *puja*, appealing for protective plentitude in the face of harsh uncertainties he murmurs to himself, waves his incense sticks, rings a small bell and crumbles whatever marigolds might be lying on the *puja* shelf in front of his images. As he does this his eyes maintain an intense visual intimacy with the gods and his body describes a gentle swaying, yearning, movement as though caught in the force field around the image. (2004: 191)

The consumption and use of such images by rural Indian villagers is primarily about bodily empowerment. Through the medium of the devotee's gaze, pieces of paper are transformed into powerful deities. The images enter through the eye and have bodily effects. The image causes the devotee to sway and move, in a whole repertoire of bodily performances involving touch and sound and smell. The power of the image is not simply, or even primarily, a matter of what it means. It arises from what it does, its bodily effects, and in the context of its use, in the process of which the sensory synaesthetic effects of worship arise.

Such an image clearly affects both mind and body. It has cultural meaning but is also about doing: the image impacts on the person. Precisely because this is a small, portable image, its actual effects in relation to the body of the devotee, as opposed to his or her mind, are relatively limited. For example, the devotee could move or sway in front of the image in any appropriate devotional way, and *all* the image is seen *all* at once. In this example, the fact that the image is printed on paper does not matter; or if it does, if it should be acknowledged that this is *just* an image on paper, this constitutes a problem, because for the devotee the image must always be something more than that. The image itself is fundamental, not the medium on which it occurs (paper) or the technique of its mass production (chromolithography). Let us go back again to the Indian calendar image (Figure 1.1). Pinney's analysis is both very informative and insightful. Those eyes do indeed have power in relation to a Hindu devotee, but they have considerably less power in relation to you and me. We are accustomed to a flood of eyes looking at us all the time in our excessively visualised culture: eyes on the front pages of magazines, newsreaders on TV, celebrities on billboards in the streets. The supposed intimacy of the contact has been drained and has little power in our own culture. The power of the calendar image in relation to the Hindu devotee, however, clearly relates to something beyond the image itself, a belief in the transforming power of images related to a particular system of Hindu mythic and cosmological belief and devotional practice. This provides the wider cultural context by means of which we can understand the inherent power of visual culture in this case.

As Gell (1998; 1999) and Pinney (2004; 2006) demonstrate, art, or material culture more generally, does not necessarily require a process of decoding, or a verbal exegesis of meaning, to have power and significance. It can be argued to possess these qualities in and for itself as a material medium (Tilley 1999). For example, Melanesian anthropologists have noted over and over again a great reluctance of people to talk either about 'art' or any other artefacts they invest so much time in making and decorating. Forge (1970; 1979) argues that the Abelam art of Papua New Guinea is so powerful precisely because people don't talk about it or discuss its meanings. Art in this context derives its significance from the fact that it is experienced while its meaning goes unsaid and is not discussed. It cannot be translated in terms that noninitiates can understand. In a similar vein, Losche (1995) argues that Melanesian art is a structure of sentiment and desire created through experience. The visual imagery has its own irreducibility. If the experience could be decoded, or talked through, it would simply lose its power. Strathern (1990) argues that the power of images resides in the event of their perception. They require no further outside contextualisation beyond themselves and the context of experience. It would seem unwise for us to simply assume that prehistoric rock carvers share our own modern propensity to want to talk about meaning, to translate images into words. Whether or not they shared this desire to chatter, we can at least be certain that they, like us, experienced these carvings through the medium of their bodies.

FROM SENSORY EXPERIENCE TO A KINAESTHETIC PERSPECTIVE ON ROCK ART

A kinaesthetic approach is rooted in a phenomenological tradition of research which, as argued above, must resist the notion that art is strictly a matter of the visual, simply sensing through seeing. It regards vision as only a part, albeit a very important part, of the sensory experience of the body. It provides possibilities for alternative ways of understanding rock art imagery, ways that break with dominant ethnocentric European and American understandings of visual and material culture which, in a consideration of art, effectively sever sight from body and allow that sight is somehow autonomous from embodied material experience. However, if it is possible to argue that even a small portable image has bodily effects, then the implications for the study of rock art are indeed profound. As discussed above, looking at any portable image or painting is usually a relatively passive process. By contrast, seeing rock art frequently requires having to move across an entire landscape, from one rock to another, or one area of the same rock to another. We typically don't stand on the canvas or walk over the painted surface when we look at paintings. But this, of course, is typical of the way in which we experience rock art. We enter, with our own bodies, into the image fields. The images in this manner become a part of us and we become a part of them, an intimate relationship. The sheer bodily impact of rock art imagery is therefore much more dynamic and powerful than the Hindu calendar example discussed above, or than in any of Gell's general claims about the agency of either portable artefacts or artworks. The agency he is referring to is solely a matter of mind rather than relating to the physicality of the human body in motion.

We have seen that Bergson developed a bodily perspective on memory, stressing one form of memory orientating the body as being purely habitual. From the phenomenological perspective adopted here, it is assumed that the body is an object and as much a material culture product as any other thing such as a house or an axe. As self-conscious sentient subjects or persons, we are aware of the objectivity of our own bodies, and the body itself plays a fundamental role in our self-conscious awareness and the manner in which we perceive and understand the world around us. The body is both a thing and an image, and our experience of both is mediated through the physicality of the body itself. As Bourdieu (1977) stresses, practical beliefs, actions, and thoughts arise from an embodied mind—or, in other words, a state of the body—rather than from an idealised world of disembodied pure thought.

Over seventy years ago Mauss's famous essay 'Techniques of the Body' (Mauss [1935] 1979) discussed the manner in which the human body itself is a primary object on which cultural and social differences become inscribed. Thus, different societies actively produce different kinds of bodies, and the enculturation of these bodies changes over the life courses of different individuals and is intimately related to gender differences. So Mauss argued that different ways of walking, sitting, or swimming and bodily postures such as the position of the hands and arms while walking or at rest are all culturally learnt and variable. Learning these techniques of the body requires time and becomes engrained habit as culturally enskilled practices. Thus, during the 1914–18 World War, English troops were incapable of using French spades to dig trenches which had to be replaced in their thousands, and their gait was at odds with a French military rhythm (Mauss 1979: 99 ff.). The body is 'man's first and most technical object, and at the same time technical means' (ibid.: 104), and body techniques extend to modes of sex, sleeping, child weaning, modes of resting such as squatting and walking, and so on. Learnt movements of the whole body, rather than of parts of it, include the actions of climbing, trampling, walking, running, and dancing, and cultural codes determine the 'natural' manner of the body's state of existence in different cultures, a product of techniques of socialisation. The gestalt of a walking body is also strongly moulded by cultural artefacts such as shoes versus bare feet or different kinds of shoes producing different kinds of characteristic movements and postures (Falk 1995; Michael 2000; Ingold 2004).

The perception of rock art images is thus as much a matter of the flesh, of sensation, of feeling, of corporeality, as it is a matter of cognition or mental process involving remembering, recognition, and iconic, indexical, and symbolic association, all culturally mediated processes. The body is not just a site inhabited by sensory organs but forms an active part of the entire sensory process. The body as flesh in Merleau-Ponty's sense of the term is sentient and sensible, something that touches and is touched, seer and seen. The manner in which perceptual thought takes place is therefore grounded in the kinaesthetic relationship among person, place, and landscape. All perceptive experience has a bodily basis in movement through and exploration of the landscape, as the site of all the sense organs and the brain, and as a sense organ in itself with the skin as its boundary. The body is both an object and subject of perceptual experience, constituted and constituting, a physical thing with needs and a social being with a biography situated within a particular cultural habitus or disposition to act in the world.

What the body can do in the space-time of landscape and the manner in which it can act have a profound effect on the character of experience and the kinds of meaning that experience affords. The eyes, ears, and nose are all distance receptors. By contrast, the nerves (proprioceptors) keep the body informed of what is taking place as the body moves around, a muscular internal bodily sense of the world intimately connected with the exterioceptors or nerves in the skin informing the body about touch and texture, roughness and smoothness, heat and cold, pleasure and pain. Visual, or any other kind of distance perceptual experience, has a fundamental kinaesthetic basis. The process of walking through a landscape, climbing a mountain, or swimming across a river makes one feel and think differently about them. They are never the same again because of this dynamic interconnection between kinaesthetic and sensory experience. That which is seen expands visually as one moves towards it; that which is continuously smelt or heard increases or decreases in intensity in relation to bodily motion towards or away from the source. In this sense, the body becomes the measure of all things. The experience of movement through a landscape continually inscribes itself within the body, from sweat to heart rate to a straining of the joints, tendons, and muscles. This is an infra-language of movement contributing in a fundamental way to thought, emotions, mood, and feelings. Such a state of awareness is thoroughly embodied. It does not require sight or touch to register that our limbs have moved, nor to register the effort that this has required.

The body can move in and through the world on the basis of its own learned perceptual instincts, which require no active perception or thinking where to go. We can consider here the notion of *proprioception*. This is not the usual sensitivity of the body to its surroundings but one that has to do with conditions of movement and encounters, resulting in a kind of muscular memory relating to habit and posture, 'thinking' in the body rather than in the mind—the coordinated movements of limbs and muscles and ligaments moving the body along in a characteristic manner (Eilan et al. 1995; O'Shaughnessy 1995). Through proprioceptive memory we can get where we are going and have little or no other sensory memory or awareness of the route we have taken, quite literally, for granted. Vision is not here a matter of an eye that sees but more a matter of its retinal musculature in relation to a moving and feeling body (Massumi 2002). Massumi posits that in such movement, sight is turned proprioceptive; the eyes are more part of the flesh than discrete organs of vision. This is the memory of a body without discrete mirroring images. Massumi notes that the memory such a body constitutes 'could be diagrammed as a superposition of vectorial fields composed of multiple points in varying relations of movement and rest, pressure and resistance, each field corresponding to an action' (ibid.: 59). There is much scope for experimentation here in the development of quite literally a 'muscular' approach to experiencing rock carvings.

Although it has been claimed by some that proprioception can be considered a sixth, specifically bodily sense (Sheringham 1973; and see discussions in Bermudez et al. 1995), here, following Gibson (1968; 1986), it is regarded as a sensory modality intertwined with and underlying all the others in a process in which self and landscape are co-perceived. Gibson argues that the nature and character of the landscape (to him, 'environment') has a profound effect on the perceptive process, emphasizing its role in structuring sensory stimulation. Sources of stimulation from the structure of the landscape become encoded within the bodies that move within it in relation to a complex of surfaces, edges, and textures perceived in relation to bodily movement. He considers the different senses not as isolated from each other but as fundamentally interrelated in terms of perceptual systems. Gibson (1968) identifies five basic sense systems: the basic orienting system related to gravity, posture, and motion; the auditory system; the haptic system associated with touch; the systems of taste and smell; and the visual system. While these are distinguished from one another analytically, the whole thrust of Gibson's analysis is to demonstrate the multisensual character of the interaction among body, landscape, and mind in perception, all of which are regarded as active co-presences in relation to one another, acting in relation to one another rather than being subject to any causal determinacy. The landscape provides a rich and structured sensory domain through which the body moves and thinks, and the manner in which this movement and thought take place is fundamentally influenced by their particular material characteristics. Thus, in visual perception, ambient reflected light in the landscape (as opposed to the blinding pure radiant light of the sun) provides information about the inclination and directionality and edges of rock or other surfaces and about their shapes, arrangements, colours, and textures. Surfaces, according to their direction in relation to one another, inclination, texture, and degree of absorption will structure, reduce, or amplify sound; and auditory perception derives its basis from the flow of sounds through the landscape from one place to another, producing different acoustic properties.

A phenomenological perspective stressing the centrality of embodiment in relation to kinaesthetics rejects any notion of the body as simply a surface in terms of which society constructs itself, because the body is not just a bearer of signs and meanings (a body-text) but is constructed through its relationship to the material and sensory landscape domains that it inhabits. Being in a landscape means that the limits of the space of the body are in the things with which it interacts. The space of the body in motion underpins the perception of things. As Gil has recently put it: 'Between the body (and the organs in use) and the thing is established a connection that immediately affects the form and space of the body; between the one and the other a privileged spatial relation emerges that defines the space uniting them as "near" or "far", resistant, thick, wavy, vertiginous, smooth, prickly' (Gil 1998: 126).

By 'kinaesthetic' what is specifically meant here is the study of the active effects of imagery in relation to the human body, its balance, effort, postures, and gestures. The entire process of experiencing rock art demands movement from rock to rock and often from one image on a rock to another. It requires a body in motion, an active body. A body in motion is one endowed with kinaesthesis, derived from the Greek *kinein*, meaning to move, and *aisthesia*, to perceive. This involves consideration of bodily positions, postures, and movements in relations to images and their positioning in place, an embodied state of awareness going far beyond the sense of sight in which the outstretched arm or leg or a crouching posture may be a more fundamental part of the experience involving an awareness of both self and locomotion. The primary research questions to ask are: What do these images *do* to an observer? What effects do they have? What kinds of bodily actions are required to encounter and see or, more widely as discussed below, sensorily experience them?

RESEARCH QUESTIONS

These basic research questions require both the description and analysis of bodily movement in relation to the landscapes in which the images occur. We can ask questions about (1) the body itself; (2) directionality of movement; and (3) relationships to the wider sensory landscape.

The Body

In order to see and encounter the images on any particular rock or rock surface,

- Do we need to move, or can they all be seen at once, requiring only a motion of the head and the eye?
- Is a static body involved or a body in motion?
- Do we need to look up at the images on a rock above us? (Are the images dominant in relation to an observer?)
- Are the images at eye level? Do we need to look down? (Is the observer dominant in relation to the image?)

In movement, what part(s) of the body are involved?

- The body as a whole?
- Movement of the lower or upper limbs?
- The secondary parts (e.g., the hand in climbing)?

What bodily muscular energies, actions, or performances might be involved?

- Rotation? Twisting? Turning? Leaping? Crawling?
- What duration or temporalities are involved in these movements?
- Are the bodily movements required free flowing or disjointed?
- How are our muscles and ligaments involved?

Directionality

- Can we see all the images off the rock standing passively, or do we need to move across it?
- Are particular groups of images concealed in hidden areas such as depressions in the rock, round corners, in places that are easily accessible, or not?
- Do we need to move across the rock in a particular direction—for example, from north to south or east to west?
- Do we need to walk down it, or climb up it, or move in a circular fashion around it? Are we involved in a kind of ballet?
- To experience certain iconic or figural images (e.g., boats, animals, people, artefacts) from a 'correct' perspective, rather than seeing them upside down, where do we have to stand?
- What might be implied, in terms of human bodily movement, by images that face, or are oriented, in a particular direction, such as animals with their heads, or boats with their prows, or shoe-soles, facing left or right, or east and west, or pointing up and down the rocks? Where do they lead? What path of movement might they indicate?
- In a wider perspective, how do we have to move from one rock with images on it to another?
- Which direction do we have to take? Do we need to climb, or walk, or crawl from one rock to another? Do we take a meandering route, or must we move in a zigzag fashion?

- Can the images on the next rock, or some of them, be seen from the one before?
- What kinds of relationships exist between rocks with images and rocks without, and how does this relate to material properties of the stone itself (shape, size, colour, texture, sounds in the landscape, etc.)?
- Do we experience different kinds of images on different kinds of rocks at the beginning or end or middle of the journey? What main directions must be taken to encounter the images?
- Might there be intermediate directions?
- How much freedom of choice might be involved?
- Must they be experienced sequentially and, if so, in what manner?
- From where can they be seen and, just as importantly, from where are they hidden?
- How does this directional movement relate to basic body experiential dyads (up/down or above/below; left/right; back/front; near/far; and in reach/out of reach?
- Does one need to walk over the rock itself and enter into the image fields, or move around it and, if so, in what manner?
- Can the images be viewed collectively, or does the type of place in which they occur only permit individual experience or encounter by a few?

Landscape

- What might be the intent of locating the images in one place rather than another in relation to the wider sensory landscapes of vision, sound, touch, taste, and smell (see discussion below)?
- How might the weather and seasonal changes in the climate affect this choice of location? And how might the climate affect the form and character of the images?
- How do the images relate to the form and localised character of the rock itself, such as shape, colour, texture, surface contours, presence of fissures, and the like?

We can thus describe, discuss, and annotate these and many more of the kinaesthetic and sensory effects of the images and their locations in relation both to the form of individual rocks, their relationship to one another, and their positioning in the landscape. We can also investigate how these effects change from one rock to another or from one rock carving locality to another. Some of the image fields on the rocks may permit very little bodily freedom in the manner in which they can be experienced: one must move up or along the rock in a particular direction, and in relation to the wider landscape they must be encountered in a predetermined sequential pattern (for an early study, see Tilley 1999: Chapter 5). Other rocks may permit a considerable degree of latitude of subjective choice: I can move this way and experience those images first, which requires that I turn around in order to move towards and see other images on another part of the rock, or on a different rock, and so on. We can thus begin to comparatively investigate paths of movement and the variable impacts of different rocks or image fields on those rocks in relation to postures of persons: an archaeology of placial embodied multisensory imagery.

A kinaesthetic approach to rock art thus entails trying to describe and discuss these effects of the images in relation to the human body in the landscape as precisely as possible. The primary research tool is the researcher herself or himself, or alternatively, observing the bodies of others in relation to the images. One can attempt to describe these bodily relations in words—the approach adopted in this book—or alternatively, some system of dance notation might be adapted to graphically describe embodied movements (see e.g., Laban 1950; 1966; Gell 1995; Guest 1997; Stewart 1998; Lopez y Royo 2005), an approach for which there is considerable scope for experimentation in the future.

IMAGES IN THE LANDSCAPE

There are two massively obvious characteristics of rock art which nevertheless are absolutely fundamental and whose significance cannot be overemphasized: (1) Rock art is (usually; see Chapters 2 and 3) fixed and immovable, part and parcel of a landscape. It cannot be taken away or decontextualised from this context. A fundamental part of its significance is thus its location. (2) Rock art is created in a durable material medium, engraved or pecked out of stone. We now consider both these aspects in more detail.

Rock art, being located in the landscape, requires movement through and in that landscape in order to experience it. We may be encountering one, or a few, stones in a particular place, or hundreds or thousands spread over many kilometres. The places where the carved rocks are found may be part of everyday lived landscapes, associated with fields, settlements, or hunting grounds, or may be in locations set apart or liminal places. To reach the carvings may require movement on land, or on water, or a combination of the two. So places with rock carvings form part of wider landscapes, and the manner in which they are approached and experienced in those landscapes constitutes part of their significance. The journey contributes to their experiential effects. Rocks in a landscape gain part of their significance through their sensory experience in that landscape. There is a dialectic at work between landscape and rock, or place: seeing—or not being able to see—a striking mountain on the horizon, a cleft in the rocks, a view of the sea.

Light and darkness are fundamental to a visual experience of rock art. Different kinds of light at different times of the day and seasons of the year may radically change the appearance of the images, illuminated (or not) by the rising or setting sun, in shade or direct sunlight, on dry rock or wet rock, at night under artificial illumination, and so on. But because landscapes are not just visual but smellscapes, soundscapes, tastescapes, and touchscapes, the experience of rock art is always multisensory. Thus the odour of flowers or seaweed, pine trees or birch trees, of freshwater or saltwater, or of the stone itself when dry, or after rain, is an integral part of their experience. Painting rocks or infilling carvings with ochre or other media creates its own sound, a different texture and smell, as well as a highlighted visual experience. Sound is doubly significant. First of all, carving or pecking the rocks creates rhythms in the landscape, according to how they were created (see Ouzman 2001 and Goldhahn 2002 for discussions of this). Furthermore, different types of rocks—granite or sandstone or limestone—have their own voices or tonal qualities. Secondly, there are the sounds generated in the vicinity of the rocks, such as the deafening sound of roaring waterfalls (Goldhahn 2002) or the beating of the waves of the sea, the roar of the wind, sounds created by birds and animals and the activities of people, the sounds of drumming and music. Such sounds may be constant or change in relation to the weather. The patterns of the weather and its seasonal changes are part and parcel of the experience of the rocks, and many other sounds are seasonal too: the cries of migrating animals and birds. Some rocks may be in quiet places. In others, the effects of echoes can be quite startling, amplifying sounds and making them bounce back and forth.

Different rocks and their carvings feel very different—rough or smooth, broken or uniform. Some carvings are deep, others very shallow. Tracing the outline of an image with the hands may be as significant as seeing it. Tactile contrasts between carved and uncarved areas are usually very significant. To feel or to stand on a rock is to establish direct bodily contact, to touch and to be touched by it, and looking may stimulate feeling or vice versa. The hammering of stone required to make rock carvings produces a particular burnt smell, and the fiery light of sparks and different kinds of rocks smell differently in this respect. The taste and odour of rocks can also be related to the types of foods and drinks consumed on them or in their vicinity. Thus, rocks might taste or smell of salmon or shellfish, roast pork or game, berries and mushrooms. The same images can have very different sensory experiential effects in relation to where they are found, the time of day, the season of the year, and the patterns of the weather.

Unlike canvas or paper, stone is never blank. It has its own colour, structure, sensory texture, and form or shape. These characteristics of the stone itself may be as significant as the images engraved on it, structuring the manner in which the images are encountered and experienced, or indeed understood as possessing meaning (Tilley 2004; Jones 2006). Once again, we return to the proposition that the material medium of rock art, the rock itself, is as fundamental a part of its significance as whatever it may signify. Whether we fully appreciate it or not, we always experience rock art in multisensory ways through the medium of our embodied experience. To regard rock art as a primarily visual medium is another prejudice that artificially separates out vision from the other senses. Rock art, through its location in the landscape, is generative of a wide range of experiences that extend far beyond both the visual dimension of the imagery and the particular rock on which the images are carved.

When we assign primary significance to meaning, to the images themselves, or to vision, we potentially corrupt a study of rock art by dematerialising the power of the imagery in relation to the material medium in which it is inscribed, and in relation to the landscape. A kinaesthetic approach is one that attempts to restore the power of imagery in relation to human agency. Images are fundamental in society not because they can be verbally described as meaning this or representing that, but because they require different forms of bodily actions in order to encounter and experience them. Experiencing the image through our bodies is powerful because these images alter us in subtle ways that may require no talk of their meaning. Describing the process of their bodily encounter becomes primary. So the significance of the image is not primarily what it stands for, or seeks to represent, but the event of its bodily experience. Understanding rock art thus links event, feeling, and form. It is concerned with human actions in relation to imagery as a multisensorial and synaesthetic (mingling or crossing of the senses) field.

Rock art images are typically multiple and complex, and they may not all be visible all at once. In the Indian calendar example discussed above, we witness the power of the eye. We can, of course, suggest that certain rock art images might also be strikingly powerful, dazzling and beguiling, sucking in the eye of the beholder and captivating him or her, in an analogous manner to Gell's description of *kula* canoe prow-boards or geometric patterns. Such images might well be understood as cognitively 'sticky', acting like traps. But such images are found in particular places on particular rocks in particular landscapes, and the manner in which they are approached and found and experienced is as much a matter of the movements of the body as of a cognitive operation taking place in the mind and goes far beyond vision.

Going beyond such 'sticky' images which arrest the eye, the phenomenal experience of any particular rock image, or panel of images, sets it in motion. When we visually focus on a single image, it inevitably becomes foregrounded in our perception, whereas other surrounding images become simultaneously backgrounded. As we look across the rock or walk over it, the image field is thus constantly shifting and changing in terms of figure and ground reversals, producing a shifting frame of reference rather than something static. Experiencing these images may require walking on the rock itself, looking down, and thus becoming an intimate participant within the image fields. It may require walking around, up and down, or moving in a boat. Different images or groups of images may require different forms of moving and ways of perceiving and experiencing. The materiality of the stone itself—its colour, feel, cracks, depressions, contours, and the like—works through and in relation to the body at rest or in motion, as important as the images themselves in creating particular bodily effects. A kinaesthetic approach to the art thus opens up the possibility of an entirely new way of appreciating its significance. We attempt to describe, discuss, and understand the manner in which the postures and movements of the body are generated and constrained by the images themselves in relation to the form and character of the rock.

From a kinaesthetic and sensory perspective, what is being stressed is the *autonomy* of the imagery. The images themselves are enough. We do not necessarily need to translate them, go beneath them, or worry about what they represent. Instead, we study the direct agency of this imagery, the bodily effects this imagery has on us and others. Images are thus regarded as significant not because they possess meaning but because they produce material sensory effects in relation to the bodies of those who experience them. In studying the imagery in this manner, our contemporary bodies, rather than our contemporary minds, become the primary research tool, together with our shared and distinctively human sensory capacities and dispositions. There is an entirely new methodology to be developed here which will involve a description of the human body and its postures and movements in relation to the imagery as sensed in multiple ways. We can document, one by one, individual carved rocks, or image fields and panels, in terms of their various corporeal powers in relation to the body and the manner in which these bodily effects are produced through a subtle dialectic between the materiality of the stone and the disposition of the images on it. We can compare and contrast what the stones in different rock art localities do to the body, and in what manner they are encountered. This is a project attempted in Chapters 2–4 of this book.

In considering the kinaesthetic effects of rock art, I would wish to claim that this offers the possibility of transforming traditional rock art studies, an opening out of an entirely new interpretive field made possible through escaping the tyranny of the image conceptualised as being simply, and primarily, a bearer of meaning. It creates both a new subject and object of analysis and requires a new methodology of study involving the detailed description of the postures of the body in motion in relation to the images. But on its own I do not believe that it is sufficient and needs to be linked back to a question of meaning, in a rethinking of semiotics and iconography.

Kinaesthetics and a Phenomenological Semiotics

The significance rock art has is intimately related both to meaning and doing. It has an inside and an outside. Kinaesthetic approaches attempt to understand the 'inside' elements of the art. These are its intimate relationship to the body and the human sensorium. The 'outside' elements relate to social and political beliefs and values, to gender, hierarchy, power, history and tradition, myths and cosmological beliefs, and so on. These are fundamental to any understanding of what it means.

However, what rock art means, I would maintain, cannot be adequately understood without consideration of what it does, the bodily effects that it creates or influences. Questions of meaning and questions of doing are two sides of the same coin which cannot be separated without losing something of essential value in the process. Although a kinaesthetic approach to rock art could be undertaken without reference to meaning, this would be deeply and unacceptably reductive since we would learn rather little about the specific form and nature of the images themselves. The type of result we are left with can be seen quite clearly in Gell's analysis of *kula* canoe prow-boards or Asmat war shields. All we are ultimately left with is a notion of visual seduction in the first case or psychologically induced fear in the second. This image agency approach, notwithstanding its brilliant insights for a general understanding of what visual forms do, the kinds of power they possess, is incapable of telling us anything of value about the *specificity* of the intricate carvings on the canoe prow-boards or the painted designs on the war shields. For example, the former have an extremely complex iconography which is intimately linked to the manner in which people perceive their island environment in the South Pacific in general, and in particular, the role of various bird species within it: the way in which they are symbolically evaluated,

understood, and represented in the art through close observation of their phenomenal physical and behavioural characteristics: 'There are specific qualities thought to
be represented by particular "animals" in the Vakutan environment which receives
formal representation in the carved lines and embellished surfaces of the board
assemblages. Form and colour provide the visual iconography to which body parts
and "animal" representations are attached' (Campbell 2001: 126). Such detail is surely
not irrelevant in relation to the agency of these prow-boards.

Almost every critical commentator on Gell's *Art and Agency* has been concerned with his apparent total dismissal of the value of symbolic meaning (see Pinney and Thomas eds. 2001). In a very useful recent discussion, Layton has pointed
out that iconicity cannot be reduced to the status of an indexical sign, which is at the
core of Gell's argument when he considers the agency of icons such as Hindu representations of the gods (see discussion above). Iconicity cannot be separated from the
symbolic, from cultural convention: 'Representational styles select which aspects of
the world they depict according to cultural tradition and the chosen aspects are
organized in conventional ways' (Layton 2003: 453). Gell does, despite his intentions
to the contrary, readmit semiotics through the back door when he assesses the significance of style. Considering the relation of individual objects to the overall stylistic tradition of Marquesan art, he comments that 'any part can stand for the whole as
in synecdoche; "representing" in this sense is clearly a semiotic relation in which the
object is a sign, and the corpus of stylistically related objects from which it is drawn,
is what is signified thereby' (*AA*: 166). Layton makes a crucial point in relation to this
when he remarks that for art objects to have agency is in part dependent on them
being 'read' or understood correctly, 'demanding a semiological approach' (Layton
2003: 460). For the thing to have power, we need to have an understanding of the
kinds of cultural conventions, or symbolism, at work. For icons to be effective, they
need to look like, or resemble, that which they represent, even if this is often heavily
stylised, as in totemic art in northern Australia (Morphy 1991: 155 ff.) or in the case
of split-representation on the American Northwest coast (Boas 1955).

There is precious little value in trying to read Gell's mind as reflected in his own
text. However, going beyond what may be just a point of playful rhetoric, I suggest
that the kind of 'symbolic' approach that Gell is principally objecting to is that manifested in a particular formalistic 'linguistic turn' within anthropological studies of art
and aesthetics in which the significance of iconography or pattern becomes reduced
to the manifestation of an underlying structure, with rules and grammars communi-
cating meaning like a language; and it is this approach that he particularly singles out
for criticism (e.g., Hanson 1983; Faris 1971; Korn 1978). He makes the point that
drawing linguistic analogies is misconceived. Lines or circles are not some kind of
'visual phonemes' (*AA*: 164). Visual forms are patently not encrypted messages
requiring someone of sufficient analytic brilliance to come along and crack the
underlying meaning of their peculiar imagistic codes. Pretending things are like
words in the multifarious texts of material culture really doesn't help. What this entire
approach neglects is, of course, precisely the very materiality of things, and of culture.

The hallmark of such an approach, as manifested in Saussure and translated into anthropological discourse by Lévi-Strauss (1966; 1969), is the notion that the signs of language, a relationship between signifier and signified, are arbitrary in a system in which only relational difference counts, a matter of cultural convention. But in Pierce's semiotic theory, discussed above, iconic and indexical (as opposed to symbolic) signs are non-arbitrary. They either look like what they represent (a deer looks like a deer) or index an action, event, or process (footprints in the sand), and for Gell such icons become indexes of agency. This can be claimed to provide a foundation for a materialist appropriation of semiotics, as Keane has argued (2003; 2005), rather than a reason to reject a semiotic perspective outright, especially as things, or images, may simultaneously possess symbolic, indexical, and iconic qualities. As often as not a 'symbolic sign' does not stand on its own, as opposed to an 'indexical' sign. In particular, all material 'signs' indexing or objectifying the agency and actions of their producers have an irreducible 'impurity' (Tilley 2006a). Words may be used to evoke smells or tastes or textures but, unlike things, have none of these material qualities. They only take on a visual form when materially transcribed into texts in which the ink may smell. The sensuous domain of things requires consideration of their carnal relations to persons and their bodies, so that a materialist semiotics is better understood under the rubric of a *phenomenological* semiotics.

Gell avoids any discussion of metaphor and metonomy in his explicit theoretical arguments for the agency of things, for he assumes 'metaphor' and 'metonymy' are linguistic terms and are thus best avoided. Yet his entire argument depends upon the skillful employment of metaphors and metonyms to the full. He tells us that Malanggan wooden sculptures from New Ireland are bodies with skins. Similarly, Maori meeting houses are houses for the body. Houses are bodies because, like the human body, they are containers with exits and entrances. He goes on:

> Houses are bodies because they have strong bones and armoured shells, because they have gaudy, mesmerizing skins which beguile and terrify; and because they have organs of sense and expression—eyes which peer out through windows and spyholes, voices which reverberate through the night. . . . To enter a house is to enter the belly of the ancestor and to be over-whelmed by the encompassing ancestral presence; overhead are the ribs of the ancestor in the form of the superbly decorated rafters which converge towards the ancestral backbone, the ridge pole. (Gell 1998: 252–53).

The superb description carries on; one body metaphor is piled on another. The whole point here is that the *agency* of the house—its mind effects for Gell—are produced through metaphorical means. The Maori house is a powerful *material* metaphor into the body of which people associate and affiliate. Gell's text, of course, necessarily must convey all this through linguistic metaphor.

This raises the interesting, and ultimately unanswerable, chicken-or-egg question. Which comes first, the material metaphor, the house, or the linguistic metaphors used to describe it? Did the Maoris think through their originary houses before constructing them, or did the material form think itself through them in the process of building? The assumption, which requires a phenomenological process of bracketing here, is one in which metaphor in language is considered to be primary and material metaphors, because they are silent and do not speak themselves, are somehow considered to be secondary or derivative and definitely less important. Through building the house we can argue that the Maori were thinking through themselves, and their ancestral relations, through the material medium of their bodies. Putting any of this into verbal metaphors was secondary, after the fact, a Derridean 'supplement' to the engaging and engaged material form. The house materially inscribed or 'wrote on the ground' central symbolic elements of their culture before these were ever spoken or put into words. If we think of the living, breathing, and sensing Maori body politic within the body-house, the manner in which that house was both experienced and understood was part and parcel of its mode of habitation, which only required, or perhaps did not require at all, a secondary verbal metaphorical exegesis.

The position taken here is that 'metaphor' is not a linguistic term. It is instead the name (perhaps with an unfortunate linguistic baggage or inheritance, but I see absolutely no point in coining a new term) we give to an analogical *process* that is manifested in language and in material forms. Elsewhere I have argued at length that metaphors are a primary and irreducible aspect of language and, following Lakoff and others (Lakoff and Johnson 1980; 1999; Lakoff and Turner 1989; Gibbs 1994), that human thought is metaphorical thought. We think ourselves through metaphors. The counterpart to linguistic metaphor is material metaphor, metaphorical *material* relations between things, or aspects of a thing (Tilley 1999). This provides a fresh way of understanding material culture and visual aspects of material forms. The metaphorical experience both of language and of things is grounded and mediated through the mind situated in and part of the sensing and sensed human body. Our experience of the world, through language or through things, has a metaphorical basis, but each is not a mimetic copy or duplicate of the other because they operate in different linguistic and material domains which do not necessarily require any translation in the terms of the other. Words and things perform different and often incommensurable kinds of social work.

The two most significant points to be made in this context, and in relation to a study of imagery in rock art, are first, that the performative character of this imagery, working its way though the body, may be held to be of the utmost significance because many metaphors are grounded in the human body itself and in human sensory experiences. Second, both metaphor and metonymy are grounded in an analogic style of reasoning and association which is not arbitrary. Metonymy expresses part-whole relations. The metonymic image represents the whole through a part (e.g., hand for body); the metaphoric image is all about establishing linkages and material connections between things or aspects of a thing. So the redness of a thing may evoke the redness of blood (a non-arbitrary sensory and material connection), or the house can be a body because both are forms of containers (again, a non-arbitrary material connection) (see Warnier 2006 for an extended argument with regard to bodies and containers and attributes of containing and being contained). A well-fed body is heavy and weighted down with food, just like a productive garden with its crops. The sea has significant experiential qualities of lightness and buoyancy and movement compared with the static character and heavy qualities typically associated with the land, and so on (Munn 1986; and see the discussion in Tilley 2006a). In relation to Pierce's trichotomy of signs, considerations of metaphor and metonymy thoroughly blur essentially arbitrary distinctions between different types of signs which may *either* be claimed to be symbolic, indexical, iconic, or not. Metaphoric representation in rock art plays on similarity and difference through and in material forms, exercising the mind at the same time as it exercises the body; concomitantly, interpretation becomes a multivalent process.

Linguistic or material metaphors, although culturally variable and infinitely creative and generative, do not arise in a disembodied and unconstrained mind able to think whatever it likes and in any way it likes. Both arise in carnal bodies, inhabiting sensuous landscapes, and so provide different experiential affordances and constraints for life and living, and in the practical exigencies of living and relating to others.

CONCLUSIONS

In relation to a study of rock art, I simply want to conclude by making the limited claim that a phenomenological approach that considers both bodily kinaesthetics and sensory synaesthetics offers, first, possibilities for a fuller and closer analysis. Second, it provides us with a new way to think about agency and movement in relation to imagery. Third, by doing so, it may provide a more subtle way to interpret the significance of the imagery and where we encounter it on the rocks. Above all, what a kinaesthetic approach emphasizes is the phenomenological thesis that the body is in the mind. Meaning arises from and through an embodied metaphorical mind which is mediated through very different forms of multisensorial encounter with visual imagery in alternative contexts. A kinaesthetic approach suggests that if we are really serious about understanding what images mean and the histories and social practices that they may be held to create as well as to represent, we need to investigate what these images do, and what they want of us, to adopt Mitchell's (1996) phrase quoted at the head of this chapter.

The central theme to be investigated in the following three chapters is the performative work that rock art requires of the body in the context of the sensuous landscapes in which it is materially inscribed and embedded. An attempt is made to describe bodily relations with regard to images in three contrasting cases. This perspective leads on to a consideration of the manner in which a kinaesthetic and sensory study feeds into and may inform a metaphorical and interpretive understanding of what meaning and significance those images possessed. This in turn provides a basis for a comparative understanding of the relationship among body, image, and landscape through the medium of what I term (in the concluding chapter) the 'phenomenological walk'.

CHAPTER TWO

VINGEN

TRANSFORMING ROCKS AND IMAGE METAMORPHOSIS IN THE MESOLITHIC OF WESTERN NORWAY

VINGEN PAST, VINGEN PRESENT

Vingen, with around 2,000 documented carvings, is one of the largest single rock carving localities in Scandinavia. Its location at the end of a narrow and deep fjord surrounded by towering mountains on three sides yet within sight of the Hornelen Mountain, the highest sea cliff in Europe, is certainly one of the most dramatic. Here we have the conjunction of two extremes: the towering heights of the surrounding mountains and the unfathomable depths of the fjords.

The Vingen fjord in the county of Sogn and Fjordane is situated on the west coast of Norway about 100 km north of Bergen (Figure 2.1). The Vingen fjord inlet itself is short and narrow, 1.6 km long and up to 750 m wide. The mountains surrounding it to the north, west, and east rise up to 600 m above sea level in a series of sheer cliffs and scree and boulder-strewn slopes. The fjord below is up to 96 m deep and is an eastern inlet of Frøysjøen, which is up to 460 m deep in some places a few kilometres west of Vingen. Just over 4 km to the northwest of Vingen the dramatic Hornelen Mountain, 860 m high, towers up above the fjord on Bremanger Island (Figures 2.19, 2.22). This is one of the principal landmarks, used in navigation, along the Norwegian coast. Historically, many myths and legends have been associated with Hornelen, a place where witches and trolls had their abode (Mandt 1999: 55; Viste 2003: 92).

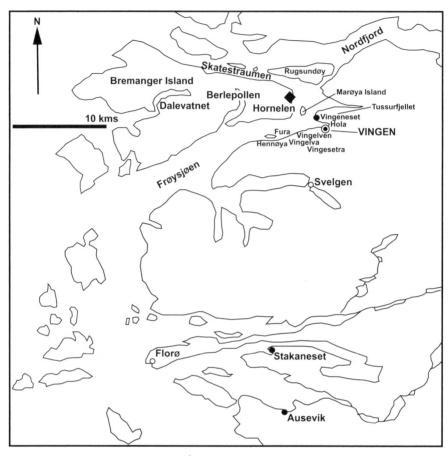

FIGURE 2.1. The location of the Vingen fjord in western Norway and places mentioned in the text.

Today, as in the past, the easiest way to reach Vingen is by boat. Walking from anywhere to Vingen is long, arduous, and difficult. A small footpath leading up the mountain and across the boggy and boulder-strewn fell before descending again to Svelgen, only 6 km away to the south, can take four hours or more, even in favourable weather conditions.

History of Research

The presence of rock carvings at Vingen was first publicised by the lawyer Kristian Bing (1912) who documented one hundred images, having learnt of their presence from local fishermen. The site was first visited by Gustaf Hallström in 1913; he undertook the first documentation of the site during a period of ten days and revisited the site for two days in 1917. This work was not to be published until 1938, as part of Hallström's (1938) study of all the northern Norwegian rock art localities, by which time many new carvings had been discovered. Johs Bøe from the Bergen Museum redocumented Vingen during a period of several months in 1925 and 1927 and subsequently published the site for the first time (Bøe 1932). Both Hallström and Bøe were assisted in their documentation by Olav Espevoll of the Bergen Museum, who must have had as intimate a knowledge of it as either man. Hallström (1938) discusses his documentation of Vingen at length and compares it with that of Bøe. Although Bøe documents a greater overall number of carvings, some found by Hallström were not found by Bøe. In general, there is a high level of agreement between their documentation of the same rocks. In some cases Bøe discovers more details; in other cases Hallström's documentation appears better. Bøe documents 778 carvings in total. Partly this was because he removed areas of turf covering some rocks, such as parts of the north face of Hardbakken and the lower part of the Kålrabi stone, which Hallström did not. Neither Bøe nor Hallström produced a detailed map of the site. Bøe provides a photograph with different localities marked on it, Hallström a thumbnail sketch. As a result, the documentation of both is of little use in finding all but the major and most obvious carved rocks at Vingen. This has considerably hampered subsequent research, which has involved trying to refind the rocks they documented.

Hallström's plates are much more organized and systematic than many of those provided by Bøe. Hallström clearly indicates which carvings are found together on the same rock or panel. This is far from clear in Bøe's documentation of the smaller boulders and rock panels, which is not very systematically organized. Sometimes the criterion employed seems to be simply where best the illustration might be fitted onto a page. In neither publication is it possible to obtain any real sense of the spatial relationships between the individual carved rocks, because of the lack of a detailed plan. The reason why neither Bøe nor Hallström could provide such a plan is easily understood. Given limited resources and time and the enormous complexity of this rock carving site, the task was quite beyond them. Hallström's work, viewed in retrospect, is a minor miracle given the short period of time he actually spent at Vingen.

The small number of rock carvings found to the west of Vingen at Vingelva and Fura were first documented in detail by Eva and Per Fett (Fett 1941).

From 1962 Egil Bakka started a fresh documentation of the Vingen carvings, uncovering many new carved areas concealed by turf, principally Brattebakken and Leitet and on the north face of Hardbakken. His visit to the site was stimulated by fresh finds of carvings on Hardbakken by the farmer Thorald Vingeleven (Mandt 1999: 65). Bakka only published a few of these in a number of articles (Bakka 1973; 1975; 1979) before his early death. Bakka's discoveries increased the number of carvings known at Vingen from around 800 to about 1,500.

Since 1996 there has been an ongoing research project at Vingen, led by Gro Mandt and Trond Lødøen, involving detailed studies of the fragmentation and weathering of the carvings and how best to preserve them (see Thorseth et al. 2001), and a total redocumentation of the whole rock carving area, integrating the work of Hallström, Bøe, and Bakka with numerous finds of further carvings. This has brought the total number of known carvings to about 2,100. In addition to this work, extensive archaeological survey—including remapping of the area, accurate measurements, and excavation—has been ongoing (see discussion below). The major results of this work have yet to be published and integrated.

A comprehensive documentation of the Vingen carvings still does not exist, nor even a detailed plan of the carving area. My own study of Vingen (excluding the smaller localities to the west, mentioned above) is based on Hallström's and Bøe's early documentation, together with that published by Bakka, personal observation of the rock carving surfaces documented by Bakka but not published by him, and some finds of rock carving surfaces made subsequently at Vingeneset and Bak Vehammaren. It is inevitably partial as a result. A fuller and more detailed analysis must await the final publication of the site (Lødøen and Mandt in preparation).

Localities, Images

The rock at Vingen is a hard, smooth, dark grey-green Devonian sandstone. Vingen is situated very near the northern edge of the area of western Norway where this stone outcrops and conglomerate blocks occur on the Vingeneset headland (Thorseth et al. 2001: 47–50). Most of the rock carvings at Vingen are found along a narrow, boulder-strewn terrace 600 m long and up to 100 m broad along the south-ern side of the fjord (Figures 2.2, 2.3). They also occur on either side of a narrow gorge created by a waterfall flowing down a fault line at the far eastern end of the

FIGURE 2.2. Looking down on the Vingen terrace from the top of Tussurfjellet on the north side of the Vingen fjord. *Photo: Trond Lødøen.*

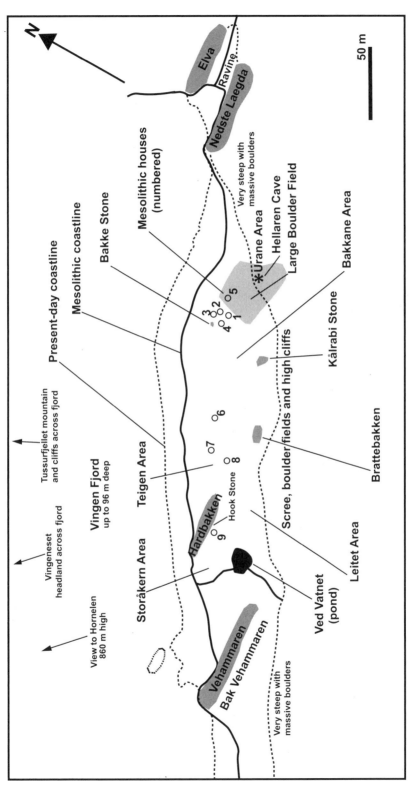

FIGURE 2.3. The rock carving areas along the Vingen terrace to the south of the fjord, showing the positions of the Mesolithic houses and other features in relation to the Mesolithic coastline.

TABLE 2.1. THE TOTAL NUMBER AND PERCENTAGES OF RECORDED MOTIFS IN THE MAIN VINGEN ROCK CARVING AREA.

Motif	Frequency	Percent
Red deer	731	34.40
Dog	3	0.14
Bear	1	0.04
Unidentifiable animals	168	8.00
'Snakes'	3	0.14
Humans	68	3.20
Hooks and scythes	511	24.10
Geometric motifs	71	3.35
Birds	2	0.09
Whales	3	0.14
Shoe-soles	2	0.09
Line fragments	322	15.19
Unidentifiable	235	11.08
Total:	2120	100.00

Source: Modified from figures given in Viste 2003: table 8.

fjord and on the headland Vingeneset to the north of the fjord at its western end. Besides at these places, a very few carvings have been found at Hola, an inlet also at the far eastern end of the fjord; to the west of Vingen, small numbers of carvings have also been found at Vingelven, Fura, Hennøya, and Vingesetra (see Figure 2.1). Table 2.1 provisionally shows the total number of known and recorded motifs from the main Vingen rock carving area.

Quantitatively, only three identifiable iconic motifs are of any significance at all: red deer, hooks/scythes, and humans. This is a strikingly restricted image reper-toire, an endless repetition of the same—deer, after deer, after deer. In the older lit-erature Vingen has been classified as belonging to the 'hunter's' rock art of north-ern Scandinavia, differentiated from agrarian art occurring to the south. This general distinction in this area of Norway is fraught with problems and is based solely on motif content since so-called agrarian carving sites are also found here.

Chronology

The dating of the Vingen carvings has been much discussed. Bøe (1932: 39) dated Vingen to the end of the middle Neolithic on the basis of shoreline displacement, noting that none of the carvings occur below 8 or 9 m above sea level. Hallström similarly dated the carvings to the end of the Neolithic while also suggesting that some might have been made at the beginning of the Bronze Age (Hallström 1938: 457). Bakka (1973; 1975; 1979) also argues, on the basis of a falling shoreline, that the carvings at Vingen date from the beginning of the early Neolithic until the end of the middle Neolithic (around 4000 B.C.), with a possible earlier origin in the late Mesolithic. He argues that the shoreline was at least 5 m above its present-day level in the final phase of carvings at Vingen, which were produced over a long period of time. He also suggests a relative chronology for the deer motifs, distinguishing four phases named after the different carving areas at Vingen on which they occur: the Vehammaren style (earliest), Hardbakken style, Brattebakken style, and the Elva style (latest) (Figure 2.4). The Elva style is dated as latest because these deer are found lowest down the rocks, at 8.25 m above present-day sea level. The Bratte-bakken and Hardbakken styles are all found higher than 9.3 m above present-day sea level, and the Vehammaren style never lower than 10 m. There are a number of problems with this analysis, since it assumes that stylistically similar animals were all produced at around the same time above the waterline. However, each of Bakka's styles could have been carved over a very long period. For example, while the low-est carvings at Elva do occur just above 8 m above present-day sea level, the high-est carvings in this group are found at a height of 18 m. So, while the lowest carv-ings at Elva might be later in date than those on Vehammaren, those higher up the rock could be of the same date, or indeed earlier. Recently Bergsvik (2002: 302) has pointed out that archaeological investigations at Skatestraumen (only 6 km to the north of Vingen) have revealed radiocarbon-dated late Mesolithic sites excavated far below the level of the supposed contemporaneous Mesolithic coastline as indi-cated by the shoreline displacement curves for this area used by Bakka.

Furthermore, Bakka's animal styles are not simply restricted to the rocks after which they are named by him, but are found elsewhere widely dispersed across the Vingen rock carving area. His Hardbakken type, in particular, has little stylistic unity, and in fact the animals he chooses as representative of this style are atypical of the majority of deer on this rock.

Lødøen (2001; 2003) has argued that the Vingen carvings are late Mesolithic in date on the basis of careful archaeological test excavations. All the archaeological material recovered from the Vingen terrace has been found to be late Mesolithic. In addition, charcoal samples from excavated cultural layers have all been radiocar-bon dated to the late Mesolithic (c. 5000– 4000 B.C.) (Lødøen 2003: 515; Mandt and Lødøen 2005: 145). There are no diagnostic Neolithic artefacts whatsoever, or even typical raw material categories or radiocarbon dates. Two small occupation areas with material of Neolithic date have been found on the Vingeneset headland to the

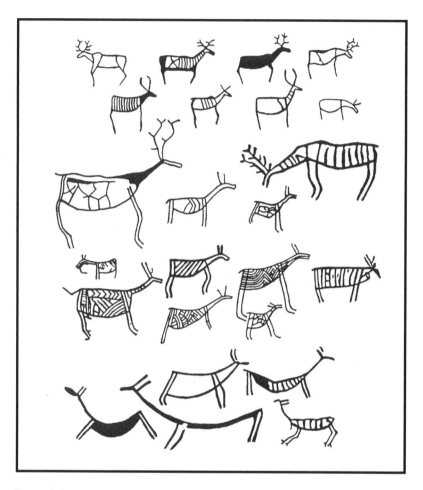

FIGURE 2.4. Bakka's typology of the deer motifs at Vingen. The top two rows are, according to him, the oldest, the Vehammaren style. Below this are deer in his Hard-bakken and Brattebakken styles, and the two rows at the bottom are in the Elva style, dated by him as latest. *Source: Bakka 1973: fig. 8.*

north of the fjord (Lødøen 2001: 221). However, these finds, unlike those of late Mesolithic date on the Vingen terrace to the south of the fjord, are not closely related to carved rocks.

Late Mesolithic Occupation and Dwellings

Archaeological survey and test excavations at Vingen have revealed the presence of circular or oval depressions interpreted by Lødøen (2001: 216; 2003: 514) as late

Mesolithic dwelling structures. There are at least nine of these, possibly more (see Figures 2.3, 2.5, 2.20). Four of these houses occur in a roughly circular cluster on the eastern edge of the Bakkane rock carving area towards the eastern end of the Vingen terrace. They can be subdivided into two pairs, houses 1 and 2, with a known midden deposit between them and houses 3 and 4. This cluster occurs immediately below a dense, tumbled boulder field and beneath a cave-like structure, known as Hellaren (see discussion below), within it. Another house only 16 m to the east (Figure 2.3: no. 5) is peculiarly concealed. It is surrounded by huge blocks and, despite its proximity to houses 1–4, is not visible from them or indeed from anywhere else on the Vingen terrace except in its immediate vicinity. Its hidden location within a dense boulder field may indicate that it had a special significance. Houses 6–9 are more scattered and occur in the approximate centre of the Vingen terrace. House 6, situated on a localised high point on the terrace, is intervisible with houses 1–4, 7, and 8. From houses 8 and 9 the summit of Hornelen is fully visible.

All these structures are between 4 and 5 m in diameter and surrounded by rough boulder and gravel walls. No obvious entrances can be seen from surface survey. They are all located within the immediate vicinity of rocks with carvings. House 3 is next to the Bakke stone, which has seven anthropomorphic motifs engraved on it. House 9 abuts the major carved rock of Hardbakken to its north and is close to the pond where there are many boulders and rock outcrops with carvings. Another anthropomorphic carving occurs on the top of Hardbakken next to house 9. Houses 6–8 are a short distance to the north of the major carved rock Brattebakken, and they and houses 1–5 occur in areas with many carved boulders and blocks. Furthermore, houses 1 and 2 have carvings engraved on their boulder walls. House 5 stands out from all the others in that none are visible from here. Houses 1–4 are only intervisible with carving areas at the eastern end of Vingen, whereas houses 7–9 are, as one might expect, intervisible with carving areas at the western end of the terrace. From house 6 almost all the major carved rocks can be seen.

None of the houses have been fully excavated as yet, but on the evidence provided by test pits Lødøen suggests that the limited thickness and unstratified character of the cultural layers excavated within these structures may indicate repeated short-term occupation. By contrast, excavation of a midden within the cluster of houses 1–4 indicates it accumulated over a much longer period during the middle and final late Mesolithic, probably as an accumulation of materials cleared out of the surrounding houses (Lødøen 2003: 515).

Unless it is argued that all the late Mesolithic material and structures from Vingen predate the use of the area for rock carving, which seems very unlikely, we certainly have here a rock carving locality with associated structures, artefacts, and midden deposits of clear late Mesolithic date.

Whether or not Vingen is classified as a Mesolithic or a Neolithic site has no relevance in economic terms, because during both periods we have hunter-gatherer-fisher societies in this area of Norway. The current evidence seems to indicate that Vingen was seasonally occupied for brief periods. On the basis of the extreme microclimate here, which is very inhospitable during most of the year, the most likely season during which this occupation took place, and the carvings made, would be during the summer and early autumn months.

Interpretations

Today this area of western Norway has the highest concentration of red deer in the country and is one of the best deer-hunting areas in Norway. Undoubtedly, the deer was a major economic resource in the past. It is in the context of the hunt that Bøe, Hallström, and Bakka tried to account for the significance of the carvings and, in particular, the overwhelming dominance of deer motifs. There is a deer migration route coming down to the Vingen fjord following the course of the river and the waterfall at the far eastern end of Vingen. As late as the eighteenth century, drive hunting took place in this area of Norway, though not in Vingen (Bøe 1932: 44). Bøe connects the carvings with hunting magic and considers that the earliest carvings were made at or near the place of the kill and later ones farther away. The carvings would attract the game, and the carvings themselves indicate the direction of the drive. On this basis Bøe argues that the carvings on the lowest half of the north face of Vehammaren and at Elva are the earliest (Bøe 1932: 45). Hallström effectively criticises this argument by pointing out that neither the Vehammaren nor Elva rocks are full up with carvings (Hallström 1938: 443). He also connects the deer depictions with the chase in a single sentence (ibid.: 454) but has nothing more to say about this. Bakka (1973: 156–57) also argues for a direct connection with a collective hunt and hunting magic, suggesting that the deer might have been driven down the cleft with the waterfall between the Elva and Nedste Laegda rocks at the eastern end of the Vingen fjord, where they met their death.

Lødøen (2001; 2003; Mandt and Lødøen 2005: 148) suggests that Vingen may have been a seasonally occupied ritual location. He points to a change from a more mobile to a more sedentary society during the late Mesolithic in this area of western Norway, which has been suggested on the basis of excavations besides Skatestraumen. Here on both sides of a strong tidal current between Bremangerlandet and Rugsundøy, more than 120 sites from the Stone Age have been documented. Over 40 of these date to the late Mesolithic (Bergsvik 2002). The material from them is virtually identical to that found at Vingen, suggesting contemporaneity. These occupation sites at Skatestraumen appear to have been reoccupied both more frequently and for longer periods during the late Mesolithic. Lødøen suggests that a greater permanency of occupation could have resulted in the need for special sacred or ritual sites and that Vingen was one of these, a place set apart for special ceremonies and rites (Lødøen 2001: 200; 2003: 518). More specifically, he suggests the art may have had an 'ideological' purpose, naturalising emerging social stratification and resolving the conflicts between individuals and groups that were occurring on account of increased sedentism. Just how this might be achieved through carving deer or scythes or hooks is left unexplained.

Mandt and Lødøen suggest a number of other interpretive possibilities for understanding Vingen. They rightly suggest that its dramatic location constituted an important part of its significance, acting as a natural frame for the carvings which were of paramount ritual and ceremonial significance (Mandt and Lødøen 2005: 152–53). More specifically, they point to the sacred significance of Hornelen Mountain, which might have been regarded as the centre of the world for the prehistoric populations (ibid.: 153). Importantly, they note that in historical times the summit was even higher than today, ending in a point or horn that collapsed during the early nineteenth century. During the summer months the Vingen carvings become magically lit up by the evening sun when it shines low in the sky over Hornelen. The entrance to the Vingen fjord could be understood as a kind of portal to another world (ibid.: 154). Vingen's very different kinds of rock carving surfaces themselves suggest different types of activities: some on or in front of which many people could gather in communal ceremonies and others in more hidden and secret locations (ibid.: 155). In a general way they suggest the carvings might be connected with rites of passage and shamanic acts (ibid.: 156; and see Viste 2003). Some of these arguments will be taken up later.

Weather

Vingen is a wet, cold, dark, and gloomy place for most of the year. The name Vingen means 'the windy place' (Mandt and Lødøen 2005: 154). For five months, from 5 October until 5 March, the sun never shines at Vingen (Mandt, cited in Viste 2003: 129). Even during the summer months, the early morning rising sun never shines here because of the high mountains to the south and east. The fjord, only open to the west, is primarily associated with the setting sun which, during midsummer, sets behind Hornelen Mountain to the northwest. During the summer months the fjord is bathed in sunlight only for brief periods. The norm here is almost incessant storms, beating rain and wind, or low clouds and softer or harder degrees of drizzle. The annual rainfall is considerable: 2,200 to 2,600 mm (Thorseth et al. eds. 2001: ix). If the Eskimo have an elaborate descriptive vocabulary for types of snow, then something similar and equally complex might be developed at Vingen for cloud and rain. The wearing of midwinter clothes during midsummer is quite normal here. Everything feels permanently damp. The ground, waterlogged most of the time, is alive with frogs during the summer. Vingen's microclimate seems quite extreme. Often in the rain and drizzle one can look out across Frøysjøen to the west and see the southern shores of Bremanger Island only a few kilometres away to the west, bathed in sunshine.

The weather at Vingen is as important an aspect of the place as the mountains or the fjord itself. It is infinitely variable, altering the character and feel of the place and the surrounding landscape. Differences in the height and density of the clouds radically affect the elemental qualities of light, water, and rock. When it rains heavily, waterfalls suddenly appear and cascade down the sheer cliffs of Tussurfjellet on the northern side of the Vingen fjord. These disappear as rapidly as they form. Heavy rain increases the force of the perennial waterfalls, whose roar is amplified. Braided flows of water may become a single torrent. The pond on the Vingen terrace expands, or shrinks, in tandem with the rain. Most of the carved rock surfaces at Vingen are relatively easy to walk up and across when it is dry. In the wet they may become slippery and treacherous, making it difficult and dangerous to climb on the steeper surfaces.

Although the weather at Vingen is predominantly wet, during dry spells the character and spirit of the place is transformed. There are days when there is no water in the pond, when most of the waterfalls dry up, times when the only apparent water is in the fjord itself. During these dry experiences of Vingen, your feet do not disappear under your body trying to walk on wet, slippery lichen, and you can walk up many of the steep and semi-steep panels quite easily. During such dry periods one can even move relatively quickly in the boulder fields, jumping from one to another and still obtaining a rather good overview of the area (Lødøen pers. comm.).

The fjord also changes its character from a glassy, mirror-like surface in calm weather to raging waves when stormy. The prevailing wind direction is from the south and west. The enclosed character of the fjord sometimes creates localised whirlwinds in which dramatic waterspouts form most frequently off the Vingeneset headland (Thorseth et al. 2001: 61–62; Lødøen pers. comm.). The water in the fjord may appear as an inky black surface, contrasting with the sometimes silvery appearance of Frøysjøen to the west and towards the open sea. Low clouds often envelop and hide the surrounding mountains completely. Sometimes the peaks of the mountains are visible and the lower slopes hidden, or vice versa. Plumes of cloud resembling smoke trails may descend into the Vingen fjord from the east or rise in that direction. Nothing remains the same for long at Vingen. It is an ever-changing place. This is a fundamental part of its mystery and power.

The narrowness of the Vingen fjord and its enclosure by high mountains on three sides have a funneling effect in relation to sound, which becomes amplified within the confines of the fjord. The waterfalls, although relatively small, produce a constant roar. Sound coming from outside the fjord itself carries an extraordinarily long distance, and during a thunderstorm, with lightning in the sky and the sound bouncing between the rocks, Vingen becomes a truly terrifying place.

IMAGES, EXPERIENCE, AND THE BODY

Following the Path of the Deer

The intention in this part of the account is to take the reader on a journey through the major rock carving areas of Vingen, following the lead presented by the most frequent images, the deer, and the dominant direction in which they face, or point, or appear to be moving. The likely path begins at the Vingeneset headland on the northern side of the fjord, leads us to the Elva carvings at the far eastern end of the Vingen rock carving area, turns to the west on the great rock of Nedste Laegda, dominated by scythe imagery, continues west along the Vingen terrace via the pond, and ends at Vehammaren at the far western end (Figures 2.1, 2.3).

Vingeneset

Vingeneset is a small, boulder-strewn headland which juts out into the Frøysjøen at the western end of the Vingen fjord on its northern side. The headland appears prominent from the main Vingen rock carving area, about 700 m distant. Above and to the east of it the barren, treeless, smooth, and boulder-free cliffs of Tussurfjellet rise up dramatically. This is an utter contrast with the boulder-strewn headland. The effect is to make Vingeneset appear as if it should not be there at all: a rocky nose stuck at the end of the mountain as an afterthought. From a distance it appears to be an accumulation of scree and boulders, fallen from the mountain and forming the headland, but actually it is a combination of outcropping rocks and fallen boulders (Figure 2.5). The headland only appears pointed and prominent from Vingen itself. From elsewhere in the landscape, whether seen from water or land, it appears insignificant. It is thus a place meant to be seen from Vingen, and from much of Vingeneset the whole of Vingen can also be seen.

FIGURE 2.5. Vingeneset seen across the Vingen fjord from the entrance to the Hellaren cave towards the eastern end of the Vingen terrace. The Bakke stone is in the centre of the picture next to the fjord. The flags mark the positions of the Mesolithic houses nos. 1-4 (*see Figure 2.3*).

Vingeneset is the only known area with rock carvings on the northern side of the fjord. While the sheer lower cliffs of Tussurfjellet, plunging down into the depths of the Vingen fjord to the east, might have been carved, they were left untouched. Vingeneset has fourteen recorded carving surfaces. These form a rough band about 300 m long running diagonally northwest to southeast across the headland, rather than parallel to the shoreline as seen from Vingen itself. Taken together, these rocks constitute the longest linear sequence in the Vingen rock carving area. The majority of the carved rock surfaces are separated from each other by only 10 m or less, but there are also three significant gaps between rocks where carvings along the sequence are between 50 and 100 m apart. The carvings consist almost exclusively of images of deer (about 59 images, or 90% of the total). Apart from these there is one small whale depiction, two or three human images, at least four hooks, a small ring, an oval geometric design (suggested to be a human vulva), and carved lines which are in all probability remains of further animals.

All the carved rocks are the lower exposed rock outcrops of the Tussurfjellet itself. Above and below these rocks there is a massive conglomeritic boulder field of a much rougher and broken character. None of these boulders have any carvings on them, despite the fact that they may be directly adjacent to or interspersed with carved rock surfaces. Vingeneset thus presents two main contrasts: (1) between the mountain and the headland itself; and (2) between the conglomerate boulder fields and the smooth rock exposures with carvings, which are of the same rock and have the same character as Tussurfjellet rising above them. The conglomerate boulders here constitute an alien stone in the Vingen rock carving area which are avoided and left unmarked by images.

Even though the rocks form a rough northwest-to-southeast sequence, movement from one decorated rock exposure to another is neither obvious nor predictable. Finding and encountering the carved surfaces elicits surprise as one moves between one and the next. This is partly due to the variable distances between carved surfaces. Also, the carvings occur on a variety of different rock surfaces—some concave, some convex, some inclined upwards at an angle of 45 degrees or more, others almost flat exposures. And even though straight-line distances between many of the carved panels are short, most are not intervisible. And finally, moving between the carvings requires negotiating a passage between huge conglomeritic boulders and moving up, down, and across the rock exposures and boulder fields at different heights.

The individual carved panels are relatively small, usually quite low down on steeply inclined rock surfaces, and constitute single visual fields requiring one to move only the head to see all the images from the bottom of the rocks. One either looks down on the designs below, or they are at eye level, or just above. Viewing these carved panels thus does not require clambering up and over the rocks themselves or walking across engraved rocks between separate images. Almost all these images occur on south-facing rocks, and one looks to the north in order to see them, with one's back to the Vingen fjord. A few of the rocks in the middle of the sequence are very low and situated on the margins of a hollow with a peat bog. It is here that the human images occur.

Hornelen is hidden from all but a few of the carved panels at the southeastern end of the sequence but is visually dominant on the skyline beyond from those at the northwest end. The Vingen rock carving area itself is out of view from the northwest end of the sequence but comes into view as one moves southeast at a point beyond which the Hornelen summit is either invisible or no longer visibly dominant from the carved panels.

The animal images on Vingeneset are all different. There are no two identical depictions. They are all highly individualised, differing markedly in size and internal body decoration. There may be as much, if not more, differentiation among the animals depicted on one panel and those on another. However, there is a strong unifying aspect that links the individual images together. All the animals, with only a couple of small and much more schematic exceptions, are depicted so as to face in the same direction: towards the east and the Vingen fjord itself. These are lively images of animals in movement, most with strongly curved backs, front legs thrust forwards, and back legs either straight or also thrust backwards (Figure 2.6). This strong sense of inland eastern movement is complemented by the solitary whale design at the far northwestern end of the carved panels, which also appears to be in vigorous movement facing east towards the Vingen fjord. This whale figure effectively marks the point at which the Vingen fjord ends and is the most westerly of all designs in the Vingen rock carving area itself.

FIGURE 2.6. Deer image on carving surface 10, Vingeneset.

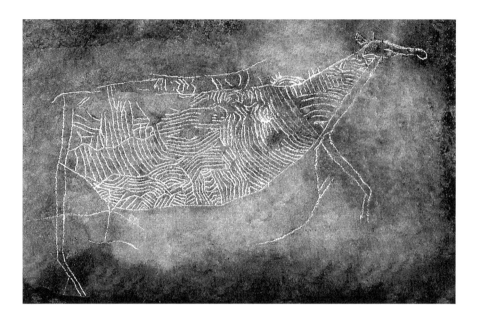

FIGURE 2.7. The largest deer (2 m long) in the Vingen rock carving area on carving surface 4, Vingeneset. Chalked in. It is now covered for conservation. *Source: Thorseth et al. 2001: fig. 3.1.*

The deer are depicted, as elsewhere in Vingen, in small groups of up to nine or ten individuals. On individual panels different animals are of roughly the same size, and single animals are not visually dominant. However, the largest animals, including the largest deer depiction in the entire Vingen rock carving area, occur at the southeastern end of the sequence on the largest single rock exposure and closest to Vingen itself (Figure 2.7).

Elva

The rock carvings at Elva, together with those at Nedste Laegda, are at the far eastern end of the Vingen rock carving area and some 1.3 km east of those at Vingeneset. Together these are the most remote localities in the Vingen rock carving area. The Elva rock carvings are located on a steep, south-facing rock slope that is today above a waterfall and a stream (Figure 2.8). They are found in two main groups. The western group of carvings are found low down the rock face immediately above the stream that now flows below them. In the late Mesolithic, this area would have been a small cove at the far eastern end of the Vingen fjord, and seawater would have lapped near to the bottom of the rock with the carvings. An observer can look across at the images on this panel from below them. The sheer rock rising up steeply beyond blocks out any view of the surrounding landscape to the north and the top of Tussurfjellet. Sound is a very important part of the sensory experi-

FIGURE 2.8. Looking towards the sheer rock carving surfaces at Elva from the west.

ence of these carvings, with the roar of the waterfall plunging down the mountainside to the east and another waterfall behind plunging down the rock slope of Nedste Laegda to the sea.

The western group of carvings are on a panel about 11 m long and consist of
eleven deer images, all facing east, apart from one at the far western end which faces
west (Hallström 1938: pl. XXIV; Bøe 1932: fig. 23, nos. 647–57). These animals are
stylistically very similar to those on Vingeneset. They face in the same direction and
appear to be in vigorous movement—inland and up besides the waterfall to the
mountaintop beyond. Again there is a high degree of individuation in these deer
depictions in terms of internal body markings. Beyond these there are another
twelve or so indistinct deer depictions, again facing east and shown in vigorous
movement (Bøe 1932: fig. 23: nos. 658–710).

The main eastern group of carvings occur on a panel about 25 m distant, covering an area 16 m long. They run obliquely across the rock face, which is about
18 m high. The lower carvings can be reached by means of moving along a small
ledge on the rock face. Others higher up are extremely difficult to reach because
of the sheerness of the rock, which is smooth and unbroken apart from minor
cracks and small protusions. To reach (or to have made) these carvings requires

being suspended from a rope above and abseiling down the rock face above the thundering waterfall, which forms a narrow gorge along a fault line below them. The danger and difficulty of such an effort appears to be the whole point of this rock surface at Elva: a feat of courage, dexterity, and technical skill that would only be possible for the young and the fit. Farther east and higher up the mountainside by the waterfall there are perfectly good and much more accessible rock panels which were left uncarved. Above these carvings the barren mountainside rises steeply, with huge, sheer slopes free of boulders and scree, and other areas above and below with broken rock outcrops and huge boulder fields. This is an awe-inspiring space dwarfing humanity.

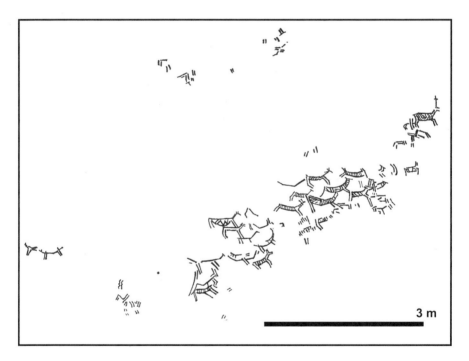

FIGURE 2.9. Deer on part of the eastern and higher rock carving surface at Elva. *After Hall-ström 1938: pl. XXXVI.*

Hallström (1938: pl. XXXVI) and Bøe (1932: fig. 24) record around 50 animals here. These run diagonally up the rock face in four diffuse groups of between ten and fifteen animals (Figure 2.9). Stylistically they are all very similar to those in the western group at Elva and the carvings on Vingeneset. All but a few of the deer face east and are displayed in vigorous movement. The flex of the back and the outward stretch of the legs are derived from a close observation of the manner in which deer move, bounding and leaping when frightened and in flight.

Nedste Laegda

To the south of the Elva deer carvings, another group of images occur which are utterly distinct, consisting almost exclusively of 'scythe' depictions. Hallström remarks that 'the differing locations . . . are remarkable. The former [Elva] down by the river bed and on a surface sloping steeply southwards, the other [Nedste Laegda] way up on the steep ridge on a surface sloping faintly northward. Perhaps the definite difference also in the contents of these carvings may have something to do with their different locations—or the other way round' (Hallström 1938: 437).

Approaching these rocks from the Elva carvings requires crossing over the deeply incised streambed and climbing a steep rock face to the south. The carvings are found across the top and northern slopes of a rounded ridge running east–west down towards the Vingen farm and terrace. They cover an area of about 23 m long by 12 m wide (Hallström 1938: pl. XXXVII; Bøe 1932: 548–646). This is by far the highest rock exposure with carvings in the Vingen area, and from here there are extensive views to the west along the Vingen terrace, with the northern face of Hammaren visible in the far distance.

The carvings are dispersed over a large rock exposure that has deeper and larger glacial striations running across it than anywhere else at Vingen. In places these form short, shallow, hanging grooves 2–3 m long across the rock surface, open to the north, somewhat reminiscent of those found in the rocks at Norrköping (see Chapter 3) but much more weakly defined. To the east of the carved rock, a waterfall runs down the mountainside and then turns to flow west through a channel on the southern side of the rock. It then turns again and flows north, plunging down to join the stream flowing down the mountain to the north of the rock and separating it from the Elva carvings. The carving area is thus bounded by running water on three sides—to the north, south, and west—and by the steeply rising mountain slopes to the east. Standing on the carved rock you can gaze northwards across the stream and waterfall to look down and across at the western and eastern groups of carvings at Elva.

There are at least nine different groups of 'scythe' depictions at Nedste Laegda, with a total number of some 92 images (Figure 2.10). The rock areas with carvings are all intervisible, but in order to see the individual images one must move across and around the rock. Some of the 'scythes' are orientated towards the west, some to the east, others to the north and the south. In addition to the 'scythes', there are at least six deer. These are markedly different in form from those at Elva; all but one isolated example (which is 11 m to the east of the 'scythes' and not associated with them) are scooped out from the rock surface, rather than pecked in outline, in keeping with the depictions of the 'scythes'. All these animals are again depicted in vigorous movement. All but one face west or outwards from the Vingen fjord.

All the animals appear right side up when looking at them from the south. By contrast, seeing the 'scythes' right side up requires much more complex body movement. Entering into the image fields and looking down on the images engraved into the rock below requires either movement from west to east across the slope, or to the north downslope or to the south upslope, or circular motion around particular

FIGURE 2.10. Scythe and deer images on part of the Nedste Laegda rock carving area. *After Hallström 1938: pl. XXXVII.*

groups of the 'scythe' images. In comparison, the Elva carvings, though they require one to climb up to them or swing down from ropes to see them from above, nevertheless have a consistent and simple orientation. By contrast, the 'scythe' images at Nedste Laegda require a 'placial' dance around and across the rock. They release the body from a fixed gaze and set it in motion. This rock surface contrasts with all others at Vingen in terms of requiring such a complex series of movements and encounters, and this is primarily on account of the particular form and spatial orientation of the 'scythe' images. Nedste Laegda was the dancing rock of Vingen, set high above the fjord and affording views across and down the terrace below to the west and across to Vingeneset.

It is worth noting that both the Elva and the Nedste Laegda carvings occur at the far eastern end of the Vingen rock carving area. Both are spatially separated from other major carved rocks and are in a rather secretive and unexpected place where the mountain, deeply incised by fault lines and parallel waterfalls, rears up to the east. This is the way in which one can climb up through the scree slopes and over the rocks out of Vingen to the mountaintop to the east, a land route out of the fjord end. Historically, this was the arduous route over which the sheep, goats, and the cattle of the Vingen farm were led up to the mountaintop for summer grazing.

This is the darkest and gloomiest end of the Vingen fjord, where the early morning sun never shines; yet it may be bathed in the rays of the evening sun during the summer. This is also the place where sound resonates most, bouncing among the steep rocks at the fjord's end. It is where wind from the west, the predominant direction, funnels up the mountain from the fjord, and where clouds descend from the east, trails of smoke, down into the fjord: special qualities of sound and light.

Urane

Immediately to the west of Nedste Laegda, an enormous boulder field runs across the Vingen terrace and up the slope below the sheer cliffs and scree slopes of the mountainside to the south. This is where the Vingen farm and its boathouses are situated. This mass of stones is composed of irregular stone blocks jumbled and jammed together and varying enormously in size. Smaller stones may be next to massive blocks measuring 5 m or more in length. The whole area is covered with stone and has very little surface vegetation apart from small pockets of blueberry, heather, and grass. Midway up this stone jungle there is a cave-like structure, known as Hellaren (Figure 2.11A). This is composed of an enormous block on the northeast side and a tumble of smaller blocks on the southwest side and to the back. The roof consists of a flattish inclined slab, partly resting on the northeast side and dipping down to the southwest. This forms an irregular space about 2.7 m wide and 3.5 m deep. At the highest point the roof is 1.10 m high. Besides Hellaren, there are numerous other, smaller chamber-like spaces and passages within the tumble of stones midway up the slope.

Within Hellaren itself there are a number of carvings. On the left hand wall of the cave, towards the back, there is an indistinct image that somewhat resembles an anthropomorph. A loose stone, found within the cave and now in the Bergen Museum, has other engravings on it. To the right of the cave entrance there is a narrow passage through the tumble of boulders, and through here it is possible to crawl in and out of the cave space. One of the stones is decorated with a series of pecked lines, making a geometric pattern. Although this image is very fragmentary, its box-like form may suggest it was intended to be a deer.

The entrance to the cave faces westwards, and from here one can look down across the jumble of stones and along the Vingen terrace as far as the upper part of the Hammaren rock. Below, a cluster of four late Mesolithic house structures is visible (Figure 2.5). The situation of the cave relatively high up the slope provides a spatial awareness of the distribution of the stones below, which is not at all apparent while moving up, along, and through them.

Besides in the cave interior, there are many other decorated stones among the blocks within the Urane area. The carvings may be found on large or very small stone blocks. Some may be carved on one of the shorter sides of a stone, others on the top or upper surface, others on the broad faces. There is a complete lack of uniformity in terms of the size, shape, face or faces, or the character of the blocks that are carved. Similarly, some carved blocks are very close to each other, while others are some considerable distance away. Because of this complete lack of predictability with regard to which stones are carved and their positioning in relation to others, finding all these carvings requires an insider's intimate knowledge of place.

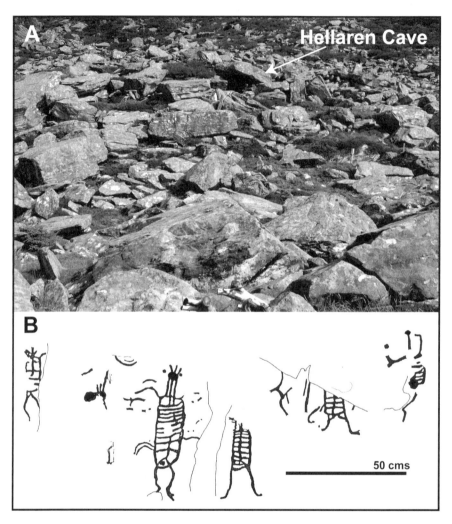

FIGURE 2.11. *A:* View upslope to the 'cave' Hellaren in the Urane rock carving area; *B:* Bøe's 'lobster people' on rock to the left of Hellaren.

Moreover, the way in which one negotiates passage through this clutter of stones determines how one encounters the different carvings.

It is impossible to move in a straight line through the boulders. One's body is constantly changing direction in the process of moving around, between, and over the stones. In addition to the larger caves, passages, and hollows between the blocks, there are numerous smaller, hidden spaces and fissures through which it is easy for a foot or a leg to slip and become trapped. This, together with the slipperiness of the stones when they are wet, makes moving through the boulder field extremely hazardous. For example, one of us, stepping backwards to look at a decorated stone, fell through a hole, one leg disappearing almost to the groin. The possibility of serious injury is ever present. Movement through the stones is therefore a necessarily slow, arduous process during which one's eyes must be constantly trained on the ground. It may require clambering with the hands. To move a short distance takes a long time.

The images on these stones are often fragmentary lines, perhaps unfinished or badly eroded designs. Apart from these, the majority of the images are of deer. These are usually depicted individually, occasionally in pairs. Stylistically they resemble the deer at Vingeneset and Elva, animals with curving backs and outstretched legs and infilled bodies, apparently in movement. The majority have their heads to the right or the west. Only a few face east or in another direction. A smaller number of stones have 'scythe' or hook designs. Clearly identifiable depictions of deer do not occur on the same stones as those with scythes or hooks. This separation of these two primary motifs replicates that encountered on the Elva and Nedste Laegda rocks.

Apart from the deer and scythe/hook images, a couple of stones depict people. Seven meters to the northeast of the Hellaren cave entrance there is a fractured slab 2.5 m long, 2 m wide, and 1.5 m high on which there are a series of five human depictions. Bøe suggests that these are 'lobster people' (Figure 2.11B). As Hallström points out (1938: 433), the animals at Vingen are exclusively shown in profile whereas human depictions are shown face on. We can perhaps best understand these images as human beings depicted in the form of X-ray images (see the discussion below). This stone is surrounded, on all but the western side, by huge tumbled boulders that effectively enclose the slab.

Bakkane

Bakkane forms part of the Vingen terrace immediately to the west of Urane and is basically a continuation of the latter. Here, however, the area is not so densely covered with boulders. Those that occur are generally smaller and not jumbled up against one another, and there are some large clear and stone-free areas in between. In part this is due to stone clearing undertaken in the recent historical past to create small 'fields'. The carvings in this area occur on larger blocks and smaller stones, some loose. The carved designs consist, for the most part, of fragmentary deer and a few hooks, usually depicted singly either on the top or the side faces of the stones. A few stones have more than one depiction although on different faces. Two stones in this group are of particular importance.

The Bakke stone is in the northeast of the area, very close to house 3. On the southwest face of this stone, which is 2 m wide, 4.8 m long, and 2m high, there are two human figures at the top and three at the bottom. At least two appear to be phallic. All are executed in a very different style from the lobster humans discussed above, with stick-line bodies and bent or wavy legs and arms (see Figure 2.12A).

The Kålrabi stone, or turnip stone, is 10.5 m long, 5 m wide, and 3 m high. The lower part of this stone was covered with soil by the last farmer at Vingen and used to grow turnips—hence its name. Bøe, during his documentation of Vingen, had the lower part uncovered, revealing a series of important carvings. The stone is inclined

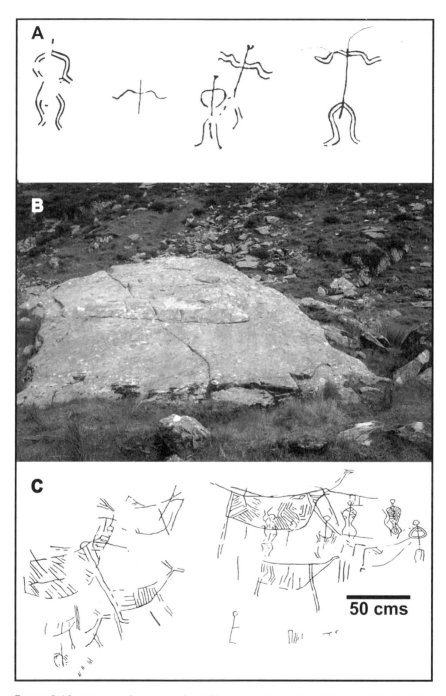

FIGURE 2.12. A: Human figures on the Bakke stone. *Source: Bøe 1932: nos. 491–93.* B: The Kålrabi stone seen from the north. C: Documentation of the bottom part of the stone. *After Bøe 1932: Taf. 18.*

from the southeast to the northwest, and the majority of the carvings occur on the lower northwest face (Figure 2.12B). This is a rock outcrop, as opposed to a fallen block, and it is surrounded by tumbled blocks on the south, west, and east sides which have tumbled down from a sheer rock face above it. A rough band of other stones with carvings runs up through the Bakkane area to this stone on the northeast side.

On the top part of the stone there are remains of some badly damaged carvings of at least four deer. Below, on the lower part of the stone, there are depictions of at least fourteen deer and five or six human figures. The latter are clustered on the western side of the panel and merge with some of the deer (Figure 2.12C). The deer are of markedly different sizes and have complex internal body decorations. All are depicted facing west. They appear to be more static than the Vingeneset and Elva carvings, and many of those on the blocks in the Urane area do not have the curving backs, although most have their front legs thrust forward. A couple of the human figures here appear more like skeletons than fleshed bodies, and they are depicted in an obviously different style from the carvings in Urane or on the Bakke stone to the south. As usual at Vingen, these human figures are shown facing front rather than in profile. These human depictions are peculiarly static, almost ghost-like in appearance. Standing beneath the stone one can see all these images at once by simply moving the head from left to right or vice versa.

Brattebakken

About 50 m west of the Kålrabi stone there is a major carved panel, Brattebakken. This is in the approximate centre of the Vingen rock carving area, and from it the summit of Hornelen is fully visible. This is the first major carved rock, moving westwards from which the Hornelen summit can be seen. Brattebakken and the Hellaren cave are out of sight from the Kålrabi stone and other carved rocks to the east. The full extent of the stone exposure is almost 30 m long and 11 m broad. The picture field occupies a much smaller part of the central and western part of the stone and extends across an area of 14 m by 8 m. To the south of Brattebakken the land rises up steeply at approximately the same angle as the rock outcrop itself. This area upslope is covered by a huge spread of tumbled boulders, and beyond this the mountain rises steeply in a series of cliff faces. To the north of the stone there is a small gully across the terrace in an area covered with smaller and larger boulders and blocks, now partially cleared to make open areas for grazing.

The images begin at the very bottom of the rock face, which is at an angle of about 45 degrees and has east–west glacial striations and slight grooves running across it, allowing easy movement up and down and across the rock, which is also crossed by a series of minor diagonal cracks. Water flows intermittently across the central part of the carving area, in precisely the area where the largest and most complex images occur, enlivening them.

The principal carvings here (about 120 in total) consist of zigzag and curvilinear lines, geometric arrangements of lines, large numbers of deer, a hook figure, and at least six human figures. Almost all the deer, with only nine exceptions, are

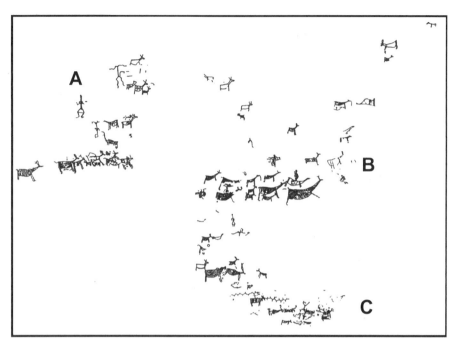

FIGURE 2.13. Carvings on the central area of Brattebakken. *Source: Bakka, unpublished documentation.* Letters refer to different groups of carvings discussed in the text.

FIGURE 2.14. Hermaphrodite human figure in area A (see Figure 2.13A) of Brattebakken.

depicted with their heads to the west. The deer facing east are all small and, with only a couple of exceptions, are carved in outline and without complex internal body decoration. The largest, most visually dominant and most complex animals all face west.

Three areas with carvings can be distinguished in the central area of the rock (Figure 2.13A–C). At the far western end, about 11 m distant from these, is another panel consisting of a group of at least ten deer all facing west. The principal motif in area A, which is 2.3 m up the slope from the bottom of the rock, is deer, three facing east, the rest to the west. Somewhat isolated from these animals is a striking human figure with bent legs and arms which appears to be a hermaphrodite (Figure 2.14). To the west of this, but extending slightly farther down the rock face, is area B, which contains the largest, most complex, and striking and visually dominant animals. These are all facing west. Two of the deer have human riders facing to the front. These, together with a more ambiguous human figure above, are similar in form to the depictions of humans on the Kålrabi stone (Figure 2.15). The deer depicted here are markedly different in style from those at Vingeneset and Elva. The backs are either straight or only slightly curved, the internal body decoration is

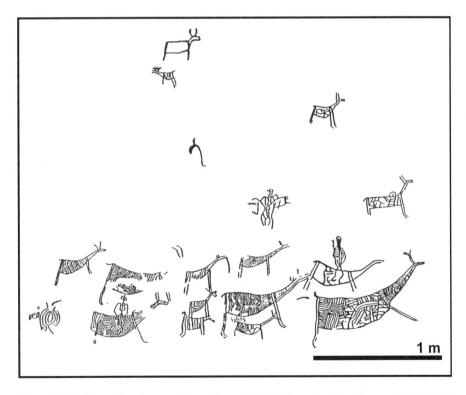

FIGURE 2.15. Deer riders in area B (see Figure 2.13) of Brattebakken. *Source: Bakka 1973: fig. 4.*

much more differentiated and complex, and the necks are more highly elaborated. The front legs are thrust forwards as if in motion, but the back legs are much more static.

Below this panel, area C has at least two human figures, one of which is very similar to the human in area A, the other a partial stick-line representation. The deer images are much simpler than those that occur above, and they appear to be peculiarly static compared with those associated with the deer riders above. These occur together with zigzag lines with offsets at right angles and geometric designs.

Standing in front of Brattebakken below area C, most of the images here are visible, along with the group of ten deer at the western end of the rock. To view the images one looks down or straight ahead, except for those farthest up the rock which require an upward movement of the head to see them. However, to see the images in detail one must move up the rock surface and, following the dominant directionality of the animals, move from east to west along the rock. This therefore requires entering into and becoming part of the image fields.

Considering the rock as a whole, small and generally peripheral animals move east, but the dominant directionality is west. At the eastern end of the rock, deer and humans are differentiated. In the centre deer riders are associated with the most complex and striking animals, the largest and most complex of which lead the herd forwards. At the western end humans are absent and the animals are simpler in form. All the deer on this panel are individualised. No two are exactly alike. This is also the case with the human figures. There is a changing progression of humans as one moves up the rock face and from the west to the east. The two lowest humans are stick figures, the uppermost with frog-like legs. The deer riders have internal body differentiation but, unlike the deer, resemble skeletal forms.

The highest human to the east, also with frog legs, appears to be ambiguously sexually marked as hermaphrodite and is spatially separated from the deer. While the deer are depicted in what appear to be close-knit kin groups—with larger and smaller and perhaps older and younger animals, male and female—the human figures are relatively isolated from one another. The two figures most closely related are those riding the deer, one towards the front of the group, the other towards the back.

Leitet

Leitet is a small area with rock outcrops about 40 m west of Brattebakken and, like the latter, is situated immediately below an extensive boulder and scree slope. Here a series of twelve engraved rock outcrops and stones have been documented, with a total of 339 motifs (Lødøen and Mandt in preparation). These fall into two main groups. A group of four north-facing panels occur in the western part of the area. These are all small and constitute single visual fields seen from below and looking across the rocks. These are separated by distances of between 1.5 and 12 m. On the largest engraved panel (Leitet 10), covering an area of about 2 by 2 m, about 26

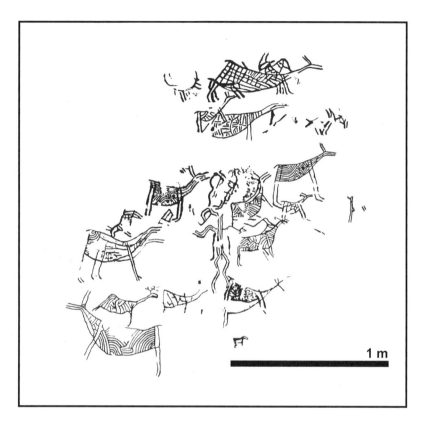

FIGURE 2.16. Leitet 10: 'Frog human' in the centre of deer images. *Source: Mandt and Lødøen 2005.*

images occur. Deer dominate, all facing west, except for the lowest animal which faces east. Their complex internal body ornamentation is very similar to that encountered on Brattebakken. In the centre of the panel is one large and striking headless human depiction with curved, frog-like legs and arms which appears to be dancing amidst the deer. This figure is located at the centre of the group of deer, all of which have a striking degree of individuation (Figure 2.16). To the west, 3.5 m away, another panel depicts a human figure of very different form and posture, together with three hooks of similar size. Twelve meters to the east of Leitet 10, another panel depicts another human figure with a strikingly large head, like that of a baby in proportion to the body size, and associated with deer.

The eastern group of panels are dominated by hook images; at least 123 images are depicted on eight panels. Only two of these panels depict deer (four and nineteen animals, respectively). These animals are smaller and have much less elaborate internal body decoration than those on Leitet 10, and the majority face to the east. There is a striking degree of superimposition of the hook and the deer motifs. The

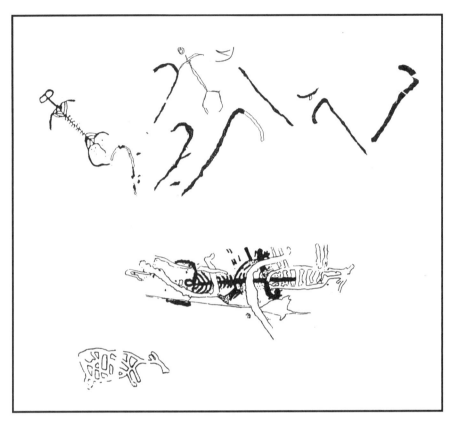

FIGURE 2.17. Human images and hooks from different areas of Leitet 8. (*Above*): Skeletal human and stick-line human with 'frog' legs. (*Below*): Skeletal human with superimposed deer and hooks. *Source: Lødøen and Mandt n.d.*

hooks in groups and rows are depicted in a wide variety of different orientations, encouraging complex patterns of movement in and around the image fields (now unfortunately—from the point of view of this analysis—covered with turf for conservation purposes). Of the eight panels, three also depict human figures. All occur highest up the slope to the south on the margins of the boulders and scree. One human occurs on the southwest face of a loose stone (on which a hook is also depicted); the figure has tentacles rather than a head, short curved legs, and long hanging arms. Leitet 6 depicts a stick-line human in close association with three hooks at the top of the panel, separated from superimposed hook and deer motifs below and a skeletal torso also associated with hooks. Panel 8 has three human images, a stick-line figure, and two striking skeletons. All are closely associated with hooks, and one of the skeletons merges with an upside-down deer motif and is superimposed with hooks (see Figure 2. 17).

Ved Vatnet (By the Pond)

The pond is located towards the western end of the Vingen terrace, roughly equidistant between the major carved rocks Vehammaren and Hardbakken. The pond is roughly circular in form and about 20 m in diameter (Figure 2.18). It is fed by a waterfall that plunges over the top of the mountain to the south and then cascades over a series of sheer cliffs before disappearing into a dense scree slope to the south and then entering the pond and flowing out into the fjord. The presence of this freshwater pond is a magical part of the experience of place at Vingen. Standing on the southern side of the pond, the peak of Hornelen is mirrored in it (Figure 2.19). If the pond were been slightly farther to the east, this would not occur. It is possible to touch the peak of Hornelen mirrored in the still waters of the pond. From the northern side of the pond, the towering mountainside above the Vingen terrace is mirrored across its surface. From the southwest Tussurfjellet appears. This is the place where the three mountains meet, touch one another, and merge in one place, where the inverted mountain peaks meet the land below, otherwise separate and remote. The Vingen fjord waters, when they occasionally become smooth and glassy, also have such mirroring effects, giving visual substance to the form of the mountains in relation to the fjord's depth. As the mountain cliffs of Tussurfjellet and Hornelen plunge down into the water, their forms effectively become visible, plunging farther downwards as reflection. The substance of water here becomes rock.

However, the pond is the place where one may touch the mountains from the land. The circular form of the pond allows movement around its perimeter, and the sight of the mountain world within it becomes transformed and brought closer. The pond, in effect, fuses together the three most striking and significant elements of Vingen as a place: the enclosing towering mountains to the north and to the south, and the sacred peak of Hornelen. The pond, unlike the fjord, provides a permanent mirror of the mountains when the weather is clear, allowing contact with the peak of Hornelen mirrored in its surface.

In brief dry spells during the summer, when the pond is no longer being filled from the cascading waterfall above, it may almost dry out. Below the water there is a mass of rounded stones and boulders. The pond and its stones have never been excavated or more than superficially examined. If there is a place at Vingen where we might expect to find votive offerings, this is surely it. Nearly everywhere around and in the pond, carvings have been found on loose stones. Some have undoubtedly been brought there in recent historical times in order to clear the land for pasture. Others may originally have been carved *in situ*. Rock outcrops to the west of the pond and to its north are also decorated. Some of these rocks too are mirrored in the pond's surface, but none are large or complex panels. The images carved on these loose boulders and irregular rock outcrops around the pond include hook or stave designs, usually single but sometimes in pairs or small groups, and deer, again usually single but sometimes in small groups. Almost all are orientated to the east. All the deer depictions are small in size, about 10–20 cm long. For the most part they are rather schematic in form and lack complex internal body decoration. The

FIGURE 2.18. The pond seen from Vehammaren to the southwest looking across the Vingen terrace.

FIGURE 2.19. Hornelen reflected in the Vingen pond.

hook/stave designs and the animals are almost always carved on different stones. They are only occasionally directly associated with each other on the same carved panel. The deer are depicted in a variety of different forms. Some are carved in outline without any internal body decoration. Others have simple straight, diagonal, or crisscross lines. A few are entirely pecked out of the rock. The majority with straight front and back legs appear peculiarly static. Only a few appear to be in motion. As in the great boulder fields of the Urane area to the east, there is an unpredictability here in terms of the sizes and types of stones or rock outcrops on which carvings occur and which sides or faces of the stones were chosen.

Hardbakken North

The great rock, Hardbakken, is situated about 20 m north of the pond. It is about 50 m long, its long axis orientated west–east. The northern face of this rock is huge, slopes down at an angle of about 45 degrees for about 8.5 m, and appears most impressive from the Vingen fjord (Figure 2.20). In the late Mesolithic the fjord waters would have lapped around its western end. The rock face has a series of glacial striations running along it from east to west, forming in place a series of parallel, shallow grooves up to 10 cm in width, along which it is possible to move horizontally along the rock face, or to climb up it. The rock face is also subdivided at irregular intervals by a series of minor and larger cracks, which run diagonally

FIGURE 2.20. The north face of Hardbakken seen from the east, looking along the Vingen fjord. The north face of Vehammaren is beyond, and house 7 is marked by the flag in the foreground.

down it from the south–southwest to the north–northeast. The 128 carved images are dispersed along the northern rock face for a distance of about 35 m from the eastern end. The western end of the rock is very shattered and broken, and no carvings have been found here. Apart from deer, which make up the overwhelming majority of the carvings, five humans, one oval, and eight hook/scythes have been recorded. All but one of the humans are in peripheral positions, low down on the rock, four at the western end. All the hooks are closely associated with deer and overlap or merge with them. There are a few minor deer images low down near the bottom of the rock, but the majority form two east–west dispersed bands: a lower band visible standing at the base of the rock, and an upper one to which one must climb. Viewing these images necessitates both vertical movement up the rock face and east–west movement along it.

The deer occur in a wide variety of different styles and postures. They are usually depicted either on their own or in groups of two to four animals. The majority face towards the west or right, but a few face east. There are two larger groups of deer. One is in the middle of the rock towards the western end of the carved area. This is the largest and most elaborate group of animals with the most complex internal body decoration, similar in style to the largest animals on Brattebakken. These are associated with hook designs pointing both west and east (Figure 2.21). One of the deer overlaps with a phallic human 'frog' figure with bent arms and legs. Next to it is another partial human figure. The second large group of deer is found near the far eastern end of the rock face towards the top. This consists of at least nine fragmentary animals with their heads to the east.

FIGURE 2.21. Deer and hook images towards the western end of the carved area of Hardbakken.

Apart from the images already mentioned, another two frog-like humans occur low down the rock surface at the far western end, associated with two deer whose heads face west. About 8.5 m from the western end, three hooks facing west and one hook facing east are associated with a central west-facing deer.

One of the surprising features of Hardbakken North is the relative paucity of carvings and their scattered dispersion across the rock surface, with large areas left uncarved. Another is the close association of hook/scythe and animal carvings on some areas of the rock surface, motifs that are usually separated.

Hardbakken South

The grassy land surface below Hardbakken dips down to the west, and the back or south face of Hardbakken is exposed over a distance of 18 m, providing increasingly large panels on which images are carved. To the east of this area, only the very top of the stone is exposed, and Hardbakken lacks a back surface. The stone is laterally divided by cracks forming a series of distinct image fields which are all meant to be viewed standing in front of the stone on the southern side. Hornelen is visible along the whole of Hardbakken, but while one must stand with one's back to the mountain to view the images on the northern face, one faces the mountain on the southern side.

The sequence of 34 images—all of which are of deer, except for a couple of small and faint hook/scythe designs and a spiral (documented by Bakka but not seen by us)—starts at the far western end with a striking panel depicting around eleven deer, many of which are fragmentary and all but one of which face east. Here the second largest deer depicted at Vingen occurs; about 1.3 m long, it is deeply incised and has complex internal body and neck ornamentation (Figure 2.22). It contrasts with the other animals on this rock, which lack internal body decoration and are smaller and much more fragmentary. This panel employs a range of scales and styles. The large central deer has bent legs but is not depicted in vigorous motion (Figure 2.22). Immediately above this panel and to the east, another small animal faces west. Another small deer is depicted on a rectangular panel facing west, 5 m from the western end of the rock. Above this a few more small and fragmentary animals face east. Beyond there are fragmentary lines and remains of another animal moving east. At 13 m from the western end, the ground surface has risen alongside the rock. This allows an observer to look down over the top of the rock and see the fjord beyond. At this point there are a group of at least six animals facing east. At 16 m from the western end, the ground surface has almost risen to the same level as the top of the stone, allowing the viewer to look down onto the top of the stone upon which is a complex scene of at least eleven deer, all facing east. These images are defined in outline for the most part; only some have vertical internal body decoration. Just over the crest of the top of the stone are two further deer images, facing west, but these are part of the north-facing slope and as such are upside down and meant to be seen from the northern side. These two groups of animals in close proximity but inverted in terms of their positioning on the rock announce the switch in viewing directionality. It is at this point that the south side

FIGURE 2.22. Large deer image at the western end of Hardbakken South. Vingeneset and Hornelen are visible across the Vingen fjord.

of Hardbakken expires and the massive extent of the northern face first becomes evident. Moving farther east along the top of the rock exposure, a series of images can be seen below, all upside down. On the very top of the rock and situated above the large group of deer images at the western end of the northern face of Hardbakken, there is an isolated and arresting skeletal human image, head to the east (Figure 2.23). Another very similar human image occurs on the south side of an isolated stone block situated 3.5 m to the south of the far western end of Hardbakken.

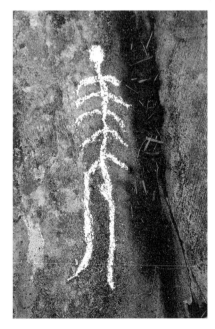

FIGURE 2.23. Chalked skeletal human image on the top of Hardbakken.

Teigen

Beyond the point at which Hardbakken loses its southern face, there are a series of three roughly parallel lines of rocks which outcrop to the south of it and to the north of the pond. Those with animal and scythe/hook images in the immediate vicinity of the pond have already been discussed. There is another carved rock here of particular importance, located immediately to the south of the approximate centre of the north face of Hardbakken. This is a massive rock outcrop on top of which one can stand and look down on the pond. The southern, higher side of this rock is reflected in the pond when one stands on its edge on the western side. Along a smooth north-facing panel of this rock 4.5 m long and 1.3 m high at the highest point, there is a striking series of images: four animals and at least 22 hook designs (Figure 2.24). The largest animal at the eastern end of this panel faces west, its body entirely pecked out. Two more schematic animals at the western end face west too, and another near the top and middle of the panel faces east. Almost all the hooks are orientated to point towards the east. This panel constitutes a single visual field. Nowhere else is there such a massing of hook designs in the entire Vingen carving area, making this panel quite exceptional. It is noteworthy that all these images occur on a small northern face of the stone facing the fjord and that they point east. None occur on the top of this rock outcrop or on its southern, higher face mirrored in the pond.

Moving farther to the east there are a series of 22 carved rocks and stones. The design fields are all small, covering areas of outcropping rocks or stones 1 m or less in size. Some of these panels depict both hooks and animals, which may face either east or west; others show only a few animals or hooks in groups. Six humans are

FIGURE 2.24. Deer and hook images on the stone surface of Teigen 1 immediately to the south of Hardbakken. *Source: Bøe 1932: nos. 405–35.*

also depicted, three in skeletal form; and as at Leitet, most are closely associated with hooks (see discussion below). As is the case in the area around the pond and in the Bakkane and Urane areas of Vingen, it is quite unpredictable which faces of which stones will have carvings on them. An insider's knowledge is required to find and move between them.

Vehammaren North Face

Vehammaren is an impressive rock exposure about 100 m in length, its long axis orientated east–west, jutting out into the Vingen fjord at its western end. The highest point, on the western part, is about 20 m above sea level. The northern face of the rock slopes down at an angle of 45 degrees and is exposed above present-day ground level for about 16 m at the western end and 12 m at the eastern end. This rock towers over and dwarfs a person standing at its base and is a highly visible landmark when seen from Hornelen and Frøysjoen to the northwest. It is in effect a larger and more dramatic version of Hardbakken (Figure 2.25). The western end of this ridge is divided horizontally by a grass-covered ledge, and above this ledge the rock face is covered with carvings. These run across the rock face from east to west, the outermost figure being only 4 m from the extreme western end of the ridge. The total length of the carvings is about 35 m, and their width up and across the sloping rock surface is about 14 m. Hallström (1938) and Bøe (1932) document around 135 different carvings on the western end of the rock.

The carvings across the rock face are, for the most part, in clearly defined groups subdivided by vertical or diagonal cracks. Running west–east horizontally across this face are strong glacial striation lines, breaking up the surface somewhat and allowing one to climb up the rock surface more easily. Thus this rock, like so many others at Vingen, has an in-built directionality not only in terms of its overall east–west orientation but also in terms of the micro-topography of its surface in relation to which the carvings conform.

The carvings occur in two main east–west bands running along the rock face. In order to see the lower band of carvings one must move east to west along the terrace and look across and up at the images. The upper band of carvings is almost invisible from below. This is because the rock is inclined at an angle of 45 degrees, and so it slopes back and away from an observer below; to see them requires moving up and across the rock surface from east to west or west to east below them (Figure 2.26). There is an asymmetry here in that the lower band continues along the rock face farther to the west, while the upper band continues farther to the east. In addition, the upper band, for the most part, is relatively narrow, with most of the deer covering only a 1-m wide band of the rock, whereas the animals in the lower band are much more widely dispersed, covering an area up to 3.5 m. The two bands are separated by an uncarved area about 4 m wide.

Effectively, the carvings in the lower band are relatively easy to see and approach from the terrace below, compared with the upper band, which is less accessible. From the top, the rock falls away precipitously. The carvings in the upper

FIGURE 2.25. Wayne Bennett on the north face of Vehammaren.

FIGURE 2.26. Looking along the north face of Vehammaren towards the west.

band are, with only a few exceptions, situated well below the very top of the rock face, about 5 m down. Movement down the rock face from the top to see these images is very difficult compared with upward movement. The horizontal glacial striations forming a series of closely set ledges and gentle protuberances can be used very effectively as a kind of fragmented ladder for moving up the rock face and along it. Due to the angle of the slope, these 'steps' cannot be so readily seen or grasped with either the hands or the feet. Approached from the top, all the images appear upside down, and one cannot view them right side up until one has moved over the image field and turned around (if moving forward down the rock). The most likely way to approach these images may therefore have been from below.

The images in the upper band consist entirely of deer images, all but four of which face to the west. The lower band also consists entirely of deer (all but two of which, at the far western end, face west), except for a bird (?) figure and a human figure at the eastern end. The majority of the deer are small, about 20–30 cm long, and relatively unelaborated in terms of internal body decoration. The only larger animals occur in the lower band. All these deer, compared with those depicted elsewhere at Vingen, appear strikingly static, with straight front and back legs. Only a few with curving front legs might be described as in motion, but even in these cases it is interesting to note that the legs curve backwards. They are not thrust forwards in the style of the depictions at Vingeneset, Elva, Brattebakken, and elsewhere. On this, the most westerly carved rock in the main Vingen rock carving area, the motion of the deer appears as arrested (Figure 2.27). As elsewhere, the deer are depicted in groups of variable size, between two to ten animals

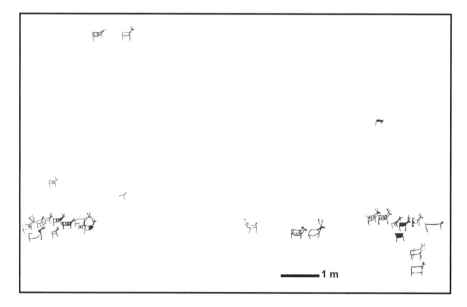

FIGURE 2.27. Part of the upper group of deer images running along the upper part of the north face of Vehammaren. *After Hallström 1938: pl. XLI.*

in the upper band of carvings. In a few cases, larger and more elaborate animals are depicted in the front of the groups.

Farther to the east there are other groups of carvings on the north, or front, face of Hammaren. These occur much lower down the rock surface and again run in clearly defined east–west bands across it. All the 31 identifiable images here are of deer facing west, except in two cases. They can be seen from the bottom of the rock but require east–west movement along it in order to follow the succession. As with the animals farther to the west, these are small and mostly static depictions.

It is possible to walk along the very top of most of the northern face of Vehammaren. Here there are two further isolated panels with carvings, separated from those previously discussed. One is a richly decorated panel 3 m wide and 1.5 m high. The images contrast markedly with those lower down on the main rock exposure. They consist of five deer in motion, with curved backs and front legs thrust forwards and all facing west. The other depicts a series of eight hooks orientated to face east. These occur on a small depression on the very top of the ridge, clearly separated from the deer images below on the northern face. Their hidden presence above the deer images, together with the difference in directional orientation, constitutes a significant contrast.

Bak Vehammaren

In contrast to the almost continuous sequence of deer depictions on the north face of Vehammaren overlooking the Vingen fjord, the depictions on the back of this rock occur on broken and separated rock outcrops, facing both to the south and the north. These occur in three or four parallel but discontinuous and rough east–west bands behind the ridgetop on more or less flat ground and running down a slope to terminate towards the west and by the sea. Immediately to the south of these carvings there is a broad band of tumbled boulders which is sandwiched between braided waterfalls to the west and the east, both of which run through dense scree slopes and fans below the sheer cliffs of the mountain. All these carvings, with the exception of a few minor images such as an isolated oval design, do not occur on the tumbled blocks derived from the mountainside to the south, but are along the southern tilted strata of the Vehammaren rock itself. These dip away at angles of up to 45 degrees but are only exposed for about 1–3 m above ground level. Clearly it was inappropriate to decorate the tumbled boulders in this area, given the enormous symbolic significance of the Vehammaren ridge itself. The tumbled blocks from the mountainside were almost entirely avoided, duplicating the situation on Vingeneset.

Here there are about 150 images in total, only slightly fewer than on the broad northern faces of Vehammaren. These occur on 35 different panels or individual rocks. The vast majority of the images are of deer: about 120 images together with sixteen hooks, five humans, one depiction of a whale, a possible single whale, and dog images, together with indistinct pecked lines. The deer face both to the west and to the east. This, together with the greater variety of kinds of images, clearly differentiates the northern and southern sides of the rock. The front face of Vehammaren presents a relatively coherent and public, certainly monumental visual display. The images on the back of the rock are both discontinuous and varied, and this is reflected in their manner and substance.

While the carvings on the north face of Vehammaren dictate a particular and rather structured pattern of bodily movement from east to west and up and along the rock face, the carved rocks along the back of Vehammaren, by contrast, allow considerable freedom in the sequence in which they are encountered and in bodily movement and posture. On the back or southern side, therefore, there is the possibility of a greater degree of polysemy in terms of the meanings attributed to any particular sequential structure of the images encountered.

The eastern end of this group is marked by a north-facing rock outcrop upon which there are a few carved hooks and lines. To the east of these, the waterfall flowing down to the Vingen pond cuts through the scree. These are, in effect, an outlier of the main sequence of designs on the front face of Hammaren. In order to reach these carvings one must climb up from the Vingen terrace below, up a fissured, sloping, and irregular rock face. From these images one moves west, climbing up a slope between fallen blocks and entering into the space of the boulder field on the south side of Vehammaren (Figure 2.28). The next image occurs on a fallen block 1.9 m high and 1.3 m wide, leaning at an angle of 45 degrees on the back of the Vehammaren outcrop. Here there is an image of a small animal facing west. Moving westwards for 48 m, twisting and turning through large fallen blocks, all undecorated, one arrives at the first major sequence of carved rocks (rocks

FIGURE 2.28. Looking east along the higher eastern end of Bak Vehammaren.

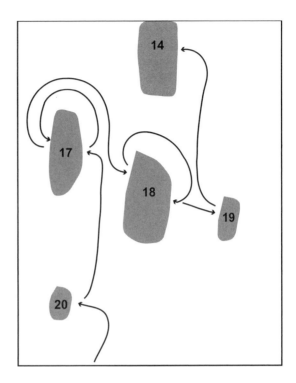

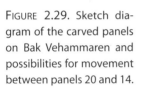

FIGURE 2.29. Sketch diagram of the carved panels on Bak Vehammaren and possibilities for movement between panels 20 and 14.

14–20) (Figure 2.29). Rock 20 is decorated with three images of hooks, all orientated to the east. One looks down on these images. From this point, a series of other rock faces with images are visible. Moving onwards from here one must start making choices regarding routes between the rocks themselves and the individual north- or south-facing carved panels on them. For example, walking farther west for 5 m one encounters rocks 17 and 18 to the left and right, respectively. Both these rocks have faces to the north and south on which there are carvings.

Particular patterns of bodily movement here between the carved panels are determined by improvised decisions to look at designs on particular rocks in sequences that are not self-evident but require subjective choices. The body-subject must decide, for instance, whether to see both faces of the same rock before moving to view another rock, which requires moving forward and turning around, or alternatively, seeing panels facing in the same direction on different rocks. Figure 2.29 shows one way to move between these panels. Here there is an obvious dialectic between, on the one hand, a degree of individual choice and, on the other, the physical positioning of the carvings dictating how it is possible to encounter them. The images on these rocks are of deer pointing either west or east, depicted together with a hook on one of the faces of rock 18.

Rock 14, with 40 figures on its surface, is the largest and most elaborately decorated panel. The rock is 12 m long with a 4-m-wide north-facing surface, 1 m high on the southern side. The northern face of the rock, across the whole of which the images occur, is broken and irregular. At the eastern end images also occur lower down on a broken part of the face. To see the designs requires east–west movement along the base of the rock to the north and between this panel and the front (northern) face of Vehammaren which, despite its close proximity, is invisible. The deer depicted here face both to the west and the east, and a small whale is depicted low down on the rock pointing west. The separate panel measuring 1.2 by 0.9 m on the eastern end of the rock can only be seen up close by standing on the rock itself and leaning backwards against the inclined mass of the main rock itself. Here there are depicted deer which at the western and eastern ends are pointing in different directions. Two humans are depicted centrally in between them. Rocks 9–12 represent a final arrangement of carved panels at the western and highest end of the back of Vehammaren. These are all north-facing panels decorated with deer facing both east and west, and rock 12 has two small stick-line human figures. The remainder of the carved rocks in the sequence are all on south-facing rocks which occur along the sides of a steep gully on the southern and far western end of Vehammaren. Here there are images of deer facing west and east; and on from rock 1, farthest to the west, there are also six hooks/scythes, all but one orientated to the east (Hallström 1938: pl. VI:97). Most of the animals on these rocks are rather small and fragmentary. There are a wide variety of different styles of depiction. Some animals are similar to those on the front face of Vehammaren: rather static and lifeless. Others, with arched backs and front legs thrust forwards, appear in vigorous motion.

FIGURE 2.30. The rocking stone on Bak Vehammaren with concealed carvings beneath it.

Apart from the images on these rock outcrops, there is a huge tumbled block, fallen here from the mountain above and resting on the dipping bedrock of Vehammaren. It is 3.3 m high and 1.5 to 2.6 m wide (Figure 2.30). When pushed hard, the rock tilts slightly. On the western side the block is slightly raised above the underlying bedrock. Remarkably, there are pecked designs concealed underneath this block: two animals and a simple human figure.

Body Kinaesthetics and the Carving Surfaces

It is striking just how different the rocks carved at Vingen are from one another. If, for example, we compare the front (northern) face of Vehammaren and Elva, at the far western and eastern ends of the rock carving area, we find that these are effectively structural inversions of each other both in terms of the choice of rock, the manner in which the images are encountered, and the character of the depictions (virtually all deer in both cases):

VEHAMMAREN	ELVA
North-facing rock	South-facing rock
Horizontal imagery	Diagonal/vertical imagery
Seawater below	Freshwater below
On ridge	Above gorge
Deer highest to west	Deer highest to east
Deer face west	Deer face east
Deer static	Deer in motion
Sea at end of carvings	Sea at beginning
Moving along the rock	Climbing up the rock

By contrast, the character of the rocks Vehammaren and Hardbakken, with their front and back faces and the way both are bodily encountered, is almost identical. Here there is repetition in terms of both the character of the rocks and the manner in which movement occurs in relation to the front and back faces: structured with limited choice on the front face, and much more latitude and freedom for moving in different ways along the back. What differs on these rocks is primarily the form and character of the carvings. On Vehammaren there is only a single human figure; five occur on Hardbakken, where a series of hook designs occur, absent from the front (north) face of Vehammaren.

We have seen that the rock carving surfaces at Vingen are constantly changing in character throughout the rock carving area. The main distinctions that can be drawn are the following:

1. Huge rock exposures versus small boulders.

2. Continuous rock faces versus discontinuous panels.

3. High rock faces versus low rock faces.

4. Carvings on outcropping bedrock versus carvings on tumbled boulders.

5. Easily accessible and visible carvings versus carvings hidden in caves and crevices and under boulders.

6. Carvings on north-facing versus south-facing rocks.

7. Carvings associated with the fjord and saltwater versus carvings associated with waterfalls and the pond and freshwater.

Viewing the images on these rocks requires radically different kinds of bodily motion or stasis, as discussed above.

DESIGN FORM

Deer Imagery

We have seen that the depictions of deer at Vingen are stylistically very different from one area to another throughout the rock carving area. Deer images are not only dominant quantitatively throughout the Vingen rock carving area, but include by far the largest, most elaborate, diverse, and complex of the individual images. On one analytical level we can refer to distinctive carving styles in terms of depictions that appear generically similar to each other. These are named after the rock carving areas on which they dominate. Overall, three main different styles of deer imagery can be defined:

- *The Elva/Vingeneset style* (Figures 2.4, 2.6, 2.9). These animals have a strongly arched back and stomach, and a long neck. The back and neck-line are continuous. The front legs are thrust forwards, while the back legs are either straight or strongly curved forwards. The entire body is usually internally decorated with straight, curving, or hatched lines, but these are not usually dense. The necks are usually undecorated. Most have two long ears or horns. These animals are the sole type at Elva and are common on the Vingeneset rock panels and in the Urane boulder field below the Hellaren cave. A variant occurs on Nedste Laegda, where entire bodies are pecked out rather than internally decorated.

- *The Brattebakken/Hardbakken style* (Figures 2.4, 2.12C, 2.13B, 2.15, 2.21, 2.22). These animals have a straight or only slightly curved back and stomach and dense and extremely complex internal body ornamentation which may also extend over the entire neck. Parallel, curved, and hatched lines are used to differentiate different parts of the body and the neck. They have two pairs of front and back leg lines. The back legs are straight, and the front legs point forwards. Most possess two long ears or tines. These animals dominate on Brattebakken, Hardbakken, the Kålrabi stone, and Leitet. Some occur on Vingeneset, including the largest deer in the entire Vingen rock carving area (Figure 2.7).

■ *The Vehammaren style* (Figure 2.27). These animals have straight or only slightly curved front and back legs. The body is usually either rectangular or only slightly curved. Many have only a single front and back leg line, others have pairs. Some have no internal body decoration. Others have a very simple series of straight, diagonal, curved, or hatched lines. The neck is usually not decorated. The internal body decoration is never intense in the manner of the Brattebakken/Hardbakken style. The back and front parts of the body are sometimes clearly differentiated by the presence/absence of decoration or different types of infill. A very few are pecked out entirely. Some clearly possess antlers. As well as on the front and back of Vehammaren, animals of this style occur on both the front and back faces of Hardbakken, on Brattebakken, in the area around the pond, in the Bakkane area, and on blocks in the Urane boulder field.

Defining such broad style groups at Vingen is an exercise fraught with problems. Some animals cannot be easily classified in terms of any of these groups. Others might be regarded as transitional between one and another. Bøe attempted to define eight different groups (Bøe 1932: 28–31), whereas Hallström (1938: 451–52) has six and Bakka (1975) four (see discussion above). All three men were interested in these questions of style solely in terms of chronology rather than of what such styles, however defined, might mean and what effects they had—which are the very different questions I am interested in addressing. The notion that chronology explains anything, that the manner in which the deer are represented is simply a matter of changing styles over time, is first of all just a presupposition. Second, it tells us precious little about the Vingen rock carvings, their relationship to the very different rocks on which they are carved, or their bodily effects, or their iconographic significance to the people who made, used, and understood them. It is, in fact, a way of avoiding having to address these questions—which is, no doubt, the reason why it has appealed to so many.

It is important to recognize that notwithstanding these very general stylistic similarities and differences outlined above, the individual images of particular animals differ significantly from one another. I have been unable to find any two absolutely identical animals in the Vingen rock carving area. On each rock panel, carved rock face, or carving area, the deer are individuated in a number of different ways. Furthermore, how these animals are individuated is related to the particular style in which they are carved. The primary ways in which they are individuated are as follows:

■ In terms of size: from about 15 cm to 2 m.
■ In terms of body posture: angle and degree of curvature of body, neck, and legs.
■ In terms of numbers of legs.
■ In terms of sex and/or seasonal indicators: the presence or absence of antlers and ears or tines.

- Whether they appear to be in movement or static.
- In terms of directionality: which direction they face.
- In terms of types and intensity and complexity of internal body decoration.
- In terms of whether they occur alone or in groups of different sizes.

The deer are both the same and different: a class of animals (the same) stylistically differentiated across Vingen but nevertheless retaining their individual differences. Although it is unlikely that deer were more important than a seasonal subsistence resource, they nevertheless provided an ideal metaphor for expressing similarities and differences between individuals in relation to social groups and social groups in relation to one another: we are all the same yet we are also different. We have our individual characteristics yet we belong to groups that share commonalities which differ from one another. The spatial positioning of the deer on individual panels (in terms of high/low; front/back; left/right; west/east; centre/periphery) may be more complex expressions of social relationships in terms of social hierarchies, gender, and seasonal movement and migration. At both Brattebakken and Hardbakken the most important and complex of the deer images occupy visually dominant central positions on the rocks. There is a clear hierarchy of images on these rocks. The most important images are precisely those that excite and attract the eye and exert their own visual power. These are the images that take the longest to look at, reflect on, and understand.

It is noteworthy how few of the deer depictions at Vingen show elaborate antlers or tines, and in only a very few cases can it be suggested that both ears and antlers are represented. For example, on the front (north) face of Hardbakken there is only a single animal with a full set of antlers. Unlike the others, it has a bent head and appears to be grazing (Figure 2.4, third row down, farthest to right). Mézec (1989: 15) argues that this suggests the deer are either young or are stags shown after the spring, when the antlers have just been shed but have not yet grown tines. Another simpler, more plausible alternative is that these are depictions of hinds (Mandt 1998; 2001). It is overwhelmingly female deer and their young being represented—more abstractly, a female principle. If we follow such logic from a structuralist line of reasoning, we might then claim that the hooks and scythes at Vingen are complementary male signifiers: deer is to hook as female is to male (see Tilley 1991 for an analysis of this kind in relation to elks and boats at Nämforsen in northern Sweden). Since stags are clearly represented at Vingen, albeit in small numbers, this is not an argument I think it fruitful to pursue. I want to suggest instead that the hooks and scythes have a completely different range of referents as local and regional landscape signifiers (see below).

Many of the deer images are clearly based on close observations of the behavioural repertoire of deer and inspired by them. Red deer are typically gregarious animals living in herds. These typically range in number from four or five, the minimal social unit, to 30 animals. They often move in single file, with the stags at the rear and the biggest stag last of all (Burton 1969: 53). Calves, usually single, are born in June after an eight-month gestation period. The young calf has a dappled coat, but after a few months it acquires the ruddy brown winter coat of the adults, so thick that it provides protection from the worst of storms. Calves usually remain with the hinds for the first couple of years. For much of the year the stags live apart from the hinds and their young. The most notable feature of the stag is his antlers, which begin to grow when the male calf is one year old, from single horns to branching antlers of up to six points in stags over six years old. These are shed in the spring but regrow fully at a prodigious rate by the rutting season in the autumn, when the stags roar loudly and compete for dominance over groups of hinds. Red deer hinds them-selves live in groups that are hierarchical in structure, with dominant hinds heavier than subordinate hinds and their offspring more likely to survive the first year. The stags typically leave the hinds and the young while shedding and regrowing their antlers, returning during the rut when they wallow in a mixture of mud and strong scented urine, dressing themselves for the occasion (Prior 1987; Chapman 1991; Clutton-Brock et al. 1982; Buczacki ed. 2002).

There are no scenes of stag fighting, rutting, or copulation at Vingen. What, above all, is being emphasized is the sociability of these animals. While it was obvi-ously only possible to carve one or a few animals on the smaller boulders and pan-els, the deer are characteristically depicted in small groups everywhere on the larg-er rock panels and surfaces too. For example, on the higher eastern end of Elva there are four main groups of six to ten or so animals. On Brattebakken there are similar-ly four main groups or clusters of eight to twelve animals. On the north face of Hardbakken there are two main groups of similar size at the western and eastern ends of the rock. On the front (north) face of Vehammaren there are six groups along the upper part of the rock, each consisting of three to eleven animals. These are clearly separated from each other on the rock both by areas without carvings and by cracks running vertically or diagonally down the rock face. Most of the images below similarly consist of groups of animals of the same size. These all fall perfectly within the normal range of deer group size discussed above. The animals are typically depicted in one or several rows, one behind the other and facing in the same direction. Furthermore, on Vehammaren dominant stags with large branching antlers are sometimes depicted following behind groups of hinds and younger males (Figure 2.27). A similar scene occurs at the eastern end of Brattebakken (Fig-ure 2.13: area A). We know this to be typical of the way deer move.

The sociability of deer, group size, male and female differentiation, dominance structure, the growing and shedding of the stags' antlers, the blatantly sexual per-formances and fighting of males at the rut, the wearing of cosmetics—perfume and 'paint' by the males—and the fact that most hinds give birth to only a single calf, all provide a strikingly rich analogical domain of metaphorical possibilities to explore and explain the relationship between human individuals and social groups. It is not surprising that there is such a rich body of folklore associated with this animal, both in Britain and Scandinavia.

Mézec has cogently argued that the deer images at Vingen might simultaneous-ly signify (1) deer as individual animals; (2) the herd; and (3) metaphorically the principle of the clan or the social group. The images may all ultimately have to do with the relationship between the individual and the social group (Mézec 1989: 21). The internal body decorations are both stylized and extremely variable. They cannot be readily understood as X-ray images depicting either internal body organs or skeletal parts in the manner of some of the elk carvings from northern Scandinavia (Hagen 1976: 134 ff.). The internal body decoration at Vingen has the primary purpose of differentiating between individual deer and groups of deer, and may thus have a primary totemic, or classificatory, significance as signifiers of different social groups and as statements of individual and group identity. These decorations also enliven or invigorate the animals, clearly differentiating various parts of the animal such as the rear and front quarters, the neck, and the head.

Following the path of the deer images through the Vingen rock carving area suggests an overall narrative theme. At the beginning of the journey, on Vingeneset, and then through Elva, the animals are lively and in full flight. Stylistically the deer are similar from Vingeneset to the depictions encountered in the Urane boulder field. Farther along the Vingen terrace, from east to west, their motion slows. On Brattebakken, in the very middle of the Vingen terrace, the style changes, and the images, while more highly internally decorated and intense, are becoming slower. Human figures riding the deer here indicate their mythic or symbolic taming. The animals on the front of Hardbakken are similar, both in style and in terms of their slowed motion. On Vehammaren the deer mostly appear as static and motionless. Along the top of this rock this arrested motion is further indicated by the fact that the animals here only possess single back and front legs. The narrative is about control and transformation. At the beginning of the journey the east-moving deer are wild and moving freely; by the end of the journey the deer have been symbolically domesticated.

Hook and 'Scythe' Images

After deer, hook and 'scythe' images are by far the most common motifs at Vingen (Figures 2.10, 2.17, 2.21, 2.24). There are 511 in total, or 32 percent of the total number of identifiable motifs. Bøe describes the hook, or stave, motifs as being like the upper part of a walking stick with the curve at the top. The scythe motifs differ considerably in that the 'blade' is considerably wider and longer, while the 'handle' may be fairly similar in form. At Vingen, scythes uniquely predominate at Nedste Laegda and occur only sporadically westwards to the pond, where hooks predominate. In some representations, however, the difference between a 'hook' and a 'scythe' is thoroughly ambiguous: one can see either or both. These ambiguous forms all occur on tumbled blocks and boulders between Urane and the pond. No scythes occur to the west of the pond on the north face of Vehammaren or on Vingeneset.

These hook and scythe-like images are almost completely unique in the entire distribution of Norwegian prehistoric rock art, apart from the presence of a possible single motif of similar form at the Ausevik rock carving locality also on the west coast of Norway, 30 km south of Vingen (Figure 2.1; Hagen 1969: locality VI: no. 224, p. 39). Other than this single image from Ausevik, somewhat similar scythe or hook-like designs are documented elsewhere at the large Nämforsen rock carving locality in northern Sweden, but here fewer than 40 examples are known (Hallström 1938: 454; 1960; Hagen 1976: 99).

These are the only images at Vingen that might be interpreted as representing artefacts. Bøe (1932: 36) regarded these motifs as representations of tools or weapons used during hunting, suggesting a general resemblance between these designs and the form of hafted picks or axes. What possible practical use they might actually have had in the context of the hunt remains obscure. Hallström, by contrast, suggests they may have had a ceremonial function. He notes that the blades of the scythes are similar in shape to the bodies of animals on Nedste Laegda and that a few of them appear to have ear-like protrusions. It is also noteworthy that hooks and scythes are depicted overlapping or merging with deer—for instance, on the north face of Hardbakken. They are never held by humans, and there are only rare cases of overlap or superimposition with human figures, such as at Leitet (Figure 2.17). On the basis of analogies with images of elk heads on poles found at Nämforsen, he interprets them as stylized animal heads on poles (Hallström 1938: 454).

It appears most likely that these hooks and scythes represent ceremonial staffs of different kinds. These are likely to have been made of organic materials that have left no trace in archaeological contexts in western Norway's very acidic soils. Hallström's argument that they represent stylized animal heads on poles requires our accepting the presence of extremely stylized motifs in the context of a rock carving locality where otherwise iconic or representational images, many very naturalistic in style, completely dominate.

There may be another, somewhat more compelling, interpretation of these motifs. The rock where the scythe images completely dominate, to the virtual exclusion of all others, Nedste Laegda, is the highest rock carving area at Vingen. It affords a fantastic view down the fjord to the west. When the fjord waters are calm, scythe blade and hook-like forms appear as darker and stiller patches of water within the Vingen fjord as a result of the confluence of currents and the shape of the fjord itself (Figure 2.31). These must have been observed in the past, as they can be today. Not only is this the case, but just west of Hornelen on Bremanger Island there are two fjords—Berlepollen, almost 6 km long, and Dalevatnet, 4.5 km long—which are almost perfectly shaped in the form of scythe blades (see Figure 2.1). Their scythe-like forms are readily apparent when seen from the mountains above them. Such scythe-shaped fjords occur nowhere else in the vicinity of Vingen and indeed are most unusual elsewhere in this area of western Norway. This, together with the fact that both are found on Bremanger Island only a short distance away from the sacred mountain and from Vingen itself, gives them added significance. The 'blades' of these fjords are orientated in quite different directions. Dalevatnet points towards the east, whereas Berlepollen swings round and points north. This great difference in the orientation of the fjord 'scythes' finds its counterpart at Vingen in the images at Nedste Laegda, where the scythe blades are also orientated in opposing directions (see Figure 2.10).

FIGURE 2.31. Scythe image appearing in the waters of the Vingen fjord.

We can suggest, therefore, that these motifs were powerful metaphors of place and identity. Vingen was occupied by people who not only lived in the shadow of the sacred mountain, Hornelen, but they also identified themselves and their relationship to place and landscape in relation to the scythe-shaped fjords sharing the same island as Hornelen. This perhaps suggests that Bremanger Island itself was considered a sacred island to the local populations of hunter-fisher-gatherers, containing as it does both Hornelen and the scythe-shaped fjords. There is little doubt that the populations at Vingen would have had an intimate knowledge of the forms of the fjords in the surrounding area and would have traveled along them and seen them from the mountains above. What more powerful way could one express one's relationship to place than to carve these images that could also be observed, in a magical way, appearing in the waters of the Vingen fjord itself?

If the scythes are material metaphors for Dalevatnet and Berlepollen, what of the simpler hook forms at Vingen? One possible explanation might be to suggest that they are stylized representations of the same thing; but to attempt such an explanation would be to ignore the specificity of their form in precisely the same manner as Hallström's argument that they might represent stylized animal heads. Again, another possibility, closer to home, can be suggested. Approached from the north, the journey to the Vingen fjord takes on a hook-shaped form. The end of the hook is the Vingen fjord pointing east, with its 'handle' running up through the waters east of Marøya Island towards Skatestraumen (see Figure 2.1). Most of the hooks carved on the rocks at Vingen are similarly orientated to point east. For example, all the eight hooks hidden away on the very top of the north face of Vehammaren point east. All but two of the 22 hooks depicted together on the single rock behind Hardbakken and near to the pond face east (see Figure 2.24 and the discussion above), as do the majority on the other rock outcrops and tumbled boulders between the pond and Urane.

The argument being put forward is that both the hook and the scythes are metaphors for journeying, social identity, place, and landscape—for Vingen as a special place in the context of a wider landscape of fjords and mountains, and for Bremanger Island in particular. These images may have multiple meanings, such as:

- Representations of actual ceremonial staffs.
- Landscape signifiers: scythe- and hook-shaped fjords.
- Expressions of sea journeys through the landscape to Vingen in the shape of the scythe and the hook. People approaching Vingen from the shores of Skatestraumen would have a hook-like journey to this place as opposed to the scythe-like journey down the extraordinary Berlepollen and Dalevatnet fjords. Another less likely possibility is that the collapsed part of the Hornelen summit may originally have had a rock overhang giving it originally the form of a hook.

Human Images at Vingen

Human images are the third most common type of motif at Vingen. Viste (2003) registers 68 certain or possible human depictions. Discounting the more uncertain examples, there are around 60. Humans are never depicted in profile, and none at Vingen hold tools or weapons of any kind. While the animals, all shown in profile, have a strong sense of directionality, facing or moving in a particular direction, this feature is strikingly absent in the human figures. What appears to be important about them is that they face towards an observer, thus establishing a more intimate relation. The deer, by contrast, never look towards human beings. Rather, they are being observed. The human figures are, in many cases, very closely associated with deer but not with the scythe and hook images. Some of these human images are strikingly different from one part of the rock carving area to another. They are absent from the major carved rocks farthest to the east, Elva and Nedste Laegda, but occur in variable frequencies throughout the rest of Vingen. Four main types of human representations occur at Vingen:

- Simple stick-line images carved with a single line. These occur on Vehammaren, Bak Vehammaren, Hardbakken North, Brattebakken, and on panels in the Leitet and Teigen areas; only one might be described as having a phallus. Those on Hardbakken and Teigen lack heads and sometimes arms.

These images appear strikingly static. They occur either on their own or are depicted in close association with deer and hooks, with little or no merging or superimposition. They never occur in groups or pairs (see Figure 2.17).

- Images with bent or curving frog-like legs and curved hanging arms or long, bent, and wavy outstretched arms. These may be carved either with single or double lines. They are the most common type of design occurring on Bak Vehammaren, Brattebakken, Hardbakken North, Leitet, Teigen, Urane, and Bakkane. Some are clearly phallic, and at least one at the eastern end of Brattebakken may be hermaphrodite (see Figures 2.13, 2.14, 2.16). Some have relatively large rounded heads, while others lack heads altogether. These humans occur either as single depictions or in pairs, while five are depicted together on the Bakke stone (Figure 2.12A). Most are closely associated with deer. On Hardbakken North two humans of this form merge or are superimposed with deer. On Leitet 10 one striking figure is surrounded by deer (Figure 2.16).

- Skeletalised representations of humans. These occur on the top of Hardbakken and on panels in Storåkern, Teigen, and Leitet (Figures 2.17, 2.23). The ribs are emphasized on some, together with the vertebrae on others. Two of these images at Leitet are particularly naturalistic in form. All except the two images on Hardbakken and Storåkern are closely associated with hooks that merge with, or are superimposed on, the skeletal forms. There is only one case (Leitet 8) where such a skeletalised figure merges with a deer. These images occur singly or in pairs. On Leitet 8 one is closely positioned near a stick-line human (see Figure 2.17).

- Human representations with enlarged torsos. These occur on Vingeneset, Urane, Brattebakken, and on the Kålrabi stone in the Bakkane area and are carved in a wide variety of forms (see Figures 2.11B, 2.12C, 2.15). Some appear to represent fleshed bodies with the bones revealed beneath in an X-ray style. In other cases the internal body patterning is somewhat analogous to the manner in which some of the more elaborately decorated deer are depicted. They occur in groups of up to five and are closely associated with deer rather than hooks; they are superimposed in relation to the deer on the Kålrabi stone, and as deer riders on Brattebakken, where they also occur on the same panel but are spatially separated from stick-line and frog-leg human depictions, some with enlarged torsos with internal divisions. A few of these appear like fish skeletons; others resemble human skeletons. The torso, with internal body divisions representing ribs, is represented in at least fifteen cases. Bøe (1932: 38) identifies some of the human figures at Vingen, those on the Kålrabi stone, as being female and other oval-shaped geometric depictions elsewhere as suggesting a vulva. Bakka (1973: 137) similarly identifies the figures on the Kålrabi stone as female and finds further 'vulvas' depicted on Brattebakken and elsewhere (ibid.: 139). He also suggests that on Brattebakken a sexual union between a human and a deer is depicted. Mandt suggests that possibly some places at Vingen were reserved for women and their activities (Mandt 1995: 283). However, only a small minority of any of these figures can be identified as either male or female, while a few might be understood as hermaphrodite (Mandt 2001: 303). States of human transformation rather than gender relations appear to be the dominant theme.

The juxtaposition or superimposition of these human figures with deer shows an intimate association between the two, both in life and in death. Some of these human figures with torsos can be understood as X-ray depictions in which we see the bones (vertebrae and ribs) beneath the flesh. Others are clearly skeletal, with the flesh removed and only the bones remaining. So, while all the deer can be understood as being fleshy, living beings, the human depictions portray various states of bodily transformation between life and death. Almost all these skeletal images occur in what might be termed the 'back spaces' of Vingen. They do not occur on the front faces of the great Vehammaren and Hardbakken rocks closest to the fjord. Here the humans with frog legs are represented. The skeletal representations occur among the huge tumbled rocks in the Urane boulder field, on the top and behind Hardbakken near to the pond, and on the important carved stones situated to the far south and on the margins of the Vingen terrace, on the Kålrabi stone, Brattebakken, and Leitet, or away across the fjord on Vingeneset. We might understand these representations and their location as suggesting that Vingen was not only an important arena for rites and ceremonies for the living, but that more specifically, it was a place connected with death rites, perhaps involving the defleshing of bodies and the deposition of the bones in Hellaren and the other chambers and crevices found in the Urane boulder field. We see the human beings in various metamorphosed states from life to death and the common link between the living and the dead with the deer who fed both the living and the souls of the dead. The association of hooks with the skeletal images without enlarged torsos is of special interest in terms of a metaphorical theme of journeying from life to death.

The notion of metamorphosis from one state to another can be suggested to link the skeletal depictions with the human figures with bent frog-like legs. There are frogs everywhere on the Vingen terrace, and they must breed in the freshwater pond between Hardbakken and Vehammaren. In other words, the frogs breed in Hornelen's mirror. This may suggest that frogs were considered sacred creatures at Vingen—hence their anthropomorphised form, providing powerful metaphors for myths of human origins in a watery existence and their current lifestyle on the land. Frogs were likely living in this area of Norway during the late Mesolithic, and the presence of frog bones might be expected in future excavations. In their life-cycle, these amphibians metamorphose from tadpoles that cannot survive on land to frogs that must breathe the air and cannot survive under the water. Beginning as strictly watery, fish-like beings, they grow into a totally different form and must then live both on the land and in the water. Tadpoles grow limbs while maintaining their embryonic heads. The depiction of human beings with frog-like legs and arms articulated in a particular way, together with a bulbous rounded head, suggests a possible conceptual linkage between a closely observed phenomenon and the lives of humans. The hunter-fisher-gatherers of Vingen similarly depended for their survival on the resources of the land and the water and were people intimately associated with both. The frog thus provides an ideal metaphor for human origins, movement, and transformation between the two domains.

Conclusions

Why Vingen?

Every place is unique, and so is Vingen. There is no single characteristic that makes Vingen stand out as a location that might be chosen over others for rock carvings in this area of western Norway. Equally suitable rocks exist elsewhere. Hornelen is visible from many other places in the surroundings, a similarly wet microclimate at the end of a fjord enclosed on three sides by steep mountains exists at Svelgen and elsewhere, and so on. It is rather the combination of these elements, together with others, that makes Vingen so special. These are:

- The impressive 45-degree sloping ridges of Vehammaren and Hardbakken, both jutting out into the fjord at their western ends: ideal rocks for monumental displays of imagery.
- The enclosed character of the Vingen fjord in which most of the surrounding world is shut out.
- The view to Hornelen to the northwest in relation to the setting of the midsummer sun.
- The particular sound effects of the winds and the waterfalls.
- The presence of the pond with its inverted image of Hornelen.
- The extreme microclimate.
- The existence of the long terrace on the southern side of the fjord.

Vingen is special because of these combined factors. They made it a good place to carve rocks. But what makes Vingen absolutely unique is the particular juxtaposition of vertical and sloping rock exposures and tumbled blocks and boulders with caves and chambers. There is no comparable single rock carving area in Scandinavia in which carvings are found in such a small area and in such a staggeringly diverse range of material contexts. Concomitantly, the bodily postures, movements, and actions required to experience these carvings are more diverse than anywhere else.

Society, Identity, Place

The populations at Skatestraumen and others on Bremanger Island lived and moved directly under Hornelen's shadow, exploiting the rich fish and fowl resources of the fjords and the deer of the land. Vingen was their ceremonial arena. Here rites took place for the living and the dead, and the carvings were made, used, and seen in connection with these rites. I have argued that these had primarily to do with marking changes of status of individuals within individual clans or social groups. The deer was material metaphor for both the social group and the individual within that group. Society was conceived and displayed through deer imagery. The hooks and scythes were metaphors of social identity in relation to place and landscape, and journeying through that landscape: the scythe-shaped fjords sharing the same island as the sacred mountain, and the Vingen fjord itself. So we have both social signifiers and landscape signifiers.

Public and Private

We can distinguish between two principal types of carving areas at Vingen in terms of front and public spaces and hidden, back, private spaces. The two primary public carving spaces at Vingen are the two great rocks of Hardbakken and Vehammaren. Both are dramatic and monumental in size and situated next to the fjord and remarkably similar to each other in form. Both can be seen from out to sea and from the Hornelen summit. In late Mesolithic times one could literally step ashore from the fjord onto their northern faces. A drama of theatrical deer imagery is being played out on their front or northern faces. Here bodily kinaesthetics are both limited and structured by the positioning and the flow of the images across the broad rock faces. Hidden behind each rock, away from the fjord on the southern side of both, the form, content, and disposition of the images are very different and much more varied. Similarly, possibilities for bodily movement between the carved rocks and panels are much more varied and differentiated. It is no longer obvious where to go or what imagery will be encountered. Situated midway between these two great rocks is the pond, with its powerful inverted image of Hornelen, surrounded with small carvings on smaller and larger boulders and rock outcrops whose locations are unpredictable and would be known only to someone with an intimate insider's knowledge of the Vingen landscape.

The other major carved rocks along the Vingen terrace to the east—Brattebakken, those at Leitet, and the Kålrabi stone—are all positioned on the far southern side or rear of the terrace. These rocks only have a northern front face or public side but are much smaller and less monumental than Hardbakken and Vehammaren. These might be described as semi-public places. The carvings in the Bakkane area and in the Urane boulder fields are, for the most part, in hidden and fugitive places. The extreme easterly location of the Elva and Nedste Laegda carving areas and those across the fjord at Vingeneset suggests that these were special hidden and reserved locations. None of these are obvious areas in which one might expect to encounter visual imagery. An outsider visiting or being taken to Vingen would no doubt be brought to Hardbakken and Vehammaren to see the public displays of imagery. They might perhaps be taken to see Brattebakken, Leitet, and the

Kålrabi stone, but the sheer extent and diversity of the Vingen carvings and the narratives told through them would remain concealed.

The Collective and the Individual

The distinction made above between public and private places for rock carvings at Vingen may further relate to a distinction between the individual and the collective. The great public rocks must have been collectively carved by many different individuals. It seems fairly obvious that the singular or small groups of carvings found on small boulders and rock surfaces around the pond and in the Bakkane and Urane areas must have been the work of individual carvers. People could be identified and distinguished in relation to the stones they carved. These stones were part and parcel of their identity and relationship to place.

While Elva and Nedste Laegda were possibly reserved and special areas at Vingen, these were nevertheless collectively carved and used in ceremonies and rites. We can thus distinguish between public and private carving areas at Vingen, crosscut between a distinction between collective and individual carved rocks. In the most general sense it can be claimed that the major public and collectively carved rocks at Vingen are expressions of social values and beliefs, with people coming together and cooperating to create the images. The carvings on the smaller and larger stones and boulders are the expressions of individuals. This might be regarded as part of a wider narrative about social fusion and fragmentation and about the relationship of the individual to the social group.

Fame and the Powers of Carving

The sheer dexterity and skill with which many of the Vingen carvings, particularly the deer images, were pecked out with a series of blows to create the final image has been noted many times. These are masterpieces of prehistoric art. The act of making them would necessitate great balance on the more precipitous rock faces but would be comparatively easy elsewhere. The old and frail, women who were pregnant, and the very young could never have carved the upper rock surfaces at Elva or at Vehammaren. These must have been the work of younger individuals and represented their prowess. It may be the case that carving such images formed part of initiation rites associated with transformations of social status. The beauty of the finished image, and the sheer achievement in being able to create it at all, brought fame and prestige to the carver who was able to execute it in such a challenging location. The act of creating certain images was a means of attaining status within the social group, in the same manner as prowess might be acquired through hunting.

Field investigations at Vingen have revealed one of the pecking tools, found in an eroding cultural layer next to a rivulet, probably used to create the carvings. This is an elongated stone with a pointed end. The diameter of the point is exactly the same as most of the pecking marks on the Vingen images (Lødøen 2003: 516). The raw material is diabase and comes from the Stakaneset quarry, which was in use during both the Mesolithic and Neolithic (Olsen and Alasker 1984), involving a 50-

km-long boat journey to the south (see Figures 2.1 and 5.2). In a symbolic sense, the origin of these images, pecked with such a stone, was exotic. The act of carving them connected Vingen with the outside world, another symbolically charged place, and a wider community of people. There can be little doubt that the carvings at Ausevik, only about 12 km away by boat, were also made using the same stone. That both of these were special places can be in little doubt, given the use of specially quarried stone tools for their manufacture, a theme further explored in the next chapter.

Metamorphosis

The images at Vingen are far more than material metaphors for clans and social relationships, identity, place, and landscape. They are about metamorphosis and transformation in a place, Vingen, which was itself always changing and infinitely variable. The weather, the water, even the rock itself at Vingen change as one moves from one area to another. The bodily kinaesthetics required to view the images radically alter as one moves from one area to another, from linear outcrops that can be viewed beside them to sheer cliffs one is required to climb, to sloping platforms one must move across, to huge boulder fields one must negotiate, to huge rock faces one must move along. In tandem, the deer change from those in violent motion to those that are static and from those with simple body decoration to those that are intensely decorated. Then there is the 'movement' (differing orientations) of the hooks and the scythes. The human depictions similarly transform from those with fleshy bodies to skeletal depictions. It is the dead humans, the ancestors, who ride and domesticate the deer, symbolically exerting control and arresting their movement. The sacred frog, the most cogent and powerful symbol of the process of metamorphosis one could hope to find, breeding in Hornelen's mirror, become anthropomorphised as human. Vingen is place and image in transformative process.

CHAPTER THREE

STONES
THAT WALK

ARCHITECTURE AND
IMAGERY IN THE IRISH
MIDDLE NEOLITHIC

This chapter considers Neolithic megalithic imagery in two of the largest and most important passage grave (temple) cemeteries in Ireland: Loughcrew and the bend of the Boyne (Figure 3.1). I prefer to use the term 'temple' in order to indicate the social and religious significance of these monuments, which is far beyond their use implied by the standard term 'passage grave'. These temples, among the largest and most spectacular known in Europe, are highly elaborated with graphic imagery. They have by far the greatest concentration of megalithic 'art' known in Europe, and one of them, Knowth, has about 45 percent of the total of decorated stones known for Ireland (Eogan 1986: 168). At the time of its construction, the decorated kerb of the Knowth temple would have presented the greatest visual spectacle anywhere in Neolithic northern Europe.

The majority of the motifs were picked on the surface of the stones in a series of pits or pickings with a sharp point of flint or quartz. This was undertaken in a variety of ways: (1) line picking, to create particular individual motifs such as spirals; (2) solid or area picking, to infill particular graphic elements such as lozenges, or fill a surface area of the stone; (3) diffuse picking over the entire surface of the stone or parts of it; (4) close area picking of parts of the stone; and (5) pick dressing of the overall stone surface or large areas of it, removing the surface (C. O'Kelly 1982: Shee Twohig 1981; O'Sullivan 2002). Sometimes almost the entire surface of the slab is picked, leaving unpicked areas to stand out in relief. In this case unpicked areas form the motif. So picking could be used to create motifs either in the positive or the negative. Picked lines were sometimes deepened by rubbing with a smooth pebble to achieve a more even groove, as on the entrance kerb stone to Newgrange

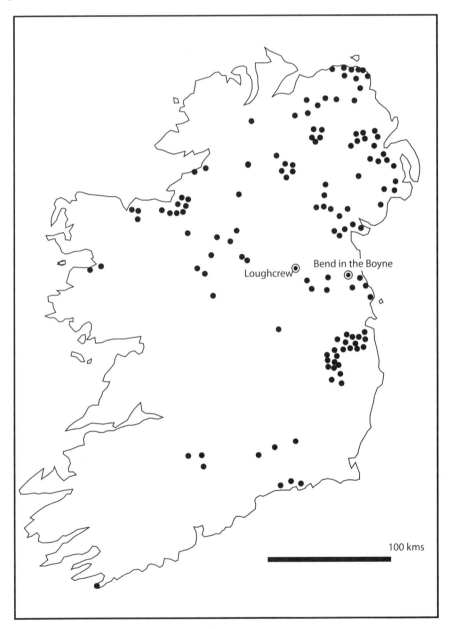

Figure 3.1. The distribution of passage graves (temples) in Ireland, showing the locations of the Loughcrew temples and those of the bend of the Boyne. *Source: After Eogan 1986: fig. 45.*

(see below). Another technique was to scratch or incise the surface. Sometimes this technique was used to mark guidelines subsequently infilled with line or area picking (Shee Twohig 1981; Eogan and Aboud 1990).

The imagery is almost entirely graphic or geometric and seemingly 'abstract' in character. The motifs present on the decorated stones in Irish temples have long been divided by scholars into ten basic categories, although many are ambiguous and indeterminate in form (Shee Twohig 1981: 107; C. O'Kelly 1973; 1982: 146; O'Sullivan 2002: 659). The main forms are curvilinear (circles, spirals, arcs, meandering lines, and dots in circles) or rectilinear (zigzags, lozenges, radials, parallel lines, and offsets or comb-devices). Besides these, there are numerous cupmarks, and every commentator has remarked that in most cases it is impossible to distinguish whether these were deliberately created or enlargements of preexisting hollows or irregularities on the surface (Figure 3.2).

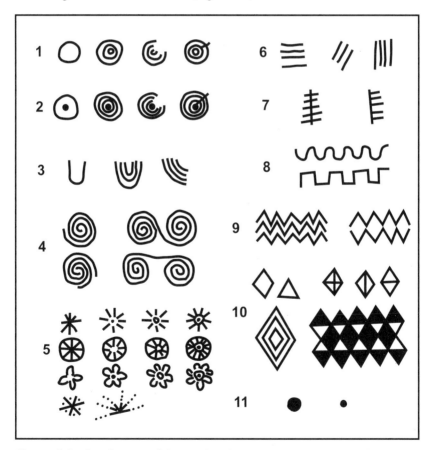

Figure 3.2. Classification of the graphic designs occurring in the Irish temples, showing the main variant forms (*after Shee Twohig 1981: fig. 11*). *1*: circle; *2*: circle with central dot; *3*: U motif; *4*: spiral; *5*: radial; *6*: parallel lines; *7*: offset motif; *8*: wavy lines; *9*: zigzags; *10*: lozenges/triangles; *11*: cupmarks.

Eogan (1986) has listed a series of fourteen different 'styles' of Irish temple 'art', but what is meant by the term 'style' is rather unclear. Most are simply defined in terms of the dominant motif used—for instance, the spiral style, circular style, or dispersed circular style. Here we have 'styles' defined in terms of single motif forms. By contrast, Eogan's 'angular style' lumps together a variety of different motifs—lozenges, triangles, and chevrons—while his 'angular-spiral style' refers to stones with both spirals and angular motifs. Other so-called styles are not based on motif form at all but are instead evaluative statements: 'lavish', 'unaccomplished', 'random' (ibid.: 153–65). As O'Sullivan has pointed out, the difficulty with all these approaches is the reduction of the imagery to a series of elementary forms, ignoring non-formal ornamentation such as the pick-dressing of stones (O'Sullivan 1986: 71).

These temples were centres for collective burial. Cremation was the predominant rite, which took place on pyres somewhere outside the temples before deposition of the remains inside the temple chambers. A close connection might be assumed to exist between landscape and architecture, imagery, and rites of passage concerned with death and the regeneration of life. These themes will be explored here in relation to the manner in which the monuments, their external and internal architectural spaces, their imagery and decorative surfaces, are experienced through the body.

In the first section of this chapter a descriptive account of the temples is undertaken, examining the relationship between the temples and their landscape settings, the imagery, and their external and internal architectural spaces. The second section discusses the material qualities of the stones and other materials used to construct the temples. In the third section the significance and power of the imagery are addressed in the light of these considerations. In the conclusions various strands of these discussions are drawn together to argue that the imagery was intimately related to embodied human experiences of stone and water, temple and landscape, processions of people and the movement of celestial bodies in the heavens.

EXPERIENCING THE MONUMENTS

The accounts below are inevitably subjective experiences, and I make no claims here that this is an objective account. I do not describe the imagery on every stone in detail, for that would simply result in a catalogue. Shee Twohig (1981), C. O'Kelly (1982), and O'Kelly and O'Kelly (1983) have provided excellent catalogues for Loughcrew, Newgrange, and Dowth, 'objectively' showing what motifs occur on the stones but often 'subjectively' not illustrating areas of pick dressing thought to be relatively unimportant. These provide extremely helpful guides to a modern visual experience of the imagery, showing one where to look. The principal concern here, however, is with the impression the imagery makes through somatic experience of it. Although this is inevitably a contemporary experience and certainly not a 'Neolithic' one, the simple claim being made here is that any human experience of these monuments, either past or present, is bodily mediated. Different persons, according to knowledge and circumstances, experience these monuments in different ways, and what ultimately is important about this are the experiences and impressions that they take away with them and remember and the narratives and meanings that they are able to construct from these experiences. Thus, the accounts that follow are memories, set into narratives. In relation to Loughcrew, Dowth, and Newgrange, the accounts are inevitably heavily influenced by the availability of detailed documentation for all the stones. For Knowth site 1, such documentation has still not been published. Eogan's (1986; 1996; 1997; 1998; Eogan and Aboud 1990) illustrations of the kerbstones and of the stones inside the temples are both partial and selective. Their scale, and the level of detail provided, act as a rather unreliable guide to an experience of the stones themselves. We can be sure that people in the Neolithic did not react to the stones through the medium of two-dimensional paper documentation and certainly did not experience everything, whether it was hidden or not. In this respect, at least, this contemporary account of Knowth may bear a greater resemblance to a 'Neolithic' experience and impression of that monument. I start with a brief discussion of the relationship of the monuments to the surrounding landscape and then consider them from the outside and the inside, starting with the Loughcrew temples first and then examining those of the bend of the Boyne.

Loughcrew

The Loughcrew ridge is situated 57 km due west of the mouth of the river Boyne. On this curving east–west ridge there are four summit areas: Patrickstown, Carnbane East, Newtown, and Carnbane West, all rising above 250 OD over a distance of 4.5 km. Clustering on these summits, a temple cemetery of around 30 temples was built (Figure 3.3). Rising up to 276 m, this ridge dominates the surrounding low-lying and undulating landscape in its vicinity (see Fraser 1998 and Cochrane 2005 for a detailed discussion of the localised topographic placement and interrelationships of the temples). Some of the higher summit temples are very prominent landmarks that punctuate the skyline and are visible from many miles around. From them there are panoramic views across Ireland, almost from coast to coast. Conwell, one of the antiquarian excavators of these temples in the 1860s and 1890s, claims that hills in 18 of the 32 counties of Ireland are visible from here (McMann 1993: 46). To the northeast the Mourne Mountains and Slieve Gullion are prominent, the Wicklow Mountains and the Hill of Tara are to the southeast, the Iron Mountains to the northeast, and the Slieve Bloom Mountains to the south. The river Blackwater, an east-flowing tributary of the Boyne, rises just to the north of the Loughcrew ridge, providing a physical connection between the temples here and those of the Boyne valley. The temples here are generally considered to be fairly late in the sequence of temple construction in Ireland, dating from the mid-fourth to early third millennium B.C. (Sheridan 1986; Cooney 2000), with the largest temples being constructed towards the end of the sequence. Imagery is documented from the inside of many of the monuments, and on two external kerbstones of two different temples, but most are very ruinous and fragmentary. The imagery in the two largest and best-preserved summit cairns, cairn L on Carnbane West and cairn T on Carnbane East, is considered here.

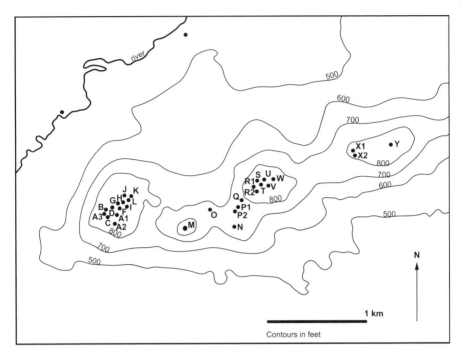

Figure 3.3. The distribution of temples along the Loughcrew ridge. *After McMann 1993.*

Loughcrew: Temple L

Temple L is contained in the second largest cairn on the eastern end of the cluster of cairns on Carbane West. It is the most elaborately decorated of the thirteen temples in the group (Figure 3.4; Shee Twohig 1981: 211–13, figs. 229–29, pls. 30–31). The kerb, consisting of 42 stones, is remarkable for the use of relatively thin rectangular slabs riddled with shallow surface depressions as if the stones had been rough-picked all over their surfaces (Figure 3.5). These are, in effect, naturally 'decorated' slabs, with the best examples chosen to flank the southeast-facing entrance and bound the southern sector of the cairn, the most important area of the temple circumference or circuit. In the north and northeast sectors this type of 'decorated' stone is missing, and the kerbstones here have a more irregular and less distinctive shape.

Thus, rough 'picked' stone surfaces, all undifferentiated in terms of the absence of any pattern, confront the observer moving around the outside circuit of the temple, 'decoration' that becomes lost in the area farthest away from the entrance. These stones require circulation past them in either a clockwise or counterclockwise fashion. They can never be seen all at once. They may be viewed at will from a greater or shorter distance away, and the observer looks down at their surfaces with the great cairn rising above them. In this high and windswept location these stones can alter and change rapidly in relation to the qualities of the light and the patterns of the weather.

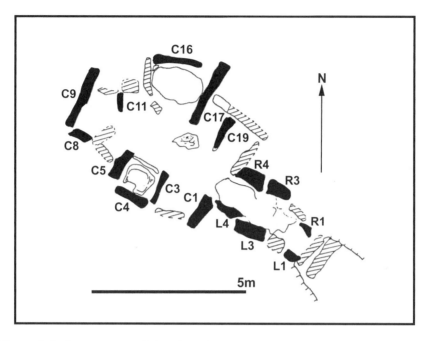

Figure 3.4. The passage and chamber of Loughcrew temple L, showing the positions of the decorated orthostats. *After Shee Twohig 1981: fig. 222.*

Figure 3.5. Kerbstone in the southern part of the cairn of temple L, Loughcrew.

The short, confined passage into temple L has four orthostats on each side, six of which (three on each side) have rough surfaces, some further enhanced by picking and deepening. These decorated passage orthostats are sparsely elaborated with motifs that often appear to be both partial and indistinct, and whose positioning alters from stone to stone. Entering the passage today requires stooping down and moving past the lower outer stones. The roof height then increases (the present roof is a restoration but probably approximates the height of the original) so that it is possible to stand upright and walk into the temple chamber from the inner part of the passage. The fourth stone and final passage orthostat on the right-hand side is covered with deeply picked cupmarks and depressions. The surface of this stone, riddled all over with hollows, has both the greatest visual and tactile impact despite the absence of geometric motifs on its surface. This and its opposite left orthostat are set inwards in order to constrict and narrow the passage so as to encourage bodily contact as one brushes past the stone surfaces to enter the chamber.

The chamber feels particularly large and spacious compared with the constricted passage, and its corbelled roof (its central part now replaced by concrete) may originally have been 5 m high. The chamber consists of a series of eight cells, two central ones on the left- and right-hand sides containing stones basins. Standing just inside the chamber space, having entered it from the passage, an observer can see only some of the decorated stone surfaces. All the designs on the western faces of the stones are concealed as one walks into the temple, but can be seen when exiting. So an observer has one perspective on the decorated stones on the way into the chamber and another on the way out. Some decorated stone surfaces are thus hidden or revealed in relation to the process of moving into and out of the temple chamber. In the passage, in order to see the decorated stones one must look either to the left or the right while moving forwards. Experiencing the designs within the chamber space requires an altogether much more complex process of bodily motion: moving forwards or backwards, turning to the right or the left, looking up and looking down, clambering over sillstones and entering between orthostats into recesses. Significantly, only some of the stone surfaces are decorated. Some are decorated on two faces, others on only one face, and there is no predictability with regard to which stone surfaces are decorated, what their form or size may be, what associations the images may have, or whether they are located on the upper, lower, or middle surfaces of the stones. One must look across at some images, down or up to see others. Just as there is a lack of predictability in image positioning, the cells of the temple chamber all differ in size and depth. The observer experiences a constantly changing sense of space and a kaleidoscope of image fields varying according to body position, motion, or stasis.

The most striking and elaborately decorated stone surfaces are not in the most obvious and easily visible places. From the passage entrance to the chamber, designs on the backstone of the opposite innermost cell (C9: Figures 3.4, 3.6) are only partially visible, and none are dramatic; on the right half are a damaged circle and some pick marks, on the left three large meandering picked lines and other

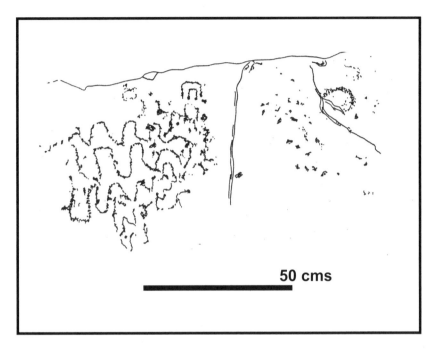

Figure 3.6. Orthostat C9 in the back cell of temple L, Loughcrew. *After Shee Twohig 1981: fig. 225.*

indistinct meandering and U-forms. The rough, indistinct, and irregular nature of the images repeats the visual and tactile experience of most of the passage orthostats. This end cell is the least elaborately decorated of the three main cells. The decorated stones inside the cells to the left can only be seen when entering these cells and turning round. The most elaborately decorated stones are to the right of the chamber. This is a fairly predictable relationship between architecture and imagery in the Irish temples, where greater emphasis is often given to the right-hand recess, and occurs at Newgrange, Dowth, the eastern passage and chamber in Knowth 1 (see below), and at Knockroe (O'Sullivan 2004: 48; Cochrane 2005). Two in particular stand out from all the others. Stone C19 is surprising because it is the thinnest orthostat in the chamber and situated just to the right of the entrance. It is elaborately decorated on its western and eastern faces with lozenges and zigzag lines, which are deeply incised. The most elaborate stone of all forms the back of the main and largest centre right cell (C16: Figure 3.7). The dominant images are concentric circles and U-shaped forms surrounding central dots, with triangles and lozenges at the top and the far right. The central motifs on this stone appear to be conceived and executed as a whole and in relation to one another so as to create a definite and coherent pattern of relationships, which occurs nowhere else in temple L. The order and relative coherence of the pattern are striking and memorable.

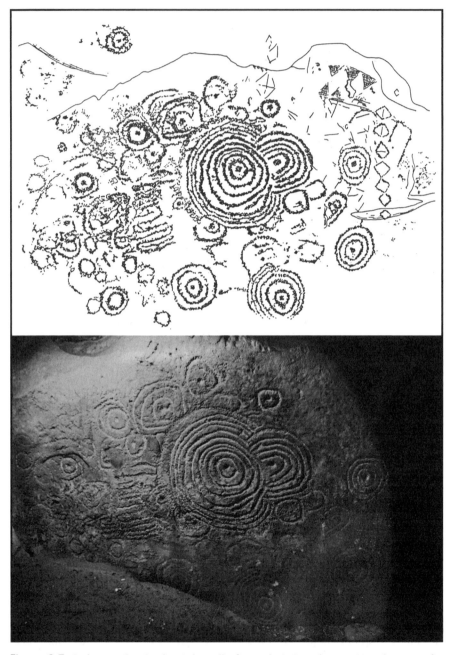

Figure 3.7. Orthostat C16 in the right cell of temple L, Loughcrew. *Line drawing after Shee Twohig 1981: fig. 226.*

As one moves through the chamber and encounters the images, there is no sense of greater elaboration or complexity as one proceeds to the back of the temple. The main differentiation is between the left or south and right or north sides of the internal space. Shee Twohig has also emphasized (1996:76) this concentration of the most striking images around the two central cells, with basins indicating their importance in funerary and other rites (ibid.). There is also a sense here of a deliberate structuring of the images, insofar as the central cells on both the left- and right-hand sides with basin stones are dominated by circular designs, and there is an absence of lozenges or triangles on the left-hand and least elaborately decorated side of the chamber throughout the temple space. This asymmetry between the left- and right-hand sides is also found in the number of cells (three to the left and four to the right). Shee Twohig notes that the central left cell has a tall, white pillar stone set in front of it to the left of the opening, impressively illuminated by the dawn sunshine in early November and February (ibid.: 76).

Loughcrew: Temple T

Temple T (Figure 3.8; Shee Twohig 1981: 214–17; figs. 232–38, pls. 33–37) is situated on the flat central hilltop summit of the Loughcrew ridge on Carnbane East. It is by far the largest temple in a group of seven temples, with six, much smaller 'satellite' cairns situated around it. The roughly circular external kerb flattens and turns in towards the entrance on the eastern side. The kerbstones are particularly massive, with the two largest flanking the passage entrance. The third largest kerbstone, known as the Hag's chair and located on the northern side, is decorated on its external face with pits and circular designs. A few other kerbstones may originally have been decorated, but the decoration is now lost through weathering. Many of the stones have surfaces similar to those of temple L.

The passage and chamber, on the eastern side of the cairn, occupies a small space compared with the massive cairn itself. The passage, which has been the subject of some undocumented reconstruction, faces due east. From the entrance, looking down the passage and directly into the chamber space beyond, the backstone of the deepest and final cell of the chamber is visible, with striking radial and circular motifs on it. Brennan reports that at the equinoxes, the rising sun shines directly into the temple after dawn, illuminating this stone and the sillstone between the passage and the chamber and gradually moving across and illuminating and animating some of the images in a striking manner (Brennan 1983: 90–100).

The passage is composed of five orthostats on either side. The third and fourth on either side are inset as jamb stones, creating a threshold between the inner and outer passage spaces and constricting entry into the innermost area before the chamber. Here a sillstone was shown on early plans by du Noyer (Shee Twohig 1996: 73). All the passage orthostats on the left-hand side are densely decorated. Two of those to the right lack graphic motifs. This contrast between the left- and right-hand sides is striking and important. Entering the passage, one must at first stoop. The first orthostat to the left is highly decorated with circular, radial, and pitted motifs covering its entire face, except at the very bottom. This stone has a smooth and flat face with deeply picked decoration. The stone opposite to the right is considerably rougher and is

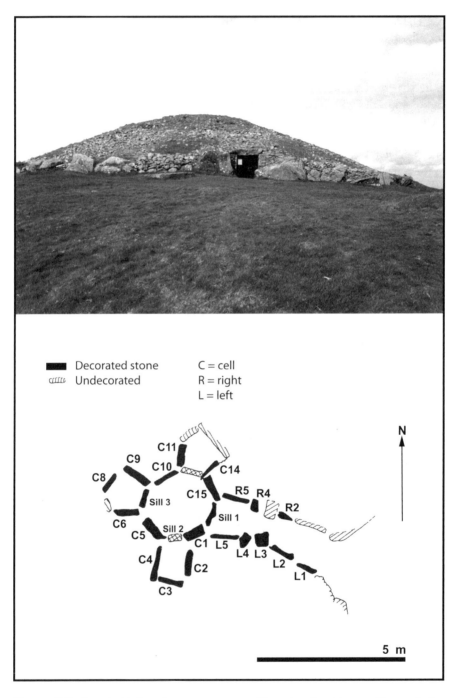

Figure 3.8. Temple T, Loughcrew cemetery. Plan showing the positions of the decorated orthostats in the chamber and passage. *After Shee Twohig 1981: fig. 232.*

undecorated. The second orthostat to the left is also elaborately decorated on the upper part of the face. Opposite it the second orthostat to the right is decorated with less elaborate and densely packed motifs. Again this stone has a much rougher and more uneven surface. The third stone to the right contrasts with the two outer orthostats on this side of the passage, being a squat, undecorated pillar which feels rough to the touch. Opposite it, the third stone to the left, with elaborate meandering designs on its inner face, is again far smoother. So entry and movement down the passage involves not only a contrast between decorated and undecorated stones and a higher degree of elaboration of the decoration on the left, but also a rough (right) and smooth (left) tactile contrast between the stone surfaces themselves.

Stooping lower through the inner door jamb and moving into the innermost and higher part of the passage, the final two orthostats to the left and right are by far the largest, and both possess significantly different surface decoration from the outer passage stones. The surfaces of both are dominated by deep holes enlarged and elaborated by picking. However, the stone to the left also has circular designs, related to and integrated with this surface of picked holes, whereas

these are absent on the stone to the right and many of its surface holes are deeper (Figure 3.9). The presence of these hole-riddled stones immediately before the entrance to the chamber repeats the positioning of a similar stone to the right of the chamber entrance in Loughcrew temple L. The depth of the pits is what distinguishes these stones. The decoration elaborates the pits that preexisted on these stones in their unaltered form; and clearly the stones were chosen to be orthostats because of the original presence of these pits on their surfaces. They signal that the inner sanctum of the temple has been reached. Looking ahead and into the chamber, the high (0.6 m) sillstone, over which one must clamber, is similarly decorated with picked decoration on its outer surface. Chamber orthostats C1 and C15 are angled to

Figure 3.9. Detail of cupmarks and enlarged holes on orthostat R5, temple T, Loughcrew.

either side of the sillstone, but whereas C15 juts out into the passage, C1 is set back. There is a further contrast here in that the outer edge of C15 is rough and covered with deep pit decoration, whereas the outer edge of C1 is far smoother, with some indistinct linear picking.

Contrasting with the chamber space of temple L, with its eight irregular stalls, the chamber of temple T is far more symmetrical in form. It consists of four angled orthostats and four sillstones, creating a polygonal space with three distinct side cells, one to the left, another to the right, and a final cell at the back. Both the cells and the passage are clearly differentiated from the main chamber, and in the same manner, by high sillstones. As in temple L, there is an enormous sense of space and height formed by the rising corbelled roof of the chamber (2.5 m in height). Ahead, the decorated backstone of the innermost cell is visible along with decorated stones C5, C10, and sill 3 (see Figure 3.8). The sillstone has, on its right, a deeply picked radial design like those on the backstone of the cell. Stones C5 and C10 possess pit and circle decorations, but C5's are far more elaborated. These stones effectively repeat the theme of deepening, elaborating on, and embellishing features already present on the stone surface, found on the innermost two passage stones. Turning round and looking to the left or right chamber, orthostats C1 and C15 contrast markedly. There is no decoration on C1, whereas C15, the tallest stone in the chamber, is covered with holes and depressions. The lower part of C15 has no obvious added decoration, while the upper part is covered with motifs that elaborate on the pits.

Moving to the left of the chamber and peering over the sillstone, the images in cell 1 become visible (with artificial illumination). This cell is rectangular, allowing one to stand inside it, but the optimal viewing distance is from outside the cell. The backstone has many circular designs that elaborate on deeply picked central pits. This stone has a smooth and fairly even surface, contrasting with the irregularity of the side stone to the left, C2, which has cracks, surface depressions, and pits elaborated and deepened with picking. The backstone has by far the most elaborate and greatest density of images in the cell. By contrast, the right stone of the cell, C4, has very little decoration, just a few circles elaborated around central pits. The dominant imagery is at the back of the cell in a very dark space within the temple. Without artificial illumination, it would only be possible to feel the motifs and pits.

The opposite cell, to the right of the chamber, has four orthostats rather than three and is polygonal in shape. Only the two outermost of these orthostats are decorated, splaying at angles to the chamber. C14 has a striking series of deeply picked geometric motifs on its smooth face. The undecorated backstone of the cell is rough, with many shallow pits covering its surface. C11 has lozenge forms and angular lines picked on the lower part of its face, some of which elaborate on cracks. Other motifs on both these stones again elaborate on natural pits. On the underside of the capstone there is a small area of decoration that remains hidden if one does not crouch or lie down and look up, consisting of parallel zigzag lines cutting across a crack.

The final and innermost cell constitutes both a surprise and contrast to those cells on the left and right of the chamber space. Its illuminated backstone, the motifs on which are only partially concealed from the chamber by the sillstone, has already been mentioned. But what is most striking about this stone is not only the relative ease with which the motifs on it may be seen, but their grouping, distinctiveness, and clarity of form. The motifs on this stone appear to be coherently ordered in relation to one another in a manner not present on any of the other passage or chamber orthostats. On the latter the positioning of many of the motifs appears to be a 'response' to features already found on the stones themselves—regular or irregular surfaces, holes, cracks, and depressions—making the overall design relationships appear somewhat haphazard. Stone C8 appears much more like a blank 'canvas' on which designs were executed where desired (Figure 3.10). The stone surface is exceptionally smooth. The flamboyant radial, star, and other geometric forms that decorate it have an exceptional clarity, standing out from rather than merging with the features of the natural stone surface—unlike on the other stone orthostats. Luminosity and clarity go hand in hand. The two flanking cell orthostats to the left and the right are far less elaborate, with comparatively little and rather indistinct decoration, acting as a foil for the visual elaboration of the backstone. The real surprise in this cell is the 'secret' decoration on the underside of the smooth, flat capstone, repeating the same types of images found on the backstone. To view these designs requires either stooping down and looking up or lying flat on one's back. So the final chamber of the temple, and the deepest in relation to the external cairn, requires the greatest and most radical change in bodily posture in order to experience and encounter the motifs, which effectively dominate an observer who must experience them from below. The images force the subjugation of the body beneath. They, rather than the observer, are dominant.

The organization of the decorated stones in this temple is clearly designed to continually surprise the uninitiated observer. There are no repetitive or obvious themes. For example, while the backstones of cells 1 and 2 are decorated, that in cell 3 is not. Cell 1, unlike cells 2 and 3, has no decoration on the underside of the capstone. What one might expect from the experience of one of the cells is not repeated in another.

The manner in which the innermost part of the passage was originally bounded by sillstones on either side duplicates the structure of the three chamber cells. Effectively, the inner part of the passage constitutes a fourth cell, rectangular in shape like cell 1. So this temple can be envisaged as having cells or internal subdivisions orientated in relation to each of the cardinal directions. Two of these (the passage and end cell) are illuminated, those to the north and south or right and left, dark. From the perspective of the inner temple chamber, the passage entrance 'cell' has the external landscape beyond the temple as its 'backstone'.

In comparison with the stones forming the passage and the chamber cells, the other chamber orthostats are relatively unelaborated with images. All the emphasis is on the front and very back spaces of the temple chamber. Two major kinds of

Figure 3.10. Graphic imagery on orthostat C8, temple T, Loughcrew. Chalked.

images may be distinguished: those that elaborate on the preexisting surfaces of the stones, enlarging or deepening holes, impressions, and cracks; and those that are executed on a 'blank' surface (which occur primarily in the innermost cell), images that are alternatively either guided by, or imposed on, the stone surface. The only clear lozenge/lattice designs occur in the right cell, whereas circular designs are concentrated on the left-hand side of the passage and chamber, a similar arrangement to that encountered in temple L. There is no clear left/right distinction of the chamber space in terms of degree of motif elaboration either quantitatively or qualitatively—a major difference with temple L—and the end chamber of temple L is little elaborated in comparison with temple T. Both the structuring of the motifs and the bodily movements and postures required to experience them are very different in the two temples. Temple T has a much smaller, simpler, and more symmetrical chamber plan than temple L, but the forms of the motifs and their positioning are far more complex.

In temple T the left (south) side of the passage is more elaborated than the right. One prominent theme is the deepening of the decoration as one approaches the chamber space, with the deepest 'cupmarks' occurring on L5 and R5, the two innermost passage orthostats. Most are simply elaborations of preexisting pits and hollows in the stones, which were chosen for this reason. They were preinscribed. Interestingly, the kerbstones are relatively free of distinguishing holes and hollows and are undifferentiated and uniform in this respect. These depressions and hollows have an inherent ambiguity about them. Most were naturally present on the unaltered stone, but they have also been modified and created through picking. Some were created 'from scratch', but in most cases it is not possible to tell.

Temples in the Bend of the Boyne

The Boyne River is the longest and most significant watercourse on the east coast of Ireland between the Wicklow Mountains to the south and the Mourne Mountains to the north and is roughly equidistant from both. Three huge Neolithic temples, Dowth, Newgrange, and Knowth, and their smaller satellites are enclosed by a dramatic meander in the Boyne.

The temples are similar in size and appearance, each consisting of a roughly circular and flat-topped cairn, over 80 m in diameter, 12 to 15 m in height, with an external kerb containing one or more passages and chambers. Set only a few kilometres apart, Newgrange is centrally located, Dowth is to the northeast, and Knowth to the northwest. They dominate the surrounding landscape and contain by far the greatest concentration of megalithic 'art' in Europe. Each is associated with a number of smaller or 'satellite' temples, seventeen at Knowth, three or five at Newgrange (including two other mounds in the valley below), and two at Dowth. Besides these, other temples are located in the bend of the Boyne. In all, 31 definite and nine possible sites have been identified (Stout 2002: 22) (Figure 3.11). Temples began to be constructed in this landscape around 3400 B.C., and radiocarbon dates show that the three great temples are roughly contemporary and were built towards the end of the sequence of temple construction, around 3200 B.C. (Eogan 1999; Cooney 2000: 153 ff.). This account considers the imagery found on the structural stones of the three great temples in relation to their wider landscape setting.

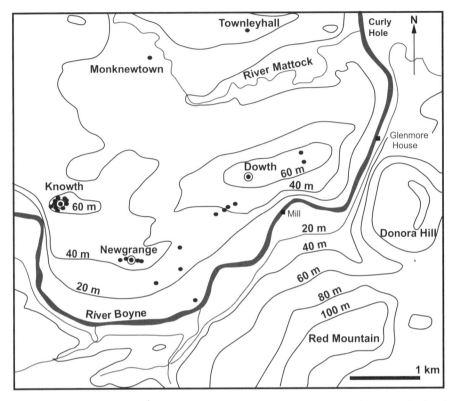

Figure 3.11. The distribution of temples in the bend of the Boyne in relation to the local topography. *After Cooney 2000: fig. 2.3.*

A View from the River

Today the tidal reach of the Boyne is to the Curly Hole at the junction of the Boyne and Mattock rivers. Five and a half thousand years ago, the sea was 4 m above its present level and may have extended somewhat farther to the west, at least up to Glenmore House only 1 km downstream from Dowth (F. Mitchell 1995). The temples, then, were located just beyond the highly significant point on the river where saltwater mingles with freshwater. The river, were it not for the construction of numerous modern weirs, would have been navigable as far as Slane to the east and beyond. Each of the temples is sited on the summit of a rise to the north of the river, and all are intervisible with one another. Dowth to the east occupies the western end of a low ridge, Newgrange a central but lower rise in the landscape, a hill island surrounded by lower ground on all sides, and Knowth, like Dowth, at the western end of a low west–east ridge, with the land sloping gently away to the south and north. Only 500 m to the west of Knowth there is a steep river cliff down to the river Boyne.

A visitor coming to the Boyne temples today does so by road, arriving at the visitor centre, crossing a footbridge over the Boyne, before being bussed to the sites.

This has the advantage of emphasizing the significance of this river, down which an outsider in the prehistoric past is most likely to have passed. From the sea the Boyne follows a tidal course running approximately east to west for 12 km before swinging sharply to the south. It then flows for 3 km to the south before swinging back again on a westerly course, then looping to the north before swinging again to the west, creating a great arc within which the temples are situated. In terms of this great southern arc of the river, Dowth is situated at the eastern end, Knowth at the western end, and Newgrange in the middle. From the eastern start of the loop at the Curly Hole to just beyond Dowth, the Boyne passes through a narrow wooded valley with steep banks on either side. Following the river course, both Dowth and Newgrange first come into view at Mill, just a little downstream from the present visitor centre. From the river one passes the great mound of Dowth without noticing it, but it can be seen looking back towards the sea at this point, with Newgrange visible to the west.

Continuing to follow the course of the river, Newgrange becomes ever more prominent and dramatic on the skyline, and it is evident that the main façade and entrance area to this temple is orientated to face towards the river at the point at which the flatlands are widest and most extensive to its south (Figure 3.12). While Dowth slips by unnoticed by a river-borne observer, Newgrange is seen to dramatic effect. Continuing along the Boyne, Newgrange slips out of view at approximately the same point as Knowth can first be seen, looking to the north. Knowth is visible

Figure 3.12. View to Newgrange from the river Boyne.

along a 700-m stretch before disappearing out of view at the point at which the river swings north to flow within a constricted valley. One slips past and beneath Knowth, like Dowth, unnoticed at the point at which the river is closest to it.

Newgrange is thus the only temple that can be seen from either the east or the west from an extensive 3-km stretch of the river. By contrast, views of Dowth are extremely restricted and relate to downstream movement, while Knowth is visible both upstream and downstream of its location from short stretches but not where the river is closest to it. Access to both Dowth and Knowth from the closest point on the river is restricted and difficult because of the steep river cliffs below them. Newgrange, however, is readily accessible across the low but slowly rising ground from the river up to it. Here there is a complete absence of river cliffs north of the river. These are marked and well defined south of the river along its entire course from the Curly Hole to Slane, far to the west of the bend in the Boyne. The river is not visible from the entrances to either Dowth or Knowth, unlike Newgrange. There is thus a special and important relationship between this, the central temple, and the river.

A View from the Temples

This landscape is totally unlike that seen from the Loughcrew temples. From there the view is to distant mountains. Here, in the bend of the Boyne, the distant horizon is much more limited by low and indistinct ridges to the southeast, north, and east. From the top of the cairns the most extensive views are due south to the Wicklow Mountains. To the west or east one looks along the Boyne valley, which is the most important and distinctive feature of the near landscape. To the west, the Hill of Slane marks the limits of the horizon from Knowth. Interestingly, this view to the west interlocks with that from the Loughcrew cairns looking east. To the northeast the sea can just be seen in the far distance from the tops of the Knowth and Dowth cairns, but not from Newgrange. The local hills and ridges give a sense of circular enclosure to the landscape surrounding all three temples. From Knowth and Dowth there are two main windows or openings to a wider world, one northeast to the sea, the other south to the Wicklow Mountains. The sea cannot be seen from Newgrange because the view is blocked by the ridge on which Dowth stands. Instead, from here the view of river cliff visible on the south side of the Boyne uniquely creates a sense of an embayment, a semicircular amphitheatre in front of the temple, which is not apparent at either Dowth or Knowth.

Dowth

Two passages and chambers are located in the western side of the cairn of Dowth (Figure 3.13; O'Kelly and O'Kelly 1983: figs. 10–26). Exposed stones in the kerb surrounding the cairn are now present in the southern and eastern sections. They are noticeably irregular in shape and size and somewhat rough greywacke blocks. Decoration is recorded on the surfaces of fifteen stones (ibid.: 148). The main motifs are zigzags, spirals, circles, and cupmarks and/or enlarged hollows. The most distinctive

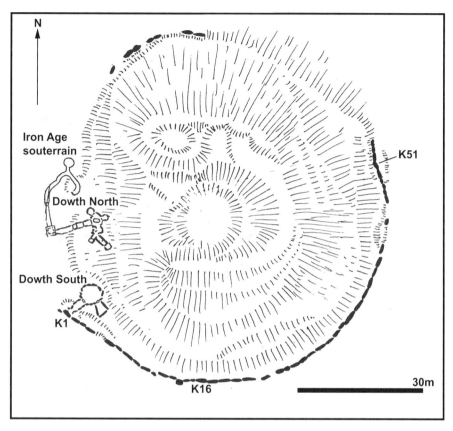

Figure 3.13. Plan of the Dowth temple. Kerbstones are numbered. *After O'Kelly and O'Kelly 1983.*

and striking stone in the Dowth kerb (K51) is decorated by a remarkable series of radial motifs, where there is an in-turn of the façade facing due east towards the equinoxal sunrise. We do not know whether or not this marks the entrance to another passage and chamber, but the solar imagery (see below) on the stone seems to strongly suggest the possibility. These images are dramatically illuminated by the rising sun on the winter solstice. The back of K51 is also covered with concealed picked motifs, circular designs, and rather more amorphous picked shapes. One of the other most highly decorated and visually dominant kerbstones is K1, outside the passage entrance to Dowth South. Motifs on the other stones—apart from K52 and K53, on which a series of large circular motifs occur—are all rather small and discrete, with no obvious structured arrangement. One, K16, has diffuse picking over much of the surface. Many of the stones are not decorated, and there are extensive gaps between those that are. Walking around the kerb from the entrance to Dowth South at a distance from which one can see the motifs on the stone surfaces, one notices that the number of kerbstones visible around the kerb varies from two or three to seven, and these may include undecorated stones. So the visual impression of the kerb, even allowing for the effects of weathering, appears to be fragmented and constantly changing, with little sense of coherence or structuring of the decorated stones in relation to one another or the landscape beyond, except in relation to the important winter solstice axis.

Dowth South

The two external passage orthostats of Dowth South are distinctly angled, restricting the space of the passage. One must clamber over the external decorated kerb stone and stoop down in order to enter. Moving into the passage one becomes aware of a distinctive trough in the centre of the face of the first right-hand orthostat, together with two wavy lines. This acts as a key for understanding the rest of the temple. The passage roof space gradually rises to the chamber beyond. Beyond the first pair of passage orthostats, the passage widens. The surface of R2 (see Figure 3.14) is quite rough and abraded with cracks. On it there is a small circular motif three-quarters of the way up the stone. Above, one must look up to see carved lines on a roofing stone. Two further passage orthostats narrow the entrance to the chamber, which is also

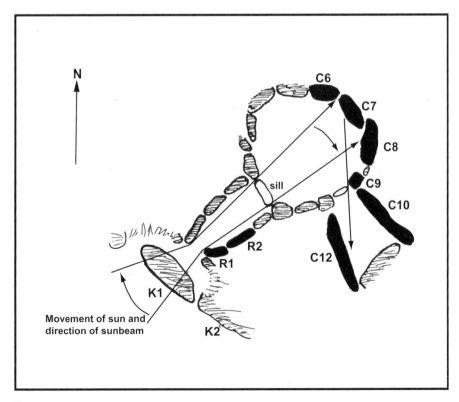

Figure 3.14. Plan of Dowth South showing positions of decorated orthostats, sunbeams, and reflections. *After Moroney 1999.*

defined by a sillstone over which one must step. On entering the circular chamber it is possible to stand up fully, and there is a sense of great volume and space. Decoration on the three central back passage orthostats, C6–C8 (see Figure 3.15), is visible ahead. This temple is orientated to the midwinter sunset, and on the shortest days of the year, from late November to mid January, at around 3 pm the dying rays of the sun move down the passage and dramatically illuminate the decorated chamber orthostats at the back (Brennan 1983: 82–85; Moroney 1999). The beam of the sun is so strong that the whole chamber is lit up. For the rest of the year, without artificial illumination the presence of the graphic imagery would be more easily felt than seen. This tactile contrast between picked and unpicked stone surfaces at Dowth appears to be as, if not more, important than the character of the motifs. There is a great contrast between the smooth areas and the picked lozenges, triangles, and lines on C7.

The surface of C7 has a curved outer surface. Acting as a mirror, this reflects the sunlight into a wedge-shaped cell on the right-hand side of the chamber, usually a dark and hidden space. The light is reflected onto the right-hand orthostat (C12), on which there is a profusion of carvings and picked areas. In February the sun's rays also illuminate the motifs on the first right passage orthostat, R1 (Moroney 1999: 41).

Not only does the sun illuminate the most important passage and chamber orthostats, there are also changing light effects:

> The colour of the sun shining into this circular chamber . . . and onto the stones is a bright beam at the beginning of this solar pattern in winter. The light turns to a warm yellow and around the time of the solstice changes to a golden pink colour. As the days lengthen again the sun rays are more honey-coloured and then become a bright, white light in February. (ibid.: 14)

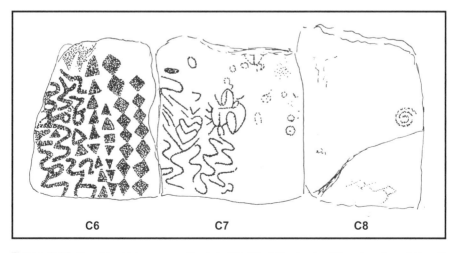

Figure 3.15. Graphic designs on orthostats C6–C8 at the back of the chamber of Dowth South. *After O'Kelly and O'Kelly 1983: figs. 24 and 25, and Moroney 1999.*

As on C7, the smooth surface of the stone on C12 contrasts with the picked areas. The natural surface of this stone is yellowish and somewhat reflective, but the picked areas absorb and dull the light, creating a dark greenish hue. In the process of picking, earlier motifs have been partially or totally obliterated. Others were highlighted by this process, enhancing them. The substantial areas dulled by surface picking now absorb light reflected from the sun's rays deflected from C7. All the emphasis is to the right and the back of this temple. Only the right passage and chamber orthostats are decorated, and the importance of the right-hand side is architecturally emphasized by the presence of the decorated cell. Unlike the chamber space, the back of the cell is undecorated. The left-hand orthostat lacks decoration but is covered all over its surface with coarse picking, roughening and emphasizing its surface. In addition, two substantial hollows in this stone have been picked deeper. By far the most dramatic stones are the two orthostats C6 and C7 at the back of the chamber.

Dowth North

The original entrance to the passage at Dowth North (Figure 3.16) is now blocked and altered, but facing southwest it too was orientated to the setting sun on the winter solstice. The passage is considerably longer than in Dowth South, and the chamber space more complex, cruciform in plan, with three side cells and a further extension, and elaboration of the right-hand cell. As in Dowth South, decoration on many of the chamber and passage orthostats is either absent or sparse. Only three of the passage orthostats are decorated, and by far the most elaborate is on the right-hand side.

As usual, the experience of the passage is of constricted space and a gradual diminution of light as one approaches the voluminous chamber. All three decorated orthostats occur at the point at which a sillstone demarcates the outer from the inner part of the passage. The distinct angling of the fourth right passage orthostat by the sillstone is designed so that the motifs on its face, deeply picked circles and linear grooves, stand out. Immediately above the sillstone, a roof lintel has some picked designs. Beyond the first passage sill, one can stand up in the passage, which gradually rises towards the chamber space. Two further sills separate the innermost area of the passage from the chamber. The remainder of the passage is undecorated. It is only when passing down the final section of the passage and entering the chamber that any further decorated stones become visible.

A huge stone basin now occupies half of the main chamber space. It is likely that its original position was in the large right-hand recess, which is alone of sufficient size for it to fit (O'Kelly and O'Kelly 1983: 152). Four massive orthostats, all different in height, shape, and form, dominate the internal chamber space. C1, sparsely decorated with a circular picked motif, is a rectangular pillar. C7 is widened and bulbous at the top with a broad internal face. C13 has a distinctive flat face; C19 is a tall column. The orthostats C7 and C19 are the most elaborately decorated in the temple. C19 has complex circular, meandering, and linear designs. C7 has at least twenty natural hollows with circular and radial designs. These flank either side of the passage, and to see the decoration one must either turn round or progress

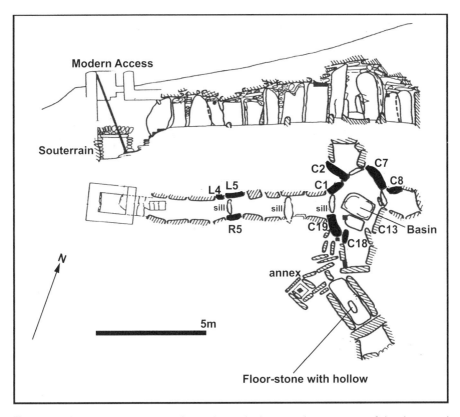

Figure 3.16. Plan and elevation of Dowth North showing the positions of the decorated orthostats *After O'Kelly and O'Kelly 1983: fig. 6.*

around the central rock basin. Neither would ever be directly illuminated by the sun. Entering the chamber one becomes aware of cells leading off it on three sides. Only the left cell has motifs on one of the stones. The right cell is the most architecturally elaborated and deep, with a series of annexes leading off it, but there is only one orthostat with a small area of irregular picking.

There is a great distinction between Dowth South and North in terms of architectural form, the kinds of motifs present, and the organization of internal space within the temple chambers, suggesting very different purposes and activities. They were perhaps visited and experienced sequentially. If this was the case, the experience of one temple would establish a false set of expectations with regard to the next. Decorative emphasis in Dowth South is on the right-hand side and in the cell. In Dowth North it is around the central chamber space. There are no stones in Dowth North with large areas of surface picking, compared with Dowth South. The structured ordering of lozenges and the like on chamber stone C8 has no counterpart in Dowth North. The latter is internally far more complex in terms of the cell architecture.

Newgrange

Newgrange, the central temple of the three great megalithic monuments in the Boyne valley, is situated on the highest point of a low hill (Figure 3.17; M. O'Kelly 1982; C. O'Kelly 1982: figs 3–6, 20, 24–55, 60–82; pl. XII). It is about 1 km to the north of the river Boyne and 15 km from its mouth to the east. The cairn has a flat top 32 m in diameter, which is 11 m high on the south side and 13 m high on the north side (M. O'Kelly 1982: 21). A kerb of 97 massive slabs surrounds the somewhat irregularly shaped circular cairn, varying in diameter between 78 and 85 m. Thirty-one decorated stones in the kerb are documented. These are concentrated in the southern sector of the cairn to the left (west) and right (east) of the passage entrance, with a few in the northwest part of the circumference and one in the northeast. O'Kelly's excavations only fully exposed a third of the cairn perimeter, so this represents a minimum number. Some may have hidden decoration on their back surfaces or tops. The entrance stone outside the passage is by far the most elab-

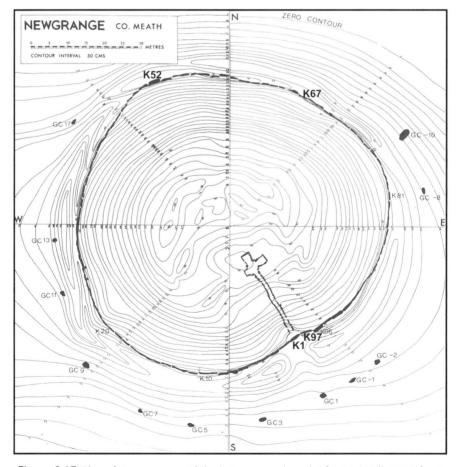

Figure 3.17. Plan of Newgrange, with kerbstones numbered. *After M. O'Kelly 1982: fig. 3.*

orate, its surface covered with rows of spirals, arcs, and interlocking lozenges (Figure 3.18A). This was carved *in situ* before the kerbstones on either side were placed

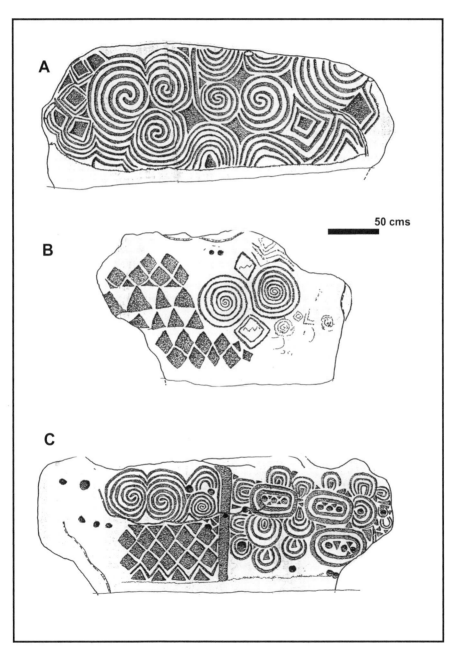

Figure 3.18. Kerbstones at Newgrange with 'plastic' decoration. *A*: the entrance stone K1. *B*: K67. *C*: K52. For locations, see Figure 3.17. *After C. O'Kelly 1982: figs. 24, 28, and 29.*

in position (C. O'Kelly 1982: 149). The kerbstones to the left and right of it are covered all over their surfaces with pick dressing. The effect is to almost obliterate the other designs on these stones—namely, zigzag lines on K2 and spirals on K97. Compared with the entrance stone, the motifs on those on either side are irregular and cover only a tiny part of the surface area. The picking, which almost hides these earlier motifs, must have been undertaken to further emphasize the extraordinary entrance stone so as to better act as a foil or framing device for it.

The motifs on the front surfaces of the other decorated kerbstones at the front of the cairn to the left of the entrance are slight and irregular. Some occur on the front faces, others on the tops of the stones. Hollows on some have been deepened. Minor picked areas occur on some, but here the intention was not to obliterate or obscure the motifs. Only a small proportion of the total surface area has any decoration at all. Four stones do possess striking and elaborate decoration. This is all concealed on their back surfaces, their front and visible faces being either totally plain or bearing decoration of an indistinct and irregular character. The same is true for the appearance of the decorated stones to the right of the entrance, except that only one has concealed decoration on the back face.

K67 in the northwest perimeter of the cairn is the only stone in this section of the cairn perimeter that has decoration on its front surface (Figure 3.18B). The decoration is in bold 'plastic style' (see discussion below), occurring in two panels, with conjoined spirals and picked lozenges and triangles to the left. No other decorated stones are visible from it. There are four decorated stones in the northwest sector of the cairn directly opposite the passage entrance. Of these, K52 is the most striking, and like the passage entrance stone, it was carved in situ. After the entrance stone (K1), K52 is the most striking and visually powerful stone in the temple perimeter (Figure 3.18C). The only other stone of similar quality and power in the kerb is K67. Unlike K1 or K67, K52 has a surface riddled with hollows that are skilfully incorporated into the design field. The kerbstone flanking it to the left, K53, has no decoration. It is one of only two yellow-brown sandstone blocks incorporated into the kerb, the rest being of the local grey-green greywacke (see discussion of the Knowth kerb below). The stone to the right, K51, is comparatively little decorated, with motifs of a completely different character. Interestingly, K51 has a fine, smooth surface, much easier to carve than the surface of K52 which is riddled with holes. The irregular surface of K52 was deliberately chosen by its carver and may have been incorporated into the kerb precisely because of its irregular surface.

Standing any distance away from the kerb of Newgrange, the only visible decorated stones are K1, K67, and K52. These are all in completely different sectors of the cairn circuit, stones that are not intervisible. A distant but erroneous impression of the Newgrange kerb would be that it contains only three decorated stones. If the passage entrance was concealed by its original blocking stone, the impression given would be of a cairn with a continuous circuit, with three entrances marked by visually dominant stones. The finest stones in the kerb in terms of both shape and size are all found in the southern part of the perimeter on either side of the entrance. In other sectors of the perimeter, the kerbstones are smaller and much more irregular in shape and size (apart from those in the immediate vicinity of K67 and K52), further emphasizing the importance of the fine stones in the southern sector and the passage entrance area. Walking around immediately outside the kerb circuit, as at Dowth, varying numbers of neighbouring kerbstones are visible, depending on the curvature of the cairn at any particular viewpoint: from some places, two or three kerbstones are visible on either side of the stone the observer is facing; in exceptional positions, six stones can be seen to the right and only two or three to the left. The norm is to experience a visual field of only two or three stones on either side of the stone in front of the observer, before the rest of the kerbstones fall out of sight. Walking close to the curve restricts the visual field of contiguous stones to between five and seven. From K52 it is possible to see as far as K55 to the right and K49 to the left, a field of vision that includes all the decorated stones in this part of the kerb perimeter. Standing in front of the entrance stone, K1, it is possible to see as far as K4 to the left and K94 to the right. However, the only motifs visible on these kerbstones are those on K2 and K97, all of which have been virtually obliterated by pick dressing.

The kerb around the outside of Newgrange, as at Dowth and Knowth, is continuous. The passage entrance is only partly visible when looking over the highly decorated stone outside it. Entering the temple itself would require clambering over this stone, about 1.2 m high, and stooping under the passage entrance lintel before walking down the passage towards the chamber. The 19-m-long passage faces southeast. It is flanked by 22 orthostats on the left (west) side and 21 on the right (east) side. Those nearest the chamber are tallest, 2 m or more above the ground. The passage is roofed by massive slabs resting either on the tops of the orthostats or on corbels above them. The passage is in two sections, the outer lower, the inner higher. Beyond orthostats R12 and L13, the roof gradually rises towards the chamber, reaching a height of 3.5 m (Figure 3.19). The floor of both the passage and chamber follows the rise of the hill on which the temple stands, so the floor level of the chamber is almost 2 m higher than that at the entrance. Moving down the passage one becomes aware of a gradually changing sense of place, with both the floor and the roof rising up, the latter more quickly. The passage is not dead straight but meanders a little, bending slightly to the left and then to the right and again to the left before the chamber is reached. The narrow and constricted passage, now with some orthostats leaning inwards, is 1 m wide, permitting only a single person to move through it. The bodily sensation is of remarkable constriction despite the changing height of the roof space; and by contrast, the corbelled chamber appears huge. Cruciform in shape, it contains three side recesses or cells, one to the left, another at the back, and one to the right, measuring up to 6.5 m along the longest stretch of the cruciform shape, all with stone basins. The largest cell is the one to the right; this has two basin stones, one inside the other (Figure 3.20). The corbelled vault, closed by a single capstone, rises 6 m above the floor. As is well known, the chamber floor is directly illuminated by the rising sun on the winter solstice, which shines through a unique, specially constructed roof box above the passage entrance

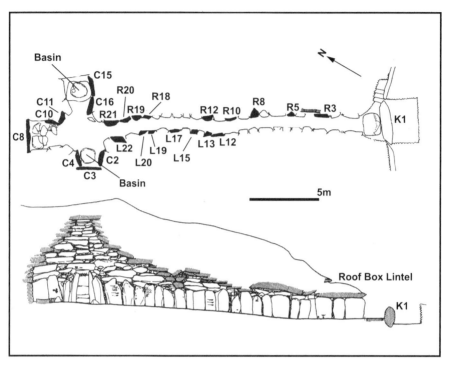

Figure 3.19. Plan and elevation of the Newgrange passage and chamber, showing the positions of stones with graphic designs. *After M. O'Kelly 1982: fig. 4.*

and crosses the floor of the main chamber as far as the back recess (M. O'Kelly 1982: 123 ff.). Light entering from the passage entrance itself extends as far back as orthostat L19 and illuminates the three spirals on it (Brennan 1983: 80). Both these light sources could be closed off or opened at will, the passage by a large slab now set beside the temple entrance and the roof box slit by the movement of two quartz blocks (M. O'Kelly 1982: 123).

Standing at the passage entrance, the first decorated stone that is visible is the front face of the lintel above the roof box, with its expertly picked lattice design. The back of the corbel supporting the roof box lintel is engraved with motifs including circles and radial designs that were always hidden after its construction. All the passage orthostat stones are pick dressed over all, or most, of their main faces, making them appear uniform and undifferentiated in both a visual and a tactile sense as one moves down the passage. There is an absence of any other visually arresting decoration except in a few cases. The only two orthostats with any visually striking or memorable designs are stones L19 and L22, which occur at or near the end of the passage on the left-hand side (Figure 3.21). Other stones display a little decoration, but this is either partially obscured through later surface picking, hidden beneath ground level, or only present on the partially exposed side rather than on the front and main faces of the stones. Some motifs are positioned towards the very top or

Figure 3.20. The stone basin in the right cell of the Newgrange chamber which rests inside another.

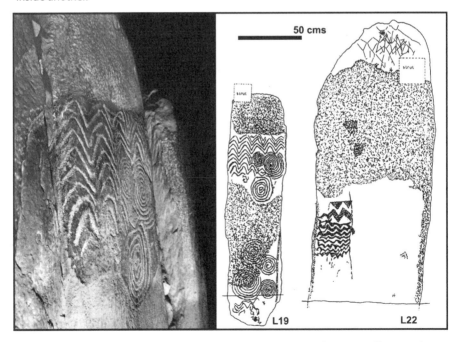

Figure 3.21. Newgrange: Passage orthostats L19 and L22. *After C. O'Kelly 1982: fig. 42.* Photograph shows detail of upper part of L19.

bottom of the main faces of the stones. In the absence of detailed, well-lighted exam-ination of the stones, the impression of the passage is of orthostats picked all over but otherwise having only two decorated stones, a puritanical simplicity of form and design. Not only are motifs picked over to completely or partially obscure them, but so also are surface hollows, depressions, and previously picked grooves. 'Natural' or 'cultural' features marking or distinguishing individual stones are all treated in the same manner, creating an overwhelming impression of uniformity.

R3 has picking all over except near the base, where there are circular decorations on an unpicked area of the stone. Most of this ornament is concealed below floor level. Some of the motifs just above the floor are also obscured by subsequent pick dressing and only partly discernible. R5 has a row of tiny triangles at the very top of the stone. R6 has some pronounced hollows on its surface and is covered with pick-ing. R8 has lozenges towards the top of the stone, virtually obliterated by overall picking. R10 has two lozenges in slight relief on the lower part of the stone, which is picked all over; R12 has picked-over grooves and a small panel of decoration on the south side rather than on the main face of the stone. The main faces of L12 and L13 have overall picking. A few motifs occur on the sides but are only partly visible. L15 is picked all over except at the top, which is smooth and decorated with three deeply picked lozenges. L19 is picked all over at the top of the stone and over much of the bottom. The central part protrudes slightly and, because of the absence of picking, has three deeply engraved spirals and zigzag lines, which appear prominently. Four other spirals at the base of this stone are partially or completely obscured by picking, and other picked lines are beneath ground level. This is the first dramatic stone in the entire passage. L20 has spiral motifs below the ground surface. R18 is decorated with some zigzag bands on part of its face, which can be traced by the fingers. R19 has two small lozenges towards the top; L20 has motifs below ground level. R20 pos-sesses some natural hollows deepened and emphasized by pick dressing covering much of its surface; R21 has picked over grooves and hollows on the main face. L21 opposite has two linear bands of picking running down the centre of the stone. L22, the final passage orthostat on the left, has an incised pattern on a smooth, unpicked surface at the top of the stone and an area with zigzag bands and triangles in an area at the base of the stone which is not picked.

If C. O'Kelly's documentation were not available, none of the decorations on the stones—apart from the panels of designs on the unpicked areas of L19 and L22—would likely be seen or felt by a casual observer. None of these motifs are especially easy to see, owing to both their position and/or the subsequent picking of the ortho-stat surfaces. To experience them at all requires very careful visual and tactile exam-ination of the stone surface, looking across and up or bending down. It also requires either being shown or knowing where to look. The final intention appears to have been to create a passage that was remarkably plain except for the presence of the surface picking enhancing every stone.

Entering into the chamber, the backstone of the end cell is visible ahead. No decoration is apparent in the chamber space, apart from picked areas on the side and front faces of some of the stones. The only visible motif is a 'wheat sheaf' motif on the east side of the right stone in the left recess. Moving farther into the chamber space and turning to the left, orthostat C1 is remarkable because of the presence of deep grooves running down the front face of the stone with picking in between. The left cell has highly visible and dramatic decoration on the backstone and on the left side. The backstone has no overall picking but has three dominant spirals in its centre. The orthostat to the left has one dominant spiral with picked and unpicked lines of lozenges above, but the latter are partially concealed because of the shape of the stone, the surface of which is smooth. The right side of this cell has a small picked area near the outer face that partially obliterates one of two spirals situated low down on it. Otherwise the surface is smooth, with only a few other picked lines present. Orthostat C5 has distinctive hollows on its main face and small areas of picked dressing. The back recess is very little decorated. Picking has obliterated one of two small lozenges near the top of the backstone, and double triangles are virtually concealed in the top right-hand corner; otherwise the cell is undecorated. Orthostat C10, on the left side of the back cell, is the only dramatically decorated stone, with a three-spiral motif picked on an undressed surface of the stone quite low down the main face (Figure 3.22). Above is an extensive area of picking, leaving untouched a faint scratched line of four lozenges but irregularly extending as far as the three-spiral motif. The motifs on this stone can only be seen when looking into the cell and not from the main chamber. By contrast, C11, whose main side faces out into the

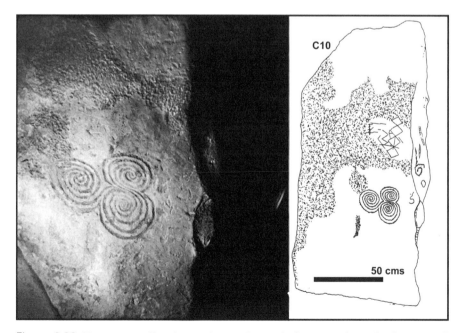

Figure 3.22. Newgrange: Chamber orthostat C10 with three-spiral motif. *After C. O'Kelly 1982: fig. 47.* Photograph shows detail of spiral and area picking above it.

chamber, is undecorated apart from one small, irregular, and indistinct oval-shaped motif near the floor. The right cell has no decoration on the main faces of the stones facing into it, but these have picking either all over their surfaces or in bands. The only motifs are small areas with picked lozenges high up the western edges of C15 and C16, which are in a very obscure and unexpected position.

The visual impression of the chamber space thus continues the theme introduced in the passage: relatively little elaboration. There are only three stones, all decorated with spirals, that might be described as striking or dramatic. Only one of these is visible from the centre of the chamber space looking in any direction. To see the spirals in cell 1 requires looking into it; those in cell 2 are best seen looking out towards the passage (Shee Twohig 2000: 95). However, entering the right cell and looking upwards at the underside of the capstone, one discovers an amazing sight. The stone is covered with spirals and interlocking circular and lozenge designs in baroque elaboration (Figure 3.23). The corbels on this cell immediately under the roofstone are similarly elaborately decorated. While these can be seen from a standing position, the roofstone is best appreciated lying down and looking up. Even so, some of the decoration is still not visible, as it disappears under the roof corbels.

The effect of the light penetrating into the chamber on the midwinter solstice through the roof box is to dramatically illuminate a space that is normally very dark. Various details of the motifs in the chamber and side cells then become illuminated by

Figure 3.23. Graphic designs on part of the capstone of the right-hand chamber cell, Newgrange.

the reflected light in a manner only possible through artificial illumination at any other time. The beam from the roof box lasts for exactly 17 minutes (M. O'Kelly 1982: 124).

Besides the stones already mentioned, certain other of the passage roofing stones and corbels in the chamber are decorated. Two corbels immediately behind the roof box have much decoration on their upper faces which was completely hidden during the Neolithic construction of the passage. Two other roofstones with hidden decoration were placed at the junction between the passage and chamber roofs; these were discovered during the excavation and restoration of the temple (M. O'Kelly 1982: 99). The last roof slab over the opening from the passage to the chamber has picked lines of triangles visible from inside the chamber looking out. All this decoration, mostly hidden, emphasizes important transitional points from the inner to the outer part of the passage and from the passage to the chamber.

In Newgrange the visually dominant visual images occur on the left passage orthostats: L19 with three spirals; on the three stones in the left recess, each with one to three spirals; on orthostat C10, with its unique three-spiral motif; and on the highly elaborate roofstone of the right (or east) cell. This again has a dominant central spiral motif together with circular motifs and ellipses. The emphasis on the spiral is the unique and memorable signature of this temple (see discussion below). The emphasis placed on the right-hand cell of the chamber and the left-hand side of the passage repeats the situation found in Loughcrew temple L.

Knowth (Site 1)

The third great temple in the Boyne valley, Knowth, contains two passages and chambers (Figure 3.24; Eogan 1984; 1986; 1996; 1997; 1998; Eogan and Aboud 1990). The original entrances and about 5 m of the passages to both were destroyed during the Iron Age and in the early Christian era. They were orientated to the east and west and, almost meeting at the centre of the cairn, were probably related to the equinoxal sunrise and sunset, although this has not been conclusively demonstrated. The western passage and chamber is of undifferentiated form, lacking side cells or recesses. The eastern one has a cruciform-shaped chamber like that at Newgrange.

The cairn containing the chambers and passages is smaller and lower than that at Newgrange. Almost 10 m high, it is more oval than circular in shape, measuring 80 m west to east and 95 m north to south. It is surrounded by eighteen smaller satellite temples, except in the southeast area of the cairn circuit, and their absence here may be a result of differential destruction. The kerb is continuous, curving in slightly at the entrances to the western and eastern passages. As at Newgrange, one would have to clamber over the entrance kerbstones to enter the interiors, which, also as at Newgrange, might originally have had removable passage blocking stones. Originally the kerb had 127 stones, significantly more than at Newgrange, but three are now missing. There is one original gap in the kerb on the northern side where the cairn was built up against an earlier temple (no. 16) whose entrance was remodelled, and an indented area on the northern side devised to avoid another earlier temple (no. 13) (Eogan 1986: 46). Of the 124 surviving kerbstones, 95 are of

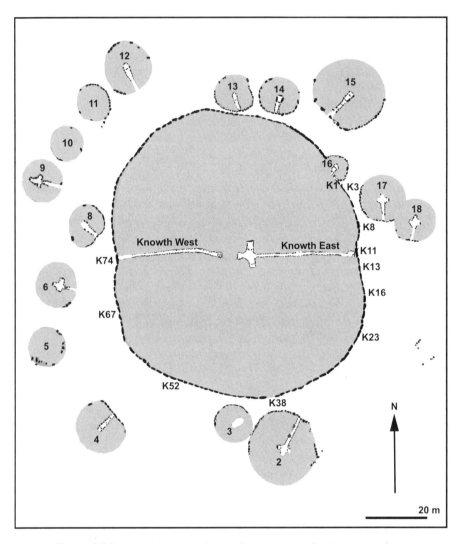

Figure 3.24. Plan of the Knowth Temple Cemetery. *After Stout 2002: fig. 8.*

greywacke, green cleaved grit, or similar rock; eighteen are of limestone, nine of sandstone. There is thus considerably more variety in the type of stone used to construct the kerb than at Newgrange.

Grey-green greywacke is the hardest and most regular of these rocks in terms of surface, texture, and shape. It has few cracks and fissures or cavities and hollows. By contrast, the limestone, grey to white in colour, has a much more irregular and fissured surface and contains many micro-fossils. The sandstone is a pinky brown, much softer, and characterised in places by numerous erosion pits and hollows. The greywacke provides a harder and more even surface for carving and is also more resistant to weathering.

Most of the kerbstones are oblong in shape, averaging 2.5 m long and up to 1.2 m high, with the largest used near the temple entrances. Great care was taken to ensure a uniform profile and equalisation of height, with sockets being dug for some stones and others sitting on a foundation of small stones built up on the old land surface (ibid.). Significantly smaller stones were used on the northern side near temples 13 and 14, where they are only 30 cm high and on average 1.75 m long. Sandstone and limestone blocks occur throughout the kerb perimeter but are particularly concentrated in the northern and southern sectors, rather than to the west and east where the temples are situated.

Because the kerb has marked irregularity in the degrees of its curves, different numbers of kerbstones become visible as one walks around immediately outside its perimeter. At some points, long stretches of kerbstones are visible; at others only two or three stones can be seen in either direction. For example, walking clockwise from stone K11 outside the entrance to the eastern passage, it is possible to see K10, K9, and part of K8 to the right and up to K16 to the left. From K23 three stones are visible to the right, two to the left. From K74, the entrance to the western passage, three stones are visible to the right and five to the left. Along straighter stretches of the kerb along the southwest perimeter and along the western side, between ten and fifteen kerbstones may be visible. In other places, where the kerb switches direction, as few as three or four can be seen. From 50 percent of the kerbstones, between five and eight other stones are visible in total.

Quite obviously, there is no point at which the entire kerb is visible at Knowth, however far away one stands. Walking beside it, there is a constantly changing visual perspective of this stone façade and of the qualities of the stones themselves— colour, form, texture, and their changing relationships and the designs inscribed on them. Looking at the kerb, one's attention is always directed at the stones themselves, to the exclusion of the wider landscape. They become, in effect, a circular conceptual landscape in abstract representation. Both entrance stones are only slightly inset from the rest of the cairn, with no pronounced forecourt areas as at Loughcrew cairns L and T. This gives a sense of a continuum, a never-ending circuit. Because of the positions of the surrounding satellite temples, the landscape beyond Knowth can be experienced only from the top of the mound.

The Knowth kerb is lavishly decorated with bold, visually striking, and often symmetrically arranged motifs. Of the kerbstones, at least 90 (73%) have decoration. Three stones are missing, another four badly damaged. Undecorated stones are concentrated in the vicinity of satellite temples 13 and 14 on the north part of the kerb, where the stones are much smaller and obviously less important. O'Sullivan has noted a general increase in the lengths of the kerbstones from the north and south towards the west and east entrance areas of the temple, with the distribution of the images following this general pattern (O'Sullivan 1998:45; 2004: 47). This decoration was meant to be seen. Of 123 kerbstones fully examined by Eogan, decoration occurs only on the backs of eleven and is 'restricted in range' (Eogan 1986: 150). There is nothing comparable to the backs of the elaborately decorated stones hidden in the Newgrange kerb. All but one are decorated with line picking, incision occurs on six, and scattered pick marking occurs on nine (ibid.: 151). Some stones are decorated on their top surfaces, but the major and most visually striking motifs are on the front faces of the stones. It is important to emphasize the sheer variety of the decorated surfaces. Although the range of motifs employed is somewhat limited and repetitive, the manner and style with which they are positioned and related to one another on the stones is unique. There are no two identical stones in the Knowth kerb. One passes in front of an ever-changing sequence of images. As some image fields on individual and adjacent stones come into view, others slip out of sight; figure and ground are constantly changing as one walks past the stones. Many stones have large and visually dominant motifs, which can be seen from some distance away from the kerb. Whereas the majority of the kerbstones at Dowth and Newgrange appear to be undecorated from a distance, the reverse is true at Knowth. Moreover, most motifs on the Knowth curve are not picked over so as to obliterate them, unlike those on either side of the Newgrange entrance stones. The Knowth kerb presents a striking visual kaleidoscope, truly one of the wonders of Neolithic Europe.

While some stones that have no decoration today might have been decorated in the past (mainly the softer limestone and sandstone blocks), the presence of decorated and undecorated stones in the kerb—of greywacke, limestone, and sandstone, with very different forms, surfaces, colours, and textures—does appear to be significant in defining discrete and related visual fields along the kerb. That is, the undecorated stones act as a frame bordering sequences of decorated blocks. The sensory contrasts and different sources of origin of the stones seem to be of great significance, a phenomenon which also occurs at the Knockroe temple in county Kilkenny (O'Sullivan 1993; 2004: 47).

Eogan has identified six framed panels around the Knowth kerb and suggests that they are strategically placed. Three are opposite the entrances to the satellite temples 4, 14, and 15; another is the entrance area to the eastern temple, and another faces towards Newgrange (Eogan 1996: 104). Others can also be suggested—for example, K1 has some areas of pick dressing but no pattern, and K3 is undecorated, acting as a frame for K2, a decorated stone with large nested arcs crossing its surface. Moving around the cairn, there are some areas with definite sequences of panels and other areas without. K3 and the undecorated K6 frame K4 and K5, which are lavishly decorated with central spirals and opposing arcs of similar form. K6 and undecorated K9 frame K7 and K8 with dominant circular and arc motifs of similar form. By contrast, from K10 to K18, a long stretch leading from the entrance area of the eastern temple to the southeast part of the perimeter, all the kerbstones are decorated without any visual break. A similar situation with panels and continuously decorated stretches occurs all round the curve except where there are many small and undecorated stones in the north where temples 13 and 14 almost abut the cairn and block a view of the kerb.

The most frequent designs on the Knowth kerbstones are circular forms, meandering lines or 'serpentine' forms, parallel lines or arcs, and arrangements of circles and spirals. Many of the kerbstones have one or two visually dominant, centrally placed motifs that stand out or arrest the eye, often of similar form to motifs on neighbouring stones (e.g., Figure 3.25: K5, K17, K11) These may be accompanied by smaller and less visually arresting motifs towards the sides, top, or bottom of the stone. Other stones have a repetitive pattern of smaller motifs of similar form, such as circles or spirals, dispersed over the entire stone surface rather than one or a few large dominant motifs (e.g., Figure 3.25: K42). Some stones combine separate motifs into a single pattern in a manner analogous to the Newgrange entrance stone. Others have unique, distinctive motifs, such as the two entrance stones to the temples in the kerb opposite each other on either side of the cairn; both have similar and distinctive decoration not found elsewhere.

Figure 3.25. Graphic designs on some of the kerbstones at Knowth (site 1).

Knowth East

Most of the passage on the eastern side of the temple is remarkably uniform in height and width (originally about 40 m long, 1.6 m high, and 85 cm wide) (Figure 3.26), and it is possible to see right down it and into the chamber from the present entrance, suggesting that the chamber and its end cell may have been significantly illuminated by the rising sun at the equinox. In the final 11-m section of the passage, the roof rises gradually until it gets to the chamber space and reaches its highest point (2.7 m) above the floor; here the soaring corbelled roof reaches 5.9 m in height. The bodily impact of the constricted passage space compared with that of the chamber is huge.

The passage on the eastern side differs from that of Newgrange by its use of sandstone as well as greywacke orthostats, the combination of which creates both a visual and tactile contrast between individual orthostats. There is also an important distinction between the outer and inner parts of the passage, with the former being sparsely decorated. A sill of three stones demarcates the transition from the outer to the inner passage space. Both the left and right orthostats immediately before the sill are decorated with picked meandering lines. The stone to the right is hard greywacke and is most visually striking, with a complex curving series of picked lines covering its surface, appearing almost anthropomorphic in form (see discussion below). The one to the left is a soft sandstone orthostat with broad bands of picking curving down from the top of the stone. Passing over the sillstones, the next four orthostats to the right have curvilinear designs covering all or parts of their surfaces; to the left there are two more orthostats. The capstone over the sillstones is also elaborately decorated on its left half with a series of zigzag lines. The rest of the passage ortho-stats are not very elaborate or visually complex. Most have areas of diffuse picking,

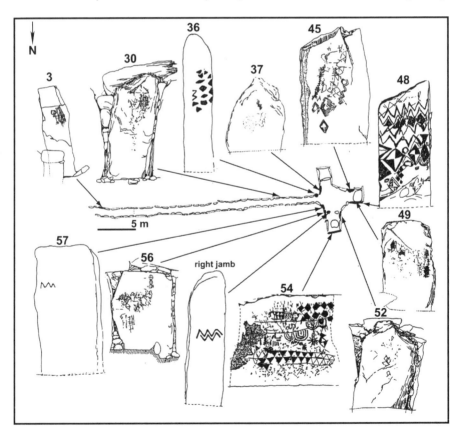

Figure 3.26. Plan of the passage and chamber of Knowth East, showing orthostats decorated in Eogan's 'angular style'. *After Eogan 1986: fig. 76.*

but there is an absence of pattern. Another sillstone in the passage floor marks the transition to the chamber space. Now high up in the roof above the second from last passage roofing stone is a corbel covered in an open pattern of zigzag lines.

Each of the chamber recesses is formed by five orthostats, two on each side and a backstone. The left and right recesses are rectangular in form, the back wedge-shaped. A sill separates the innermost part of the left cell from the rest of the chamber space. The backstone of the left cell consists of three layers of horizontal rectangular blocks. The uppermost of these is sandstone and feels incredibly smooth in comparison with the greywacke that makes up the other stones in this cell. The backstones lack graphic motifs. The innermost orthostat to the left has some areas of dense picking on its face. This cell is almost entirely unelaborated, except for the outermost corbel which has a meandering zigzag line, a circle, and other irregular picked forms.

The end cell has no sillstone but contains the remains of a stone basin covered with large areas of diffuse picking. A chamber orthostat to the right of the cell has linear or curvilinear decoration over its surface, similar to that found on the orthostats in the transitional inner passage space. The first left orthostat of the cell has a double row of bold zigzag lines running down its face and areas of very fine scored lines forming irregular patterns and lozenges. The surface of this stone is incredibly smooth; the faint scratched lines cannot be felt, only the bolder picked lines. It is only discretely decorated. The inner left orthostat contrasts utterly with the outer. The surface is rough and large areas are covered with picking, but there is an absence of pattern. Diffuse picking is also present on the corbels above. The backstone is also comparatively rough and covered with areas of picking in the vicinity of enlarged hollows towards its top. The corbels above also have diffuse picking.

The lack of decorative elaboration found to the left and back of this cell contrasts markedly with the striking motifs on the innermost orthostat to the right (no. 48). This has an almost perfectly smooth surface apart from five hollows enlarged or deepened by picking. The surface is covered with zigzag bands and lozenges in interconnected patterns. The outermost right orthostat of the cell (no. 49) has a comparatively rough surface, with slight scratched designs and small areas of picking. Picking and scratched marks occur on the corbels above. The imagery on this backstone, as in Knowth West, resembles that which occurs on the entrance kerbstone.

The right, or north, cell contrasts with the two others because access to it is restricted by the presence of two external jambs 2.2 m high. The space between them, through which one must squeeze, is only 50 cm wide. This necessitates moving into this cell sideways before being able to turn round and look ahead. So one cannot look straight at the backstone when moving into the cell. The presence of the two jambs also conceals the back of this cell from the main chamber space. Through the two jambs it is possible to see part of an elaborately decorated sandstone basin (Figure 3.27). Eogan has noted that this is so large it must have been in position before the passage of the temple was constructed and the jamb stones to this cell put in place (Eogan 1986: 42). These two jambs contrast markedly with each other. The

Combined overlays

Angular incised

Angular picked

Dispersed area picking

Close area picking

1 m

Figure 3.27. The decorated stone bowl and backstone in the right cell of Knowth East. The line drawing shows the succession of overlays on the backstone (orthostat 54) according to Eogan. *After Eogan 1997: fig. 12.*

one to the left is boldly decorated with vertical and curvilinear bands of picking, resembling that found on the left and right passage orthostats flanking the sillstones into the inner passage area. It also has an area of close picking at the bottom. The front face of the right jamb, by contrast, is decorated only by diffuse picking without pattern. Orthostats to the left and right of the cell have some faint scratched lines and areas of dense or diffuse picking. By contrast, the backstone (no. 54) is elaborately decorated over almost its entire surface with diffuse picking, bands of scratched and infilled triangles, lozenges, U-shaped motifs, picked and scored lines that overlap, and radial motifs. The corbel above is decorated with picked circular designs. This backstone is the most elaborate and complex stone in the Knowth East temple. It is also the most inaccessible physically and visually, being situated in the darkest area of the temple and requiring sideways movement through the most constricted space in order to reach it. This perhaps suggests that it was the last orthostat to be seen, the culminating point of a journey. The radial designs on it are unique in this chamber and passage (Figure 3.27). Others occur elsewhere but not in this pattern, combination, or organization on the stone face. The decorative elaboration of this backstone is matched by that of the stone basin. Roughly circular in form, the sides are decorated with deeply cut concentric lines running towards five concentric circles at the front of the basin facing the entrance to the cell. The inside is decorated with arcs and radiating lines. Turning round to squeeze out of this cell, more decoration becomes apparent: two lines of zigzags on the inner face of the left jamb. The inner face of the right jamb is undecorated. This reverses the presence and absence of pattern on entry into the cell.

Some other orthostats and corbels forming the central chamber space (rather than the sides of the recesses or cells) have some small areas of geometric decoration or picking, but none are elaborate or visually striking, except for a single corbel with a striking curvilinear zigzag pattern.

At Knowth East the greatest decorative elaboration occurs in the transition to the inner passage, and in the back and particularly the right cells. The central chamber area and the outer- and innermost parts of the passage are relatively plain in comparison.

Knowth West

As at Knowth East, the external part of the passage at Knowth West is remarkably uniform in height and width, a long, linear, 60-cm-wide tunnel moving from light to darkness as one stoops down to move along it (Figure 3.28). After three-quarters of its overall length (originally about 34 m), the passage bends to the right. The outer part of the passage has comparatively little decoration and only a few distinctive stones. As in Knowth East, in addition to the use of greywacke, some of the orthostats are of sandstone, which feel and look distinctively different. A few orthostats with decoration occur to the right and the left of the outer part of the passage, with spirals, concentric circular, and zigzag lines. Some have bands of picking but no pattern, others score marks, and none are very elaborate or visually striking.

This relative lack of visual elaboration alters dramatically at the point at which the passage starts to bend to the right. Here the orthostats on either side of the passage are decorated in a very different manner, with picked areas of meandering designs over their faces, their forms suggesting fragmentary circles and arcs. Just beyond the point at which the passage starts to bend there is a high sillstone. The space in front of the sillstone is constricted by two inset orthostats and a low roof lintel. At this point the light at the entrance to the passage is no longer visible. Beyond the sill the passage roof becomes successively higher as one moves towards the inner chamber. From here onwards, all the passage orthostats to the left and right are elaborately decorated all over their surfaces with a startling series of picked decorated bands. The decorated bands on these inner passage stones are significantly deeper and wider than anything encountered in the outer passage. They also create a sense of motion as they bend and turn across the faces of the stones. Horizontal slabs heightening the passage roof above the orthostats have diffuse picked decoration over their surfaces. Orthostat 49, to the right of the passage immediately after the sill, appears uniquely anthropomorphic in form (Figures, 3.28, 3.29) (see discussion below). Opposite it, to the left, is a totally different stone, its face covered with areas of picking but without clear pattern. On orthostat 49, it is possible to trace with one's hands the outlines of the linear and curvilinear grooves. The tactile impression of the stone opposite is, by contrast, indeterminate and diffuse because distinct lines are lacking. The stone to the right possess-

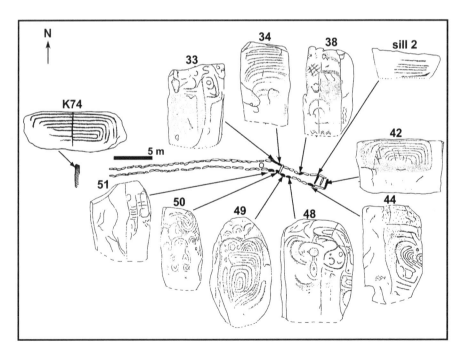

Figure 3.28. Plan of the western chamber and passage at Knowth, showing orthostats decorated in Eogan's 'rectlinear style'. *After Eogan 1986: fig. 84.*

es visual and tactile clarity in comparison with the indeterminacy and ambiguity of the picked stone to the left. The next passage orthostat to the right (no. 48) is decorated in a similar style, but the pattern is very different in form, with meandering lines and circles and semicircles covering the surface. Opposite to the left is another orthostat with an area of close picking towards the top of the stone. Above this and the next passage orthostat is an extremely large horizontal slab supporting the rising roof. The first part of the front face is picked with zigzag lines, and there are numerous score

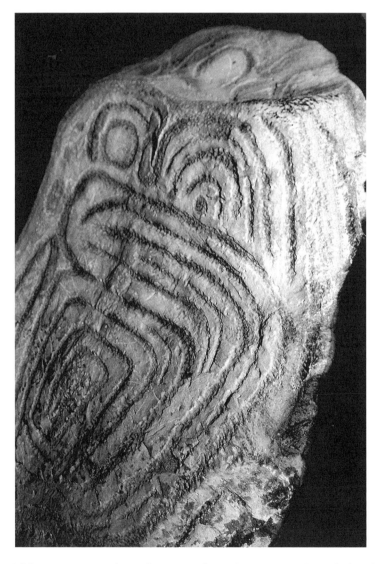

Figure 3.29. Knowth West: The anthropomorphic orthostat 49 on the right-hand side of the passage.

marks. The rest is scored all over with unpatterned horizontal and vertical lines. It is possible to trace the picked zigzag lines with the fingers, but not the score marks. In a tactile sense they are invisible. The next two passage orthostats narrow the space of the passage so that one can just squeeze through into the end cell of the temple. The left stone has broad bands of picking but lacks pattern; the right stone has diffuse picking. This constriction of the passage width contrasts markedly with the rising ceiling above. Orthostats 39 to the left and 45 to the right, opposite each other at the end of the passage, both have broad faces. The passage now feels significantly wider. Rather than brushing against the stones, one must now reach out to them on either side. Orthostat 39 differs from all the previous stones in that it has clearly distinguished broad horizontal bands of picking on the upper part of the face with smooth bands in between. The lower part of the stone has more diffuse irregular and curvilinear picked areas. The orthostat opposite is rough over most of its surface, and areas of the stone, which bulge out, are covered in picking following raised areas of the stone surface. In the middle of this stone on the right part of the face there is an area with a remarkably polished, silky smooth feel to it but broken by diffuse rough picking. The next right orthostat (44) is similar in dimensions, but its surface is utterly different. There is a significant hollow on the lower part of the stone which has two distinct faces; the first, on the right, is somewhat recessed, with a central sinuous groove dividing the face deep enough to run one's fingers through it. The right part of the face is covered with bands of curvilinear and semicircular motifs and a single lozenge whose outlines can be traced with the hands. The left side of the face has scored lozenges low down and is otherwise undecorated, apart from areas of close picking with no recognizable pattern. A horizontal corbel slab above has diffuse picking. The orthostat opposite on the left (40) is one of the most distinctive and unusual in the temple. Its face is covered with bands of triangles and lozenges resembling orthostat 6 in the back of the chamber space at Dowth South. Smooth areas in between the picked motifs have diffuse picking. This picking on these negative forms activates their shapes and makes the entire surface appear alive in artificial illumination. The stone surface also has another layer of earlier scoring of the same designs but on a much smaller scale.

The final two stones to the left and right of the temple are differentiated from the other orthostats by a sillstone decorated with horizontal grooves across its front face (sill 2). Beyond is another sill in front of the backstone. In antiquity the stone basin that once stood in the end cell was moved to its present position, stuck about a third of the way down the passage where it begins to turn to the right. Orthostat 41, to the left of the chamber space, has a broad, flat face covered with motifs utterly different again to anything previously encountered. There are very broad bands and areas of picking and more closely picked meandering and curvilinear designs with occasional lozenges and zigzags 'emerging'. There is a contrast between the decoration on the upper part of the stone and that on the lower part, where rows of triangles and zigzag and wavy lines occur. Diffuse picking covers other areas of the face, and unpicked areas are left. To the right, orthostat 43 contrasts significantly. The surface is covered with diffuse areas of picking, but there is no pattern. Diffuse picking also occurs on the corbels above these orthostats on either side of the chamber and on the capstone and two horizontal slabs forming the back of the chamber above the backstone.

Compared with the massive orthostats to the left and right of the chamber space, the chamber backstone is a relatively small and insignificant slab. The expectation gained from the experience of other temples—that one might find a massive stone here—is unfulfilled. The decoration on this slab is somewhat similar to that found on the entrance kerbstone (see Figure 3.25: K11). However, there is no central line and, unlike on the kerbstone, the lines do not curve round at the bottom to fill the central space. It consists of a series of nested picked lines forming an arch, becoming increasingly smaller towards the centre. Picking covers the lower surface beneath. The overall visual effect of the design is to create a sense of finality and disappearance from the worldly domain into another reality. At Dowth West it seems possible that the ancestral spirits of the dead exited the chamber through this backstone to emerge and be reborn through Dowth East in the direction of the rising morning sun.

At Knowth West we find a general distinction between the inner and outer parts of the passage, with the inner passage far more elaborately decorated. The theme is one of movement past sparsely decorated stones with static motifs to stones heavily decorated with meandering patterns full of vitality and movement, from thinner picked lines to much thicker bands. To simplify the journey down the passage and into the chamber space involves encountering circular, then meandering, then zigzag and triangular/lozenge motif fields, a series of stylistic transformations in the manner in which the stones are decorated. The consistent surface picking of the stones, which may be either diffuse or dense, creates pattern or not, means that there is consistent ambiguity with regard to whether motifs or patterns are present or not. On some stones pattern can be felt with the hands and visually recognized as motif. On other stones decorative alteration, or work, can be felt, but pattern or design remains elusive. Key decorated stones may be encountered on either the right or the left of the passage. Where the passage bends round to the right, the more elaborate stones with meandering lines are encountered. Precisely at the point of transition from light to darkness, the stones become deeply picked. Stones with or without motifs may sometimes be paired. In the end chamber, it is the left-hand (north) side of the end cell that is most elaborately decorated. The backstone returns one to a design form first encountered on the entrance kerbstone.

CONSTRUCTING AND USING THE TEMPLES: STONES, MATERIALS, AND THEIR LANDSCAPE SIGNIFICANCE

The Newgrange cairn was built in alternate layers of turves and water-rolled pebbles. The amount of turf stripping involved was massive, effectively taking out of agricultural use a large area in the vicinity of the cairn (M. O'Kelly 1982: 127 ff.). This also happened at Knowth, and turves were used as well to construct the Knowth and Newgrange satellite cairns (M. O' Kelly 1982: 128; Eogan 1986: 31).

The pebbles in the Newgrange cairn were derived from the lower river terrace immediately north of the Boyne, in all probability from what is now a permanently water-filled, figure-8-shaped pond 750 m due south of the cairn (M. O'Kelly 1982: 117). The greywacke orthostats of the passage and chamber and the roof corbels and the kerbstones (apart from four of brown sandstone) were brought from the area north or east of Newgrange and Knowth where this rock outcrops, 3–5 km or more away. Some were found on the surface; others probably were quarried. Some may have been collected from the coastal cliffs at Clogher Head located some 10 km north of the mouth of the Boyne (Stout 2002: 30).

Gaps in the passage roof of Newgrange were packed with a mixture of burnt soil taken from a habitation area containing fragments of animal bone in the vicinity of the cairn, and sea sand brought from the mouth of the river Boyne 20 km downstream (M. O'Kelly 1982: 101). The granite basins within the chamber recesses of Newgrange were brought from much farther away (probably from the Mourne Mountains 50 km or more to the north). In this respect, it is interesting to note the resemblance between these shaped stone basins and the natural stone solution basins (rounded erosion hollows characteristic of granite) that are so widespread on the summits of the granite mountainous areas to the north.

Five types of nonlocal cobbles were used to embellish the façades and entrance areas of both Newgrange and Knowth. At Newgrange a huge amount of white quartz was discovered around the entrance area and used by O'Kelly to imaginatively reconstruct the present striking façade. Flecked with white mica, its origin is in the Wicklow Mountains 50 km to the south. Much smaller quantities were brought to Knowth. Dark, oval and rounded cobbles of granodiorite found at the entrances to Newgrange and Knowth are from the Mourne Mountains, gabbro cobbles are from the Carlingford Mountains (probably collected on the shoreline of Dundalk Bay), and granite at Newgrange from the Mourne Mountains. Banded siltstone cobbles were derived from the shoreline of the Carlingford Mountains to the north (F. Mitchell 1992; Meigan et al. 2002) (Figure 3.30).

While virtually all of the kerbstones and internal orthostats of Newgrange are of greywacke, we have already noted that there is considerably more variety in the types of stone used in the kerb at Knowth, together with the internal use of some sandstone orthostats. Since everything else about these monuments is carefully ordered and planned and the labour involved in constructing them was massive, it is highly unlikely that the inclusion of these structural stones was the result of mere chance or the contingencies of local availability. If the builders of Knowth had required only greywacke, they would have acquired it. The whole point was to differentiate between Newgrange and Knowth in various ways. The limestone at Knowth was probably obtained from 1 or 2 km to the north or from local outcrops some 7 km to the east; sandstone was available in the immediate vicinity.

Some of the kerbstones of the satellite temples at Knowth are glacial erratics found locally. In other words, this was exotic rock found in a local context. During the Ice Age there was no movement of material from south to north, so all these erratics were derived from the mountains to the north. The small temple Knowth 14 located to the north of the great cairn had ten different types of rock in the surviving parts of the kerb, including local greywacke, limestones, conglomerates, sandstones, and glacial erratics (Eogan 1984: 83).

Outside the entrances to both passages at the great Knowth temple there are a series of stone settings. Seven occur outside the entrance to the eastern temple: two U-shaped settings to the left and three to the right adjoining the kerbstones, and two

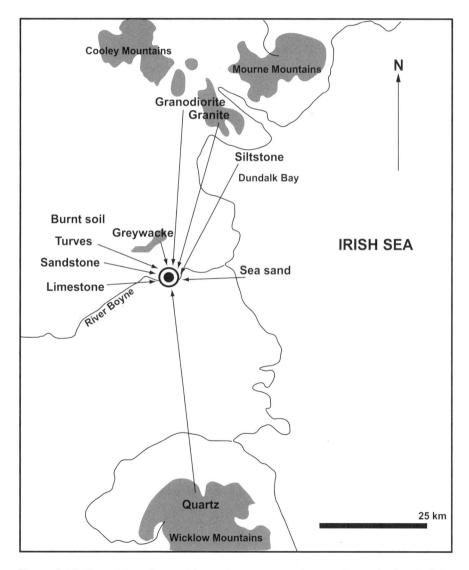

Figure 3.30. The origins of materials used to construct the temples in the bend of the Boyne.

circular settings just to the east immediately outside the passage entrance. Setting 1 was the most complex, 4.5 m from the entrance kerbstone. It was scooped 0.2 m deep into the old ground surface and was paved with small stones and a square limestone block in the centre. Overlying these stones was a layer of quartz chips surrounded by two rows of stones. The innermost row was composed of glacial erratics, the outer of clay ironstone nodules. Setting 2 was also edged by glacial erratics, its interior paved with rolled stones (Eogan 1986: 46–48). Outside and immediately to the right of the entrance to Newgrange, a similar oval setting was discovered. Within it there were 607 water-worn quartz pebbles, 'each the size of a medium potato', 103 granite stones, and 612 angular fragments of quarried quartz (M. O'Kelly 1982: 75). A stone setting or a quartz façade may have existed outside the entrance to Loughcrew cairn T. Conwell described a layer of quartz from 3 to 4 feet high and 2 feet thick extending around the kerbstones, and a local landowner uncovered three 'circles' or paved areas of white quartz outside the cairn and another to the southwest (McMann 1993: 27; 1994: 527). Chalk balls found in cairn L by Conwell (McMann 1993: 35) represent another exotic import at Loughcrew, possibly derived from the far northwest of the Irish coast. Conwell also reported finding hundreds of water-rounded pebbles in the Loughcrew cairns.

The presence of the exotic stones has been interpreted as a manifestation of social contact with areas way beyond the Boyne valley (Stout 2002: 31). Cooney suggests they had a metaphorical significance, representing two contrasting scales of social life and landscape important to the cairn builders (Cooney 2000: 136). But their significance extended much further than a distinction between near and far, local and exotic. The stones forming the kerbs, façades, stone settings, and internal layers of the cairns were brought from an amazingly diverse set of locations in both the distant and the local landscape. They were gathered together in the circular form of the cairn. The symbolic significance of these materials—their different forms, textures, and colours—were related to their points of origin in the landscape beyond the temples. The wider landscape could be indirectly experienced or objectified through these materials. It could be encountered in an ambient circular body motion —that is, in an idealized form. The materials themselves were derived from mountains to the north and the south. The latter, the Wicklow Mountains, were visible in the far distance, the former—the Mourne, Carlingford, and Cooley Mountains—hidden. These mountain sources of white quartz and dark hard stones are very different. The Wicklow Mountains have mainly rounded summits and ridges. Deep U-shaped valleys cut through them with snake-like meandering streams in their bottoms. Two conical peaks formed of quartzite rock, Great Sugarloaf and Little Sugarloaf, appear as if permanently snow covered from a distance. The Mourne Mountains to the north constitute a bleak and even more dramatic landscape, with sharp and jagged peaks, boulder-strewn areas, and rock stacks with solution basins.

Materials used to construct the temples were also brought from the sandy beach at the mouth of the Boyne, from the river floodplain, from low ridges to the north, from coastal cliffs and pebble beaches, and from tilled and settled areas around the cairns. They were derived from the highest and most rugged places and the lowest-lying land, from deposits associated with saltwater and freshwater, marsh and dry land. The associations between seawater and freshwater and different types of stone were fundamental in the Neolithic and related to ways of exploring and expressing states of bodily transformation in life and in death (Fowler and Cummings 2003). The Boyne temples were located at or just beyond the point of the river where saltwater and freshwater met. During the restoration work at Newgrange, a spring was discovered welling up (now artificially drained) in the right side of the passage beneath orthostat R8 (M. O'Kelly 1982: 113), allowing water to flow down the passage. If Newgrange was built on the site of a spring, might this relate in an interesting way to the meandering form of the passage and the use of spring water in rites of transformation?

The Boyne temples were not so much a mimetic representation of a landscape in microcosm, as found elsewhere in Scandinavia and southern England (Tilley 1994; 1996), but rather represent a radical cultural reordering of that landscape. The people who collected and used the glacial erratics to build the kerbs round the smaller satellite temples at Knowth and the stone settings outside the temple entrances clearly recognized this material as nonlocal and exotic. Like the modern geologist, they also must have had a pretty good idea of where this material came from: the distant mountains to the northeast. But how did this material reach the Boyne valley? Who or what deposited it there? In bringing together all these materials, the temple builders were merely emulating the work of ancestral or supernatural forces that had acted in the past, beyond human memory. The materials used to construct and decorate the temples had inherent value in terms of their specific qualities. They were never neutral materials but highly charged with cultural meanings. The act of bringing them together and organizing them and inscribing motifs on some in a specific place made them supercharged with magical significance.

The presence of riverine and beach pebbles in the cairns and outside the kerbs suggests that areas outside the cairns were symbolic beaches, transitional spaces between one world and another. The relationship between sea and land was a metaphor for the relationship between the outside and inside of the temple, a watery and changing external world and a dry and eternal inner world associated with the dead. Quartz was a magical stone of special significance in this context. Fowler and Cummings have beautifully discussed the manner in which the sparkling and reflective qualities of quartz are akin to the properties of water. Although a hard stone, quartz may produce ripples when struck. They suggest in the context of their discussion of quartz in megaliths on the east coast of the Irish sea that 'the practice of bringing glistening stones from the glittering sea may itself have been significant and aimed at producing a certain similarity of effect between parts of the megalithic complex and the reflective surface of the sea' (Fowler and Cummings 2003: 7). They go on to argue that those depositing quartz at a monument were 'making it wet', marking it out as an appropriate context for acts of transformation (ibid.: 14).

THE SIGNIFICANCE OF IMAGERY

Motifs in Numbers

The standard approach to analysing the motifs has been to compare and contrast different temples in relation to a quantitative analysis of the motifs. So, C. O'Kelly has remarked how each Boyne temple has a repertoire of motifs or style peculiar to itself (1973; 1982: 147). While the overall motif repertoire is held in common, some are preferred at one temple, others at another. For example, O'Kelly remarks how concentric circles are common at Dowth, and lozenges occur not at all in Dowth North and only on one orthostat in Dowth South. She also notes the manner in which radials and dots in circles are consistently found in hidden or obscure places at Newgrange (C. O'Kelly 1982: 149). Eogan very usefully shows how common motifs are typically positioned in different areas of the temple interiors. The 'angular' style occurs on the chamber backstones in Dowth South, in the chamber of Dowth East, in the passage and on the chamber orthostats in Dowth West and Newgrange. The 'rectilinear' style, by contrast, is confined to Knowth and concentrated in the inner parts of the passages and chambers of Dowth East and West (Eogan 1986: 187 ff.) (see Figures 3.26, 3.28).

One of the implications of the emphasis on different repertoires of motifs at different temples is perhaps that each temple had its unique or characteristic 'signature' relating to the social identity of the group that constructed it. But for O'Kelly, and for Shee Twohig (1981; 1996; 2000), the motifs are ultimately 'geometric' and 'abstract'; that is their meaning and we can understand them no further.

Thomas (1992) has analysed the imagery on the Loughcrew cairns in a more general way, noting that there is little similarity among the individual monuments here in terms of which motifs are used or the way in which they are combined. He examines the numbers of separate motifs used on the stones and their depth inside the temples away from the entrances. He shows that stones bearing seven or more separate motifs are only found three or four paces into the temple, and those with eight or more are deep within the temple interior or chamber. In Loughcrew cairn T, the most complex stone is the capstone in the right recess (Thomas 1992: 149). He rightly suggests that only those who could access the deep recesses of the temple interiors would be able to experience the images; therefore, given the ambiguity of the motifs, the general difficulty in decoding their meaning implies they could mean many different things to different people and would be subject to constant interpretation and reinterpretation by ritual specialists—a perfect vehicle for the exercise of power through knowledge.

But quantifying and grading 'complexity' in this manner is rather problematic. This typically modernist form of analysis bears no relationship to how a person entering a dimly lit or completely dark chamber space actually experiences the motifs. Put simply, Thomas' gaze is singularly disembodied. Looking at Shee Twohig's (1981) documentation, one can see 'everything' at once, and all the motifs on paper, large or small, faint or bold, are equally distinct. However, as the account of the temples already undertaken has attempted to demonstrate, different stones have contrasting material properties, and the motifs and areas of picking on them are bodily experienced in a very different manner from paper representations. We can count the motifs inside Newgrange, as C. O'Kelly (1973; 1982) and Shee Twohig (2000: 96) do, and find that quantitatively, lozenges and zigzags are the most common motifs. However, the spirals are actually far more important and prominent in terms of the manner in which the temple is bodily encountered and experienced. It is highly unlikely that Neolithic people went about counting motif frequencies or combinations on every stone. Instead, the imagery would leave an impression on them through the observers' bodily experience of it. Some things would be remembered, much would not. Statistical analyses by Thomas (1992) and others (e.g., Dronfield 1996) are, of course, reliant on an atemporal scheme in which all the motifs are there all of the time, whereas there is good evidence for a significant amount of temporal alteration of the stones (see below).

Style and Changing Traditions

O'Sullivan notes that the analysis of the motifs found in virtually all studies of Irish megalithic 'art' reduces the imagery to a collection of formal elementary forms. Non-formal decoration, such as extensive picking of the surface, tends to be considered peripheral and unimportant (O'Sullivan 1986: 71). He has produced an outstanding recent analysis completely revolutionising a study of the imagery of the Boyne valley temples (1986; 1996; 1997). He argues in relation to a study of Knowth that there are two basic styles of ornament: a 'depictive style' and a 'plastic style'. The former is earlier and contemporary with the construction of the temple. The latter was added later and sometimes superimposed on the earlier ornamentation. A similar sequence is identified at Newgrange and Dowth. The 'depictive style' relates to stones that simply display a range of conventional motifs superimposed on the surface without any attempt to produce a unified or coherent pattern. It may be produced either by incision or picking (O'Sullivan 1996: 83). The important point is that the imperative is to produce the individual motif(s) rather than relate these to the form of the stone. The 'plastic style', by contrast, refers to stones in which the application of motifs is clearly related to the physical form and shape of the stone itself, such as picked lines that follow the sinuous stone outline or solid picking following the form of the stone, emphasizing such features as shoulders or edges (O'Sullivan 1986: 75). This plastic style of ornamentation occurs primarily within the passages and chambers of Knowth West and East and also on some of the kerbstones. O'Sullivan notes that the depictive style occurs on surfaces of stones that were both accessible and inaccessible (i.e., hidden) after the construction of the temple, whereas the plastic style occurs exclusively on stones that were accessible after temple construction. The implications are clear: the plastic style is a later embellishment, modification, or alteration. Where the plastic style occurs on stones as depictive ornamentation, it is invariably superimposed. It seldom extends to within 30 cm of the bottom of the stone within the temples and tends to relate to the side of the orthostat visible as one enters the passage (ibid.: 76). In the western temple at Knowth, virtually every stone in the chamber area is modified by dispersed picking, often spread evenly over the surface. This is significant because rather than concentrate decoration on individual stone surfaces, it represents an attempt to decorate the entire architectural space of the temple as a whole. The focus is away from individual stones.

O'Sullivan (1996) argues for a four-stage development. In the first stage, motifs are applied to stones but unrelated to their forms. In the second stage, much more ambitious designs are integrated in relation to the surface of the stone. Kerbstones 1, 52, and 67 (see Figure 3.18) at Newgrange and many at Knowth are representative of this. In the third stage, standard Irish geometric designs are absent and, instead, meandering or more ordered linear designs cover the surfaces of the stones, as on the orthostats of Knowth West and East and on the entrance stones. The designs reflect the outlines and contours of the stones. O'Sullivan notes that 'many of these designs make only partial sense as two-dimensional images. Their aesthetic logic is more apparent in the context of the three-dimensional form of the stone' (ibid.: 86). The final phase produces displays of picking, which do not form recognizable patterns but closely relate to the contours of the stones and the overall architecture of the monument.

At Loughcrew, the imagery is almost entirely from O'Sullivan's stage 1. At Knowth, phases 3 and 4 are blurred, occurring together on many orthostats. At Newgrange, phase 3 is absent but it represents the most extreme development of phase 4, which also occurs on some of the Dowth orthostats. If phase 4 was first introduced or experimented with at Knowth, it was applied in the most vigorous manner at Newgrange.

We have seen that the techniques used to embellish the temples with imagery differ significantly from one temple to another. At Dowth there is a virtual absence of overall pick dressing of the stones, while at Newgrange virtually every orthostat is pick dressed, creating a uniform as opposed to a differentiated surface (O'Kelly and O'Kelly 1983: 158). This overall pick dressing at Newgrange occurred after the orthostats were in place. Pick dressing of this character is only found at Dowth in the right recess or cell of Dowth South. Incised decoration is rare at Loughcrew, except in cairn L and on the roofstone of the right cell in cairn T; and false, relief, pick dressing or smoothing of picked lines is not recorded (Shee Twohig 1981: 106; Eogan 1997: 218).

The Decorative Act

Frequently one finds in the literature a frustration with regard to some of the more 'poorly' executed images, such as those on most of the Newgrange kerbstones which are referred to as 'doodles', 'scratchings', 'randomly placed marks', or 'graffiti'. C. O'Kelly comments with regard to Newgrange that 'one finds motifs carved without apparent regard to the suitability of the surface or to their position on it; one finds a single insignificant-looking motif on a stone of perhaps three square metres in surface area; one finds motifs scratched or picked on the sides of orthostats while the main face remains unadorned' (C. O'Kelly 1982: 148). Her suggestion is that the actual act of carving in these cases was perhaps the significant thing. She notes that the positioning of stones with hidden motifs was meaningful. One forms the back of the roof box; others are at the junction of the passage and chamber roofs. Whether seen or not, decorated stones were employed in particular and important transitional spaces. Some stones were carved before being positioned and were intended for specific places and areas in the temples. Others were decorated in place.

Time and Memory

Overlays involving the substitution or replacement of existing motifs by imposed ones occur principally at Dowth, Newgrange, and Knowth. Sometimes earlier motifs are incorporated into new compositions (Eogan 1997). Eogan argues that at Knowth, incised angular motifs (triangles, lozenges, zigzags) are the earliest and sometimes bear no relationship to areas picked over to create the same motifs on which dispersed area picking also intrudes (ibid.: 223). Eogan has shown how some of the orthostats in the Knowth West and Knowth East temples have a succession of up to five different overlays of motifs or decoration in different styles, which he refers to as (1) angular incised, (2) angular picked, (3) dispersed area picking, (4) ribbon art, and (5) close area picking (Figure 3.27). Faintly incised angular motifs occur on thirty stones in the chamber and passage of the Knowth East temple and on eleven stones in the chamber and passage of the Knowth West temple. Faint angular incised motifs are only present on six (5%) of the Knowth kerbstones (Eogan 1986:150), and other picked curvilinear designs are superimposed over them. A further overlay of picked ornamentation occurs on fifteen stones (12%) (O'Sullivan 1986: 77; Jones 2004: 204–5). There are then either two or three events of superimposition on a minority of the Knowth kerbstones, and these usually enhance rather than obliterate or cut across preexisting motifs.

Motif overlays also occur inside the Dowth and Newgrange temples. Incised angular motifs do not occur on the Newgrange kerbstones but are present on six internal orthostats. At Dowth North, incised angular motifs occur on three chamber orthostats, in Dowth South in the right recess. Eogan's argument is that these motif overlays represent distinct chronological styles. The evidence for all three Boyne temples is broadly similar. The motifs on the kerbstones were mainly produced in a single phase. By contrast, many orthostats in the temple interiors were added to and reworked many times.

Jones (2004) relates the image overlays to mnemonic practices of remembrance. He rightly argues that stones embody the significance of place and suggests that the work, or activity, of image production was of central significance. Reworking images on the stones in the temple interiors was a 'technology of remembrance' intended to recall sentiments of place and identity. But Jones' perspective is generalized, and he does not tell us how these different images did so. He usefully points out that the reworking of the stones over time has its counterpart in the bringing of stones to the temples from the surrounding landscape. Both were repetitive acts, objectifying the significance of place and landscape. This reworking either obliterated and replaced or enhanced preexisting images. It need not have taken place in single episodes of activities throughout the entire temple interiors. It is far more likely that individual orthostats may well have been reworked at different times and on different occasions, each with its own biography of image production.

Hiding Stones

The presence of stones with hidden motifs at Newgrange and in the western and eastern temples at Knowth has led to the suggestion that many of these may have been recycled from an earlier monument (Eogan 1998; 1999: 426). Eogan suggests that the likely position of such a monument was underneath the great Knowth cairn, and stones from it may have been extracted to construct both the Knowth temples and that at Newgrange. Another possibility is that both Knowth and Newgrange were constructed on the sites of earlier monuments, since there is some evidence of a pre-cairn sod mound at Newgrange (M. O'Kelly 1982: 71–72). In Knowth West, three of these stones served as capstones and four as orthostats. All are in the outer part of the passage. In Knowth East, Eogan has identified three capstones and one orthostat in the outer part of the passage and two corbels in the chamber (Eogan 1998: 162). Except for one orthostat in the eastern temple, this decoration was entirely or partially hidden. When these stones were reused as orthostats, most were placed upside down in relation to their former positioning (ibid.: 166). This also appears to be the case for some of the Newgrange orthostats, such as R3 in the outer part of the passage. Those orthostats in the front of the Newgrange kerb with extensive hidden decoration (K4, K13, and K18) (Figure 3.31), and K4 with its decoration on both main faces, could have formed the sides of cells in an earlier temple similar in internal form to Loughcrew cairn L.

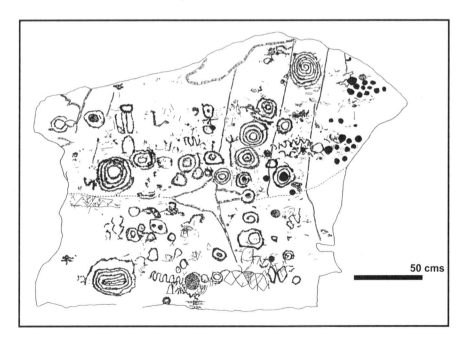

Figure 3.31. Hidden designs on the back of kerbstone 13, Newgrange. *After C. O'Kelly 1982: fig. 26.*

Entoptic Images

It has been proposed that the motifs were produced during altered states of consciousness, as 'entoptic images' (Bradley 1989a; Lewis-Williams and Dowson 1993; Dronfield 1995a; 1995b; 1996; Lewis-Williams and Pearce 2005). This is imagery spontaneously produced in the brain either by neural structures or by practices aimed at achieving altered states of consciousness, such as induced fatigue, sensory deprivation, and the use of narcotics. Dronfield claims that Irish temple art was induced through mind-altering techniques and substances. The architectural structure of temples provided 'an ideal environment for isolating the subject from auditory and visual stimulation' (Dronfield 1995b: 263). Three major stimuli might have been at work: flickering light, hallucinogenic fungi, and migrainous syndromes. His analysis is highly selective and is based on isolating particular motif forms, eliminating their spatial relationship to others on the stones, and aesthetic compositional principles (Dronfield 1995a: 543)—that is, precisely those features that might be regarded as meaningful and socially significant. In his statistical analyses (Dronfield 1996), he also lumps together motifs occurring on the external kerbstones—where presumably, according to his argument, sensory deprivation would not occur—and those found within the passages and chambers. The result of this lack of sensitivity to the context of the motifs detracts considerably from the value of the analysis. He suggests a general association between 'concentric' motifs and passages leading into the temples, but these are absent from the two kerbstones outside Knowth. Again there is a lack of sensitivity to differences between the temples and context. Another association claimed by Dronfield is between angular motifs and death rites in the temple chambers. But again, this is far from exclusive and is a far more pertinent observation in relation to the interiors of Knowth East and West than Newgrange. Non-formal decoration is ignored, as are temporal differences in the production of the images.

All the statistical analyses conducted are self-evidently paper-based and not related to any sensory analyses of the temples; nor are there considerations of those motifs that are visually dominant, hidden or not, their relationship to the shapes and forms of stones, and so on. Such an analysis derived from paper only gains a degree of plausibility by being printed on paper. Lewis-Williams and Pearce (2005: 264) declare that they are entirely satisfied and convinced by Dronfield's analysis, which is not so surprising since Lewis-Williams' earlier work inspired it in the first place. They state that 'the art shows that Irish Neolithic religion indeed entailed causing the level of consciousness to slide towards the introverted end of the spectrum, and then by placing meaning and value on selected mental percepts perceived in these states. Neolithic people carved those meaningful percepts on tombs, in the process standardizing them' (ibid.: 265). Of course, the art itself shows no such thing. Such a perspective is entirely derived from a deeply reductive neuropsychological perspective. A fundamental aspect of the imagery is that while a limited number of basic motif forms do occur, they are far from standardised and occur in complex and distinctive compositions or associations, differing from stone to stone and temple to temple. An 'entoptic' approach, rather than explaining what the art might mean, seems to explain it away as essentially meaningless, an effect of drug-induced states, sensory deprivation, and the like. Lewis-Williams and Pearce stress over and over again that the process of selecting and depicting 'entoptic' images was not automatic. People were not photocopiers producing exact copies of their visions but selected and modified those images that were significant to them (e.g., ibid.: 277). In other words, entoptically induced imagery, if it ever existed, bears little relationship to what people actually chose to depict in practice anyway, precisely because it is not meaningful.

Recognizing Iconicity: Celestial Bodies, Temples, and Landscape
Numerous attempts have been made to further decode the meanings of at least some of this 'geometric' art (see O'Sullivan 1986 for a historical review) in a much more specific way. The imagery may appear to be entirely 'geometric' and 'abstract' in character, but one line of argument is that it actually has iconic significance. For example, the wavy or meandering lines have repetitively been referred to as 'serpentine' in the literature. The circular and especially the radial motifs have been consistently interpreted as sun symbols and/or sundials (e.g., Coffey 1912 [1877]).

The most comprehensive recent attempt has been made by Brennan (1983). In effect, he tries to understand all the motifs in terms of calendrical, solar, and lunar imagery. Differences between image forms are understood as representations of (1) the sun and the moon; (2) the differing positions and movements of these celestial bodies across the sky in relation to the seasons; and (3) the monthly cycles of the moon as it waxes and wanes and changes shape. He suggests that both the crescent and the wavy lines represent the moon and the lunar cycle and counting or reckoning units measuring time. For example, referring to Knowth kerbstone 5 he writes, 'A set of 6 circles (6 months of the year?) extend across the right half of [the stone] from above the centre of a spiral with 6 turnings. The circle and crescent (far left) also suggest the moon' (Brennan 1983: 137) (Figure 3.25:K5). The twists and turns of meandering lines represent lunar cycles: 'Luni-solar images are frequently circles and crescents merged in a single emblem' (ibid.: 175). Circles describe the shape of celestial objects and their movement: 'The circle of the horizon surrounded by the circular dome of the sky gives rise to a model of the universe as a series of concentric shells' (ibid.: 189). Quadrangles are understood in terms of linking opposing cardinal directions, becoming 'emblematic of the four corners of the earth. Thus, sunrise, sunset, midday and midnight, the equinoxes and the solstices . . . are all bound together in the unity of the symbol' (ibid.: 182). The spiral is understood in terms of an 'archaic astronomy' in which the heavens were viewed as spiralling: 'The sun moves in a clockwise spiral and the stars revolve anti-clockwise. The moon's path is not a true circle but a spiral whose successive loops cross the ecliptic in a westward, anti-clockwise motion opposed to the direction of the sun and the planets' (ibid.: 189). He argues for an overwhelming preoccupation with measuring time, sundials, and calendars: 'Time is invisible and its images are necessarily abstract. The sun and moon appear as schematic symbols, frequently integrated with representations of days, months or years' (ibid.: 179).

Given that we know that the architecture of the temples was intimately related to significant points in the solar calendar, which must have been based on detailed observation and knowledge of the heavens, some of Brennan's interpretations of the significance of the imagery are plausible. Indeed, it would be quite surprising if solar and lunar imagery were absent. However, the problem with his approach is the attempt to explain everything in these terms. In the case of some particularly striking and bold motifs, such as the radials on the eastern side of the Dowth kerb, some stones in the Knowth kerb, and the rear cell of Loughcrew temple T, a fairly straightforward claim can be made that these are either iconic representations or concerned with seasonality, time, and lunar and solar cycles. Such a claim cannot be made in relation to angular designs, spirals, nested arcs, many circular motifs, parallel lines, or offsets, except in the most abstracted terms; and the more Brennan tries to force everything into the same frame of reference, the more implausible his account becomes. Cupmarks and the significance of diffuse and area picking of stones are simply ignored, as in other accounts.

Munn's (1973) and Morphy's (1991) research on Aboriginal graphic designs and their significance has amply demonstrated an enormous degree of fluidity of meaning in relation to even the simplest graphic designs such as nested circles, which are susceptible to a great variety of different interpretations related to age, gender, cosmological beliefs, and the social contexts of their production and use. All have multiple meanings, and the ambiguity with regards to what they mean and to whom, and where and why, is the key to understanding them. The demand that very different graphic designs should have a single set of significations seems rather peculiar.

What both Munn's and Morphy's research has demonstrated is that one set of meanings attributable to Aboriginal graphic designs is as representations of landscape features and ancestral doings and interventions in that landscape. For example, concentric circles can represent ancestral campsites. The central area is conceptualised as a hole from which the ancestor emerged. The circles 'synthesize the notion of a place where the ancestor slept (made camp), and walked around with concepts of emergence (coming out), procreation (progeny go into the ground) and death (ancestor goes into the ground)' (Munn 1973: 138). Given that both the local and the wider landscape and movements of stones, people, and materials in it were fundamental parts of the significance of the temples, it would be surprising if, like solar and lunar symbolism, representations of landscape and temples within that landscape and paths or routes of movement through it were not part of the meaning ranges of the motifs. So, for example, we could understand the meandering lines (see Figure 3.2: no. 8) both as relating to seasonality and solar and lunar events and movements and as meaning watercourses (rivers like the Boyne that meander) and perhaps snakes (a standard 'iconic' understanding). Meandering designs more abstractly can be understood in terms of movement downriver or around closely grouped temples with variable spaces in and between them, as at Loughcrew (see Fraser 1998). Various circular forms could be understood as meaning temples and their chambers, or kerb circuits, or the relationship between hills and temples, the kerb and the chamber, the temple and the horizon, or relate to expanding ripples in water, and so on. The concentric circular designs that are so common could represent the circularity of the cairns and their kerbs. There is no way in and no way out. What this may imply is that the cremated remains of the ancestors put to rest in the temples cannot return to the living. They are caught in an eternal trap. Some images, like those found on the backstone in the central right cell of Loughcrew's cairn L (see Figure 3.7), bear a striking resemblance to a representation of the Loughcrew temple cemetery itself, with larger temples and smaller satellite temples perhaps being depicted by the circles with central dots (chamber spaces). The banded silt-stones brought to Knowth have striking patterns of arcs looping around their surfaces: these stones were pre-decorated with the same patterns as found on some of the temple kerbs and orthostats. 'Angular' designs, such as triangles, might refer to distant mountains or passage and chamber orthostats. Spirals might be associated with the passages of the temples, with the processes of going in and going out signifying movement and transition, as Lewis Williams and Pearce (2005: 268) have suggested. There is only one way in and one way out. They are about the process of transition into and out of the passage and chamber.

The striking linked three-spiral design in the back of the Newgrange chamber (Figure 3.22), illuminated by the solstice light, can be understood as a representation of Newgrange, Dowth, and Knowth and linked ceremonial processions that took place in, around, and between these temples (the spatial 'representation' of the three great cairns is correct). It is interesting to note in this respect that such is the visual power and intricacy of this design that it is the one that everyone remembers from Newgrange, while forgetting the rest. This true memory of Newgrange (as opposed to 'false' paper memories documenting every stone) has come to stand not only for Newgrange as a whole, but for the study of Irish and British prehistory. It appears on the cover of M. O'Kelly's book (1982) and is the adopted symbol of the British Prehistoric Society. Even more widely, it has been popularly appropriated as a symbol of ancient 'Celtic' spirituality (Stout 2002: 45).

The arcs and circles on the roofstone of the right recess at Newgrange and on the backstone of the right cell of cairn L at Loughcrew can be understood in a similar way as representations of megalithic cemeteries, forecourt areas, movements around and between them, and so on. Lacking informants, we cannot know with any greater specificity, and it really does not matter simply because there is no single, original or unitary meaning for us to attempt to recover. And, as Cochrane rightly points out, there may be elements of the carnivalesque at work here, with an escalation of everyday experiences within the temples (Cochrane 2005: 17).

Seeing People

An early attempt at an anthropomorphic interpretation was advanced by Breuil (1934), but it was based on highly inaccurate and schematic drawings. Herity claimed an 'angular god' can be seen in lozenge and zigzag designs at Dowth South (Herity 1974: 106), while Crawford saw an 'eye goddess' in the triple spiral motif on orthostat L19 at Newgrange (Crawford 1957). Eogan, in his account of first entering the Knowth West temple, writes: 'Coming to a stone sill, we illuminated the orthostat on its inner right side and beheld what seemed to be an anthropomorphic figure with two, large staring eyes. This ghostly guardian suggested that we were reaching the inner sanctum'. The reaction Wayne Bennett and I had on our first entry into this temple was exactly the same. We had never seen a decorated stone like this before, inside or outside any temple, and its appearance was both wild and frightening (Figure 3.29). Furthermore, the orthostat (no. 49) is situated at a crucial point of transition between the inner and outer part of the passage, and on the right-hand side, which we know had particular importance in many temples. The anthropomorphic likeness has also been remarked on by others, if only to suggest it is purely fortuitous (Lewis-Williams and Pearce 2005: 218). O'Sullivan (1996:92) has recently argued again that this may indeed be understood as a 'schematic pseudo-human image'. He also remarks that orthostat 69 in the eastern temple, in a similar position, has a comparable, if a somewhat less anthropomorphic, design. Orthostats 49 and 69 are unique to Knowth (though are much more common in the megalithic temples of Brittany; Thomas and Tilley 1993; O'Sullivan 1996; 2002). In both temples, similarly decorated stones with meandering ribbon designs (which Eogan refers to as the 'rectilinear style') occur solely on the innermost parts of the passage and in the chambers (Eogan 1986: 194–95).

A macehead discovered in the right recess of the eastern temple in association with the decorated stone basin and cremated human remains is also strikingly anthropomorphic in form, resembling a head and face. Since there is a definite stylistic similarity between all these stones with rectilinear decoration in both temples, it can be suggested that, in connection with the two anthropomorphic stones, they are part of a narrative of bodily change and dissolution occurring in the context of the mortuary practices within the temples (cf. Thomas and Tilley 1993 for an analysis of Breton megalithic imagery). But if this is the case, it only provides an understanding of some of the orthostats in Knowth West and East. However, in the light of these observations, the significance of the picked-over grooves on orthostats R12 and R21 on the right of the Newgrange passage may have a particular resonance. Both stones are situated at transition points, R12 between the inner and outer part of the passage, R21 at the point of transition between passage and chamber. Metaphorically, these are the ribs of the stone showing through the overlay of pick dressing. Otherwise the imagery in the temples appears to be resolutely non-anthropomorphic, at least if we want to see direct iconic representations in it.

Based on the discussion undertaken so far, we can suggest the following. All the graphic designs had multiple meanings. The motifs had conceptual power as material and visual metaphors. In their 'abstractness' and their 'generality' they were capable of linking together entirely different domains of human experience and action in relation to architectural space, rituals, the human body itself, landscape, and cosmology. They were significantly related to the movements of the sun and the moon in the heavens, to the passage of time, and the seasons. They were significantly related to the architectural features of the temples themselves and movement into, out of, around, and between them. They were significantly related to the local and wider landscape, its topography, freshwater and saltwater, and the movements of stones and materials in it both in the past (ancestral time) and in the Neolithic present. They were significantly related to the human body, sensory experience of the temples, and the death rites that took place within them. Finally, they were significantly related to structures of societal power and authority.

CONCLUSIONS

The notion that at least some of the stones and the images upon them are related to the human body can be taken much further than simply pointing to possible anthropomorphic representations.

We can suggest that, in a general sense, the stones themselves were considered to be subjects rather than objects in the Neolithic. Brought from the surrounding landscape, each orthostat or kerbstone had its own biography and history and its own personality. These stones were like people. The process of decorating and redecorating them summoned forth their sonorous voices in the context of the temple. Furthermore, these stones could walk; they could move by themselves. Evidence for the manner in which stones could walk was present everywhere in the landscape of the bend of the Boyne. The glacial erratics so carefully chosen for inclusion in the kerbs of the smaller temples and the stone settings outside Knowth had clearly moved from the mountains to the north. How else could they have got there? If stones could walk, they were clearly animate beings. Decorating these stones enlivened and emphasized their inherent powers, and they could be helped to walk again by taking them from one temple to be used in the construction of another. If the stones were metaphorically like persons, then picking a stone was dressing its skin, creating a new personal identity for it, one that was frequently related to its pre-existing unaltered identity—hence, the pick dressing of 'natural' hollows and depressions. We can then envisage the long lines of stones flanking the passages, and those encircling the chambers, as being persons standing opposite each other, or in relation to each other, like lines of decorated people. The individual kerbstones and orthostats can be understood as objectifying the identities of those responsible for picking their surfaces. Part of them and their identity was permanently left on the stone and immortalised. Many of the Knowth kerbstones and the three kerbstones in 'plastic' style outside Newgrange appear to have been the work of one individual stonemason. By contrast, the internal orthostats with layered motifs appear to be the result of collective work undertaken over a period of time. In this manner, the collective rather than the individual identities of stones was being stressed within the temples, entirely appropriate in the context of collective burial rites emphasizing the significance of the temple-using group.

A considerable number of the motifs documented at Newgrange are either completely or partially hidden in various ways. Indeed, Newgrange might be described as a textbook example of the art of concealment, employing the full range of possible techniques available:

1. Completely hiding decorated stones during the building of the temple, either in the roof or in the floor, making sure that these images could never be seen or experienced.

2. Decorating stones in obscure areas where the images are likely to be missed— high up or low down or near the corners and edges of stones.

3. Placing parts of decorated stones over others so that the full extent of the image field remains invisible—for example, the roof slab in the right or left recess.

4. Positioning images on the sides rather than the main faces of orthostats.

5. Concealing images on the side faces rather than on the backstones of the cells.

6. Picking over images so as to partially or completely obliterate them.

7. Picking over and around hollows, depressions, and grooves on the stone in the same manner as images, so as to create further ambiguity with regard to what is or is not decorated and supposed to be there.

8. Using the relative lack and changing quality of natural light in the chamber and passage to enhance all these techniques and effects, the most striking visible images being in the deepest and darkest areas of the chamber which are never directly illuminated by the rays of the sun, even on the winter solstice.

Subterfuge and visual deception appear to have been an important element in relation to the external kerbstones too. We know that Knowth has two passages and chambers, each marked externally in the kerb by similar stones that are distinctive from those appearing elsewhere. Dowth also has two, and possibly a third, marked by another distinctive stone. The three stones in the Newgrange kerb decorated in 'plastic' style suggest the presence of three passages and chambers in the cairn, but we know that two of these are false. This can perhaps be understood in the context of group strategies of emulation and power, altering the monument to make it significantly different from both Knowth and Dowth.

One way of contrasting the Loughcrew temples and those of the bend of the Boyne is to understand the former as mountain temples associated with the domain of the sky, and the latter as water temples linked to the domain of the river and the sea. The stones embodied the individual significance of both the particular temple and the wider landscape. Decorating the stones can be regarded as a means of activating them, emphasizing the link between stone, landscape, place, and social identity, as Jones (2004) has suggested. The reworking of these stones over time has its counterpart in the bringing of stones and materials to the temples over time. Both were repeated acts reinforcing memories and identities.

The landscape itself is always experienced as differentiated and dispersed. In the form of the cairn kerbs of the Boyne temples, it became idealised and cosmologically ordered, gathered together as a whole. While the great temples gathered together and ordered materials from local and distant landscapes, from the mountains, the rivers, and the sea, they also ordered and integrated that landscape with the heavens above, with the passage of the sun and the moon and the stars in the sky.

Celestial and Human Bodies in Motion

The entrances of Newgrange, Dowth, and Knowth are related to the most significant points in the solar calendar: the equinoxes and the solstices. If we take into account the alignment of the Knowth passages in relation to equinoxal sunrise and sunset and the motion of the sun and the moon as they move across the sky from east to west and in the south from left to right, this suggests that movement around the Knowth kerb was clockwise, like the movement of the sun, from the western to the eastern entrance and back again through the symbolic night represented by the northern temple perimeter. This provides a model to understand motion in relation to the other temples: movement around them, too, was clockwise and to the right.

Inside the temples themselves the dominant emphasis is movement to the right. This is emphasized in the manner in which the Knowth West passage bends to the right and in the elaboration of imagery in the right cell of Loughcrew cairn T, in Newgrange and Knowth East; in the right orthostat in the end cell, the presence of a single cell to the right, and elaborated with imagery in Dowth South; and in the architectural elaboration of the right cell in Dowth North. Movement to the right (following the course of the moon and the sun in the sky) was the propitious direction both in relation to the external kerbs and in relation to the passage and the internal chamber spaces. It is interesting in this respect to note the prevalence of 'iconic' solar and lunar symbols on the Knowth and Dowth kerbstones and on the illuminated backstone of Loughcrew cairn T, discussed above.

The bodily motion involved in moving around the temple kerbs in an unconfined space is utterly different from that experienced inside the temple, where movement is linear and differentiated through constrictions and widening and changes of directions of the passages, chamber spaces, and cells. Within the temple, movement is linear, finite, and directional. One reaches a destination, an end point of the journey. Moving around the kerb is an expression of the endless and the infinite, a journey that has no beginning and no end. Given the association between the temples and death, we can suggest that the passages and chambers objectify a journey from life to death and another world beyond in which experience is transformed through their bodily effects. By contrast, movement around the kerb is a journey for the living and the ceremonies associated with life.

Death and darkness are associated within the temple interiors, a journey taking one away from the sun to a darkened interior. At the great temples of the Boyne valley, one has to cross over an external barrier, the entrance kerbstone, in order to enter into the passage, physically climb over the external membrane of the kerb secluding and protecting the temple interior from the outside world. The decorated stones could only be experienced by those entering the temple, and they remain hidden and relatively inaccessible. The somatic experience of the passage orthostats is very intimate insofar as their presence is constantly felt, impinging on the body that cannot help but brush beside them, a constant physical contact. The spaciousness of the chambers requires physically reaching out to contact the stones. The corbelled roofs create recessive and concentric rising spaces, becoming more and more confined as they rise up above. Decorated stones in the passages are always more visible when travelling out of the temples, as the light from the entrance falls against the designs when the body no longer blocks the light from behind. Tactile orientation and experience would be more significant on the way in than on the way out.

Light, Darkness, and the Transformation of Experience

The temple interiors were designed to transform human bodily and sensory experience, creating different experiential states and sensory skills and capacities. Bradley (1989b) has suggested that light and darkness were important features of the design of megalithic temples. He contrasts temples L and T at Loughcrew, arguing that while most of the motifs at cairn L were hidden in dark areas of the temple interiors, in the cells, the backstone of the end cell of temple T is illuminated. He suggests that by increasing the length of the passage on Irish monuments, it was possible to focus the sun's rays on the central chamber and specific motifs within them. Lewis-Williams and Pearce suggest that the overwhelming effect of being in the temple interiors was one of sensory deprivation: 'If one stays still for long enough the silence and darkness envelope one; they seep deeper and deeper into one' (Lewis-Williams and Pearce 2005: 208). But such 'sensory deprivation' only relates to vision and the experience of the outside landscape. The reverse can be argued: rather than creating conditions for sensory deprivation, the experience of being inside the temple heightens sensory perception in relation to the burial and other rites that take place. Inside the temple a person is removed from everyday experience and transported into a world in which normal sensory faculties are altered. Touch and feel become essential and heightened because the spatial and visual orientation afforded by the outside world is lost. Temple air is still and silent, but smell and sound are intensified within this confined space. Lewis-Williams and Pearce themselves make the important point that the sound of the orthostats being picked, and the manner in which that sound would have been amplified within the temple, would have been an important sensory dimension of its experience. Hammering a stone may have been a way of connecting with it, activating it, giving it potency—hence the presence of picking of some kind or another on virtually every orthostat within Newgrange and Knowth. In this respect, it is interesting to note O'Kelly's comment that the original shape of Newgrange, with its flat top, rounded sides, and façade was that of a huge *drum* (M. O'Kelly 1982: 73). The temple interiors both enriched and altered sensory perception in important ways.

The outer stones of temples with short passages, such as cairns L and T at Loughcrew or at Dowth, can be seen very clearly without artificial illumination, but as one moves down the passage into the chamber, the visibility of the motifs becomes successively diminished, and experience of the stones changes from being predominantly visual to tactile. This goes hand in hand with the sound effects inside the temple interior. Those associated with the moving and active body become amplified, the sounds associated with the weather, animals, birds, and people outside successively diminished. Sight within the temple becomes intimate rather than a distanced gaze. It is restricted to the stones themselves.

By contrast, the kerbs are meant to be seen rather than touched. The encounter with them is primarily visual. The experience of the decorated stones within the temple may have been as much tactile as visual—motifs whose presence was felt rather than seen. The kerbstones are public 'front' spaces designed to impress. It is highly likely that they were not just meant to impress the cairn-using group, but also outsiders or strangers. The temple itself was a reserved space for insiders—hence the very different form and organisation of the motifs. We have noted that many of the kerbstones at Knowth appear to be consciously designed as framed units. The same is not true of the decorated stones in the passage temple interiors. These have additive and improvised qualities, subject to alteration and change over time. Outside there is an endless repetition of the same themes, whereas inside one experiences unique differentiation of the stones to a much greater degree.

It is probable that many of the decorated orthostats and corbels deep within the dark chambers were never meant to be seen, or perhaps only occasionally. In this respect, there is not such a great distinction between imagery that was entirely hidden within the temple structure and that which was not. They could only be visually experienced by means of artificial illumination. The flickering of the flames that would be required would make the images move and dance. In the final stages of the application of decoration to the temple interiors, we witness a movement away from depicting individual motifs to a concern with covering both the surfaces of individual stones and the temple interiors with picking, either diffuse or dense, emphasizing the surfaces and contours of the stones. This may be understood as putting increasing emphasis on feeling and form as opposed to visual sensory perception. It may also relate to an increasing importance on acoustic experience in the drum-shaped Boyne temples. Altering the stones was intimately related to the bodily impact they had on people entering and exiting from the passages and chambers. They orchestrated and altered their somatic experience in a radically different manner.

The external kerbstones open to public view and inspection at Knowth and Newgrange now provided an entirely unreliable guide to what would be encountered inside the temples, and this may relate to an increasing separation between ceremonies for the living taking place outside and ceremonies for the dead in the internal architectural spaces. The new emphasis given to decorating the entire internal spaces of the monuments contrasts with that put on framing, emphasizing, and differentiating between individual stones on the outside. The external kerbstones are visually captivating in a way that most of the internal stones are not. Inside the temple spaces there are relatively few arresting images. Another way of understanding this is to suggest that the experience of the outside of the temples was primarily placial and related to the landscape beyond, that inside the temple primarily temporal and related to movement from the domain of life and the living to that of death and the ancestors. More 'work' and time is required to experience the temple interiors, while the kerbstones can be experienced in a much more passive manner.

The graphic imagery can be understood in terms of the bodily and sensory transformation of experience in relation to both temple and landscape. For example, it has been suggested already that the spiral may be a material metaphor for a journey from the outside to the inside, into an ever more involuted space, the circle a never-ending circuit of movement around the cairn kerbs. There is no literal narrative, just as there are few, if any, literal (truly iconic) images. The dominant motif forms are polysemous, incorporative and conceptual devices susceptible to a wide range of meanings and referential links. They are about ideas and conceptual links rather than representations of real things in the world. They are expressing conceptual connections between temple and landscape, going in and going out, the dematerialisation of human identities in the mortuary process, crossing one space to another, transitions, seasonality, route-ways, journeying in life and in death. So the imagery is not an expression of things or material realities so much as a concern with conceptual space-time relationships and transformations on a nested and ever-widening geographical and social scale.

These are:

- The temple exterior and the temple interior.

- The relationship of temples to one another.

- The relationship of the temples to their surrounding landscapes and local geography.

- The relationship of the temples to the wider landscape and social geography of Ireland.

- The relationship of the temples to others across the Irish Sea.

O'Sullivan's (1996) model of temporal development suggests both significant change in the character of the decoration and important differences among Dowth, Knowth, and Newgrange. At Newgrange the pick dressing of the orthostats seems to have been deliberately designed to neutralise and remove the power of preexisting motifs within the temple. The personalities of individual stones had to be collectively subsumed, whereas at Knowth subsequent pick dressing was often additive. At both temples there appears to have been a changing emphasis from the decoration of individual stones treated independently from one another to a concern for decorating the entire architectural space, conceived as a whole, rather than as a series of independent and separate elements (orthostats, chamber recesses, and so on). This created an even greater contrast between the external kerbstones and the internal architectural spaces in terms of differences between their relative heterogeneity and their relative homogeneity, respectively, and concomitantly their somatic effects.

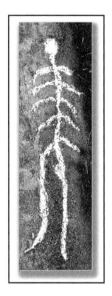

CHAPTER FOUR

THE BRONZING OF THE ROCKS

GROOVES AND EMBODIED IMAGES IN THE BRONZE AGE OF ÖSTERGÖTLAND, SWEDEN

In the northern part of Östergötland, just west and south of Norrköping, there are a remarkably dense series of rock carving locales on either side of the Motala River. To the north of the river, 61 places with rock carvings on 227 separate rock surfaces (a total of 4,475 motifs) have been documented in an area less than 2 km long and no more than 1 km wide. South of the river 103 places with rock carvings on 286 separate surfaces are known, with a total of 3,763 motifs in a band across a landscape that is only 3 km long and 1 km wide (Figure 4.1). This spectacular and massive concentration of rock carvings, the second largest in Sweden, in such a limited area marks this out as a very special cultural landscape during the Bronze Age. Beyond these spatially restricted bands of rock carving locales, few others are known, apart from rocks decorated only with simple cupmarks, which are more widely dispersed to the west, north, and east (Selinge 1989; Hauptman Wahlgren 2002).

During the Early Bronze Age, the sea level was about 20 m higher than it is today. As a result of land uplift, it was at this time that a series of rapids were formed on the Motala River at Fiskeby, cutting off the sea from Lake Glan, which was transformed from a saltwater inlet to a freshwater lake. Thereafter, the shoreline around Lake Glan more or less stabilized where it is today. By the end of the Bronze Age,

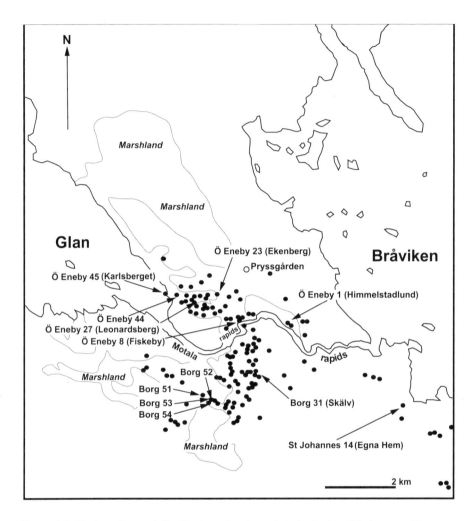

FIGURE 4.1. The location and distribution of rock carvings in the Norrköping area. The map shows the earlier Bronze Age coastline 15 m above present sea level. Marshy areas and rapids on the Motala River are marked, as is the location of the Pryssgården settlement. *After Hauptman Wahlgren 2002: fig. 3.* Rock carving locales discussed in the text are numbered as follows: *1*: Borg 51; *2*: Borg 54; *3*: Borg 53; *4*: Borg 52; *5*: Borg 31 (Skälv); *6*: St Jonannes 14 (Egna Hem); *7*: Ö Eneby 45 (Karlsberget); *8*: Ö Eneby 44; *9*: Ö Eneby 27 (Leonardsberg); *10*: Ö Eneby 23 (Ekenberg); *11*: Ö Eneby 8 (Fiskeby); *12*: Ö Eneby 1 (Himmelstadlund).

sea level was around 15 m above present-day levels, and a second series of rapids formed at the river mouth, draining into Bråviken in what is now the centre of the old industrial part of Norrköping; accordingly, the water currents down the river further intensified in strength. During this period and up to the present day, the river cut down into the land surface as it rose up, so that it now twists and winds through a minor steep-sided gully beyond Fiskeby before reaching the lower rapids. These events had a pronounced effect upon navigation. What had formerly been free passage by boat from the Baltic Sea inland became successively blocked by the formation of the rapids (Borna-Ahlkvist et al. 1998: 150; Hauptman Wahlgren 2002: 27).

IMAGES

The image repertoire, as elsewhere throughout the distribution of Scandinavian rock art, from Denmark to the Arctic, is limited and restricted. Fourteen main classes of designs can be distinguished (Table 4.1). Cupmarks constitute the most frequent design class, followed by boats, animals, shoe-soles, and human figures. Boats make up 16 percent of the total number of designs and no less than 40 percent of the figurative carvings in the area. They are extremely varied in size and type. The animals depicted are both domestic and wild, with the latter being more common. Red deer, wild boar, domestic pig, and horse are all depicted. Less frequent images are of elk, cattle, birds, dogs, and sheep or goats. A unique series of bear footprints occur at Himmelstadlund. Shoe-soles are depicted either in pairs or singly. Human figures make up 7 percent of the figurative motifs. Most are simple stick-line representations, and gender is impossible to identify in most cases. Narrative scenes generally include people, and they are closely associated with animals and ships.

By comparison, most other designs are quantitatively infrequent but nevertheless important. Depictions of swords and daggers, which are life-size and not carried, are unique to this area of Östergötland. Elsewhere in Scandinavia they occur only as scabbard images on human figures. Ceremonial hafted axes are also depicted. The only other area of Scandinavia where axes of similar type are equally frequent is in the Simrishamn area of southeast Sweden. Spears are far more common in Östergötland than anywhere else in Scandinavia (Malmer 1981: table 8). So there is an unusual and unique emphasis on weapons and metalwork of ceremonial significance. Depictions of swords and axes are always much larger in scale than other figures on the same rocks, thus emphasizing their significance. While the swords are depicted singly, axes are typically displayed in groups. Spears differ from axes or swords in that they are typically carried aloft by humans, sometimes in hunting scenes. Frame figures are almost unique to the Norrköping area (two other examples have recently been found in southeast Skåne). They are rectangular or oval in form and internally divided with vertical and diagonal lines or chevron patterns and resemble nets or traps (Nordén 1925; Selinge 1989: 152). Other motifs include circle crosses, concentric circles, and spirals (Table 4.1).

There are significant differences between the distribution of the designs to the north and south of the river (see Table 4.1). North of the river the carving locales are generally closer together, while to the south they are more widely distributed.

TABLE 4.1. FREQUENCY OF DIFFERENT DESIGN CLASSES IN THE PARISHES OF ÖSTRA ENEBY, NORTH OF THE MOTALA RIVER, AND BORG, SOUTH OF THE MOTALA RIVER.

Image	North of the River	South of the River
Cupmarks	1,691	2,558
Boats	1,126	455
Animals	397	147
Shoe-soles	210	110
Humans	243	32
Circle cross	68	17
Ring	36	34
Axes	59	13
Swords/daggers	53	1
Spears	50	4
Frame/net figures	17	22
Concentric circles	13	13
Tree	9	15
Spiral	9	4
Other & unidentifiable	494	347
Total:	4,475	3,763

Source: Hauptman and Wahlgren 2002: appendix 1 with some modifications.

Cupmarks are far more frequent south of the river, and they are virtually the only class of design to be found on rocks beyond the restricted landscape bands to the south and west of Norrköping (Figure 4.2). Figurative carvings are far more frequent north of the river. Every rock carving locale north of the river contains, on average, double the number of figurative carvings that occur south of the river (Hauptman Wahlgren 2002: 98).

All but one of the sword images occur to the north of the river, where they are concentrated on a few carved rock surfaces with a high diversity of other motifs.

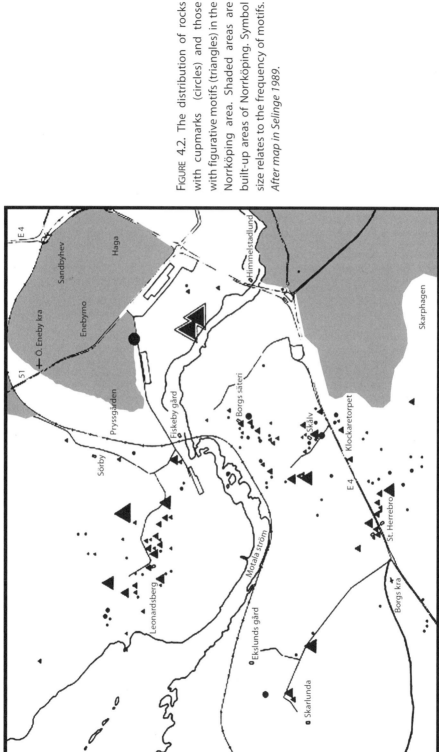

FIGURE 4.2. The distribution of rocks with cupmarks (circles) and those with figurative motifs (triangles) in the Norrköping area. Shaded areas are built-up areas of Norrköping. Symbol size relates to the frequency of motifs. *After map in Selinge 1989.*

Similarly, all but four spears, and the majority of the axes, occur north of the river. Humans also are more frequent north of the river, while shoe-soles, rings, frame figures/net designs, concentric circles, and tree figures are more common south of the river. Boats, animals, and spirals are equally frequent in terms of percentages of figurative designs both north and south of the river (ibid.: 100). However, of the total of 544 animals, almost three-quarters occur north of the river, and of these, 263 are found in only one carving locality, Himmelstadlund, where no fewer than 150 occur on one single rock carving surface (Rock 1A), almost as many as the total number found south of the river (ibid.: 107). Humans are similarly concentrated north of the river, where 90 percent of the total occur. Frame/net figures are among the few motifs that are more frequent, in terms of the total number of designs, south of the river, but the largest and most elaborate of these occur at Himmelstadlund.

The sword and dagger depictions have been dated to an early phase of the Bronze Age, Period II or III, on the basis of the similarity of some to securely dated bronze grave finds elsewhere (Nordén 1925). Swords produced during the later Bronze Age are notably absent. The axes also appear to be of earlier Bronze Age date. That the designs were successively added to the rocks over a long period of time is without question. Nordén (ibid.) argued that the carvings were produced during a short period, perhaps no more than a few hundred years during Periods I to II of the Early Bronze Age, around 1600 to 1500 B.C. Larsson (1986) is in agreement with this short chronology, arguing that the absence of typical Late Bronze Age weapons or axes suggests that the function of rock carvings depicting such artefacts (see below) was no longer relevant (ibid.: 143).

Hauptman Wahlgren suggests a much longer period of use and reuse of the same carving localities, from Period II onwards to Period VI, throughout the Bronze Age, a time span of about 1,000 years (Hauptman Wahlgren 2002: 176 ff.). Despite the massive number of carvings that occur, if we divide them equally over the years during which they might have been carved, we get a figure of only around two or three new figurative carvings per year over a 1,000-year period, or seven or eight over a 500-year period, to make up the total number known (ibid.: 179). What is certainly the case is that some cupmark sites occurring below the 15 m contour, areas under the sea during the Bronze Age but outside the main rock carving area, must be at least of early Iron Age date, indicating the great longevity of this particular tradition of inscribing the rocks.

On the basis of the frequent observation that some carvings are deeply cut whereas others on the same rock surfaces are comparatively shallow, Hauptman Wahlgren suggests that such a difference might be due to recarving of the same images (ibid.: 183), which, if the act of carving was important as part of the rituals taking place at the rock carving sites, would reactivate their significance in a particular ceremonial context. A similar effect might be produced by filling in the carvings with contrasting colouring materials such as red clay and soot (ibid.: 184 ff.).

Old carvings would then become new—which would render meaningless the idea of dating a carving to a single event in time.

SETTLEMENT EVIDENCE

In recent years a small number of settlement areas have been excavated in the Norr-köping area, notably at Pryssgården (Borna-Ahlkvist et al. 1998) and Ringeby (Kaliff 1995a) as a result of rescue excavations in advance of motorway construction. Most of the material dates to the Final Bronze Age or later.

At Ringeby post holes have indicated the presence of three probable houses in different areas of what was an island during the Late Bronze Age and which seems primarily to have been used as a cult place for mortuary activities connected with the cremation and burial of the dead (Kaliff 1995a: 21–25). The Pryssgården settle-ment, which lacks any burial remains, is of an entirely different character. It is locat-ed only 1.3 km northwest of Himmelstadlund and 1 km to the northeast and north, respectively, of the major carving locales at Ekenberg and Fiskeby, north of the river. This is one of the largest prehistoric settlements known in Sweden, with an exten-sive Late Bronze Age and early Iron Age settlement (Borna-Ahlkvist et al. 1998; Borna-Ahlkvist 2002). The area excavated, 90,000 sq m, is merely a cross section of a much larger area that undoubtedly extended to the south and even closer to the vicinity of the rock carvings, where excavations currently being undertaken have recovered more settlement remains.

Prior to these discoveries, a common interpretation was that the rock carving locales with figurative carvings were situated in areas peripheral to settlement, whereas cupmark sites and the presence of heaps of fire-cracked stones in the landscape indicated settled areas elsewhere. A pastoral economy was widely assumed. The discovery of a major settlement area only a short distance away from the most important rock carving sites has dramatically altered such a per-spective.

Analysis of the material from Pryssgården has identified twenty-one long houses, twelve smaller houses, and remains of two huts dated to the Bronze Age. The oldest long house, which had two aisles, is dated to Period I of the Bronze Age. It was 32 m long and 6 m broad, with its long axis orientated west/northwest to east/southeast (Borna-Ahlkvist 2002: 30). Two three-aisled houses are also of Early Bronze Age date (Period III), while the majority are of Late Bronze Age date (Periods IV–V). The orientation of the long houses throughout the Bronze Age is repetitive and consistent, and the majority are orientated approximately northwest to southeast. The entrances, in the approximate centre of the southern wall, faced south towards Fiskeby and the river, with only one exception (ibid.: 62). Pryssgår-den continued to be occupied during the Iron Age and into the Viking period. Most of the long houses during this time were now orientated northeast to south-west.

The evidence thus suggests long-term settlement continuity, with a great expansion of the settlement area towards the end of the Bronze Age, when it would have contained a number of farms and households. Borna-Ahlkvist argues that during the Late Bronze Age, at least three farms existed within the excavation area, at a distance of 70 to 140 m from each other. Fireplaces in the Late Bronze Age houses were consistently in the western part. This appears to have been the living area of the house, while the eastern part, often with a large pit, was used for storage and as a working area. House offerings of ceramic vessels and cranial parts of domestic animals frequently occur adjacent to the hearth at the western end of the houses. Evidence for Early Bronze Age agriculture at Pryssgården is extremely limited but included the cultivation of naked barley in garden plots. During the Late Bronze Age, cultivation in the vicinity of the settlement was extensive and varied, with crops including hulled barley, breadwheat, spelt, rye, and flax. The recovered bone material, which was quantitatively small, represents cattle (52%), sheep/goat (35%), pig (13%), and horse and dog among domestic animals, and deer, hare, birds, and a variety of fish species (Borna-Ahlkvist et al 1998: 160–61). A few Late Bronze Age pottery finds and a ceramic figurine from the settlement area have been interpreted as possible evidence for long-distance contacts and exchange with the so-called Lausitz central European urnfield culture (Stålblom 1998: 129 ff.).

The difference between the scale and extent of the Late Bronze Age settlement and that in the Early Bronze Age, together with the paucity of evidence for agriculture during the earlier period, might be interpreted as a change from a much more mobile and temporary settlement structure during the Early Bronze Age in the Norrköping area, in which hunting, fishing, and gathering may have been very important, to a more stable settlement pattern with large, permanent settlements with garden plots developing during towards the end of the Bronze Age.

CAIRNS AND BURIAL

No Early Bronze Age barrows or cairns are recorded from the Norrköping area in the direct vicinity of the carving locales. A few single examples are known from the Kolmården area north of Bråviken and to the south of Lake Glan. The nearest large concentration occurs in Vikbolandet, to the south of Bråviken, about 15 km distant to the east, a markedly different landscape broken up by wooded rocky hills and ridges (Figure 4.3A, B). The cairns here are placed high up in the landscape with extensive views across it. Many extensive Iron Age gravefields are documented in the rock carving area, and excavated cemeteries at Fiskeby, Klinga, and Skälv (Carlsson 1960; Lundström 1965; 1970; Stålblom 1994) have shown that many of these cremation burial areas first came into use during the Late Bronze Age and then expanded considerably during the early Iron Age.

During the Late Bronze Age, Ringeby was an island at the far western end of Bråviken. Around 1000 B.C. it began to be used as a cemetery, which lasted until

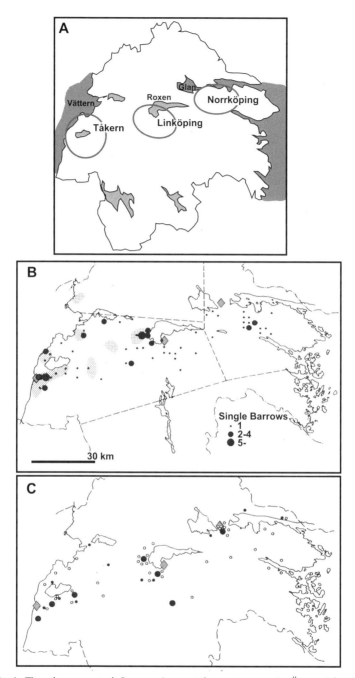

FIGURE 4.3. *A*: The three central Bronze Age settlement areas in Östergötland. *After Borna-Ahlkvist 2002. B*: The distribution of Bronze Age barrows in Östergötland. The dots show the distribution per 1/4 Economic Map sheet. Diamonds indicate rock carving areas and hatching the distribution of Late Neolithic gallery graves. *After T. Larsson 1986: fig. 88.* *C*: The distribution of Early Bronze Age metalwork in Östergötland. Unfilled circles = 1 tool find. Filled circles mark weapon finds (small dot = 1 find, large dot = 2 finds/parish). Diamonds show rock carving areas. *After T. Larsson 1986: fig. 89.*

about 400 B.C. About 60 probable burials have been identified here, 44 of which contained cremated human bones either placed in an urn or burial pit or scattered in the grave. The cleansed bones were taken from repeatedly used central cremation places (Kaliff 1995a; 1995b).

Artefact Finds

Of Östergötland's nearly 100 known 'loose' finds of bronze, most of which lack find context information, only about 20 were made in the Norrköping area. The older Bronze Age is represented by two finds of flanged and palstave bronze axes. Two are from the Motala River. One flanged axe was found near Himmelstadlund, and one palstave was recovered near the lower rapids at the river's mouth which formed during the later Bronze Age (Hauptman Wahlgren 2002: 168) (Figure 4.3C). Two sword finds are also of Early Bronze Age date, one from Resebro bog south of the river at the far southern end of the band of rock carvings, and the other from Krokek in the Kolmården area just north of Bråviken. This also may have come from a marshy area, and both were probably votive deposits (ibid.: 169). From Klinga a spearhead is documented. From the later Bronze Age a few shaft-hole axes are known, and two neck rings are documented from marshy ground south of the Motala River at Eksund where the Motala River flows out of Lake Glan. Compared with other areas of Sweden, the finds are very meagre indeed. The association of these finds with the running water of the Motala River and marsh and bog areas does appear to be significant, together with their rarity throughout the Bronze Age.

Documentation

Rock carvings in the Norrköping area have been known since at least 1760. The first systematic investigation and documentation of the sites was carried out in the later part of the nineteenth century by Nordenskjöld (1870–73; 1876), who discovered and drew the carvings on many sites. The first attempt at a comprehensive documentation of the rock carvings from the Norrköping area was produced by Nordén (1925) and, in many respects, this is still today the best source. Subsequently many, but not all, of these rocks were documented again by Burenhult (1973). Since then, a major new inventory of the rocks was conducted by the Central Board of Antiquities during 1979–80. This resulted in the discovery and documentation of an increased number of locales (Jönsson 1980). The documentation of the sites by the Central Board of Antiquities consists of written descriptions, but a special inventory, with plans, was made of those carving sites lying along the course of the then-proposed (now built) E4 motorway, running through the centre of the carving area (Broström and Ihrestam 1993).

Generally, Burenhult's method of documentation shows more carvings than those documented by Nordén on the same rocks. However, the method Burenhult used tends to systematically blur detail and produces a rather crude representation of individual designs. Nordén's work, produced at a larger scale, is much more sensitive to variation and detail in the individual designs and thus is the preferred reference used by the skilled professionals who maintain the carvings today, preserving them as a tourist attraction. In some cases, notably at Himmelstadlund, panels of designs documented by Nordén are absent in Burenhult's representations of the same rocks, although they are clearly present and painted in for tourists. Furthermore, there are panels of designs not documented by either Nordén or Burenhult, including an important boar-hunting scene, now widely used as a promotional logo by the city of Norrköping and the local rock carving museum.

As is typical in the documentation of rock carvings, the plans produced reduce the surface morphology of the rocks to a blank two-dimensional white space on which the motifs are starkly superimposed. The rocks themselves, on which the carvings occur, and their situation in the landscape are scarcely mentioned or described. Nordén (1925) does, however, depict both larger cracks and splintered areas of surface rock that have obliterated part of the designs, and again, in this respect his documentation is superior to that of Burenhult (1973). The latter documentation lacks maps or plans, so it is impossible to find or identify the rocks being depicted without cross-referencing back to Nordén's earlier work. Here small plans of particular rock carving areas are usefully provided (see further discussion in Selinge 1985).

There is clearly no 'ideal' or total documentation of these carving locales. However, the very idea of such a totalising documentation, with everything shown, is a dangerous myth that has inhibited interpretive work. Using a combination of the materials available today, both visual and written, undoubtedly provides a sound basis from which to work and discuss individual carving locales in the landscape.

The Significance of the Carvings

Nordén (1925) argued that Östergötland as a whole could be divided into three central areas where most prehistoric monuments, rock carving locales, and metalwork were found: in the east around Norrköping, in the centre around Linköping, and to the west around Lake Tåkern; this idea has continued to have relevance to archaeologists up to the present day (e.g., Kaliff 1999: 47; Larsson 1986; Borna-Ahlkvist 2002) (Figure 4.3A). For the Norrköping area, Nordén attempted to identify various carving locales with the styles of individual specialist carvers, suggesting that the motifs were created by a limited number of persons. Based on his evaluation of a similarity of style among the carvings at different places, and a short chronology, he claimed that, north of the river, those at Himmelstadlund were the work of a single master carver, those at Ekenberg another, with a third at work at Fiskeby. At Leonardsberg, by contrast, the variety of carving styles suggested to him that a number of different individuals were at work. At least two carvers were at work at Herrebro in Borg parish south of the river, while the carver at work at Borgs säteri was probably responsible for the main rocks at Skälv (Nordén 1925: 145). The forms of the carvings were thus, in part, expressions of individual style.

Nordén argued that the carvings were part of an agricultural cult. Shoe-soles, circle crosses, trees, axes, swords, and spears all played important roles in this cult, as did depictions of anthropomorphic gods. Certain 'over-dimensioned' motifs in association with humans suggested that religious and magical power was differentiated: 'one had a spear power, an axe power and a sword power, that is to say, power whose holy symbols were the spear, axe and sword' (ibid.: 148). Similarities with carvings in northwest Spain and Portugal, where daggers and axes are also depicted together with concentric circles and certain types of frame figures, suggested a diffusion of ideas and long-distance trading contacts involving copper and tin (ibid.: 158 ff., 166–67).

The striking and unique sword and the comparatively numerous axe carvings in the Norrköping area have stimulated much discussion. Malmer (1981) has pointed out the strong inverse relationship between the number of actual metal finds in different areas of Scandinavia and their depiction in the rock art. He suggests that the depiction of these bronzes in the carvings largely acted as a substitute for their ritual deposition in votive deposits and in hoards in southern areas of Scandinavia rich in metalwork (ibid.: 50).

In more recent literature, a near consensus has been reached that the presence of rock carvings in the Norrköping area in the vicinity of the Motala River can be understood in relation to long-distance alliances, trade, and prestige goods systems. Larsson (1986) argues that there is a spatial correlation between finds of metalwork and three major rock carving areas in Östergötland. These are the Norrköping area to the east, Gärstad at the western end of Lake Roxen in the centre, and the Hästholmen carvings on the eastern shore of Lake Vättern to the west. These areas are linked by the Motala River (see Figure 4.3A). In each of these Early Bronze Age settlement areas there was access to metal on a limited scale, people buried some of their dead in barrows, and the rock carving sites acted as religious and ritual centres (ibid.: 141). The majority of the metalwork is found within a 10-km radius of the carving sites: 'One immediate interpretation of this phenomenon could be that a direct relationship between the supply of bronze/bronze objects and the social function of the rock carvings as *central places* existed' (ibid.: 141). Larsson envisages a chiefly elite living in the vicinity of the sacred rock carving sites controlling both ritual activities and the supply of products such as bronze. Because of the remoteness of Östergötland from the flow of bronzes from the south of Scandinavia and beyond, the aristocratic elite controlled and consumed the flow of both weapons and tools. By contrast, in Skåne, in the far south of Sweden, the relatively good access to bronze significantly reduced the prestige character of all metalwork (ibid.: 142). The very low supply of bronze to Östergötland gave these artefacts a very high value— the ultimate symbols of power and prestige. However, 'the power and prestige given to important individuals or groups . . . expressed by certain types of metalwork . . . could not take the same mode of manifestation in Östergötland [as elsewhere] because of the scarcity of bronze. Instead it had to be expressed in other forms—by making pictures of the desirable objects and controlling the activities connected to the engraving ritual' (ibid.: 143). Thus in Östergötland, pictures of bronzes had the same significance as the real objects elsewhere. They were both manifestations of, and legitimised, inequality and social power. For Larsson, depictions of pigs on the rock carving sites, principally Himmelstadlund, indicate that feasting and ceremonies took place here, principally related to the status and position of those in power rather than ordinary people. The pig could act as a meat reserve used on important occasions in connection with ceremonies and exchange (Larsson 1993: 111, 134).

The connection between rock carvings and water transportation routes has been discussed by a number of researchers. Wigren (1987) has pointed out a close connection between the distribution of rock carving sites in Södermanland, north of Östergötland, and Weiler (1994) has similarly discussed this in relation to those to the west in Västergötland (Wigren 1987). In Östergötland it has similarly been argued that the Motala River acted as a major route of communication inland from the Baltic Sea to the west. Kaliff stresses the importance of the Motala River acting as an artery for goods and ideas, joining the Baltic to the east and Lake Vättern to the west (Kaliff 1999: 15). Borna-Ahlkvist describes the Norrköping area as 'probably one of the most important cultural crossroads around the Baltic. Here it was possible during prehistoric times to join the Baltic with the Kattegat and the North sea through Motala Ström [river], lake Vättern and the waterways of Västergötland' (Borna-Ahlkvist 2002: 194). She argues that control of the rapids on the Motala River at Fiskeby was vital; in order to pass them, people would have to either transfer their cargoes or drag their boats past, moving either inland or seaward. The presence of the major carving site at Himmelstadlund and the large Pryssgården settlement nearby are explained in terms of their being strategic meeting points, ceremonial centres, and places for exchange.

Larsson (1995) compares the overall distribution of metalwork finds in western and eastern Östergötland and shows that while the frequencies of axe finds are broadly comparable, weapons and ornaments are far more frequent in the west. Following his earlier model, dividing Östergötland into western, central, and eastern regions, each with a central area having rock carvings, metalwork, and barrows, he argues that the western area was in the past, as it is today, by far the richest in terms of arable productivity. This would allow the production of a surplus which could provide the basis by which a powerful local chiefdom could import prestige goods such as bronzes. Such prestige goods would travel to the west of Östergötland from the Baltic through Bråviken and along the Motala River: 'The large collection of rock carvings in Norrköping, together with the strategic position of Himmelstadlund as "the crown jewels," shows how important water communications were and that the symbols that were carved in the rocks really should have a direct physical contact with this communication net' (ibid.: 1995: 11; see also Larsson 1993: 112). These prestige goods accumulated at different points in the landscape but primarily in the region that was richest agriculturally, around Lake Tåkern in western Östergötland. Here excavations at Vistad revealed, in Larsson's interpretations of the finds, an exceptional Early Bronze Age settlement with remains of at least five square or rectangular houses situated high up on a plateau area surrounded by a palisade fence. Larsson (1993; 1995: 12) interprets this as the settlement of an important local chief or big man controlling long-distance exchange. Other chiefly centres in central and eastern Östergötland had, according to this scenario, a lesser significance. The style of the Vistad settlement is unknown elsewhere in Scandinavia, although common in central Europe. Finds of special pottery styles and ovens have also been argued by Larsson to suggest central European Lausitz urnfield influence or contacts.

There are a number of problems with the influential Larsson model of centres of chiefly power (and unequal status) connected with control of the rock carving sites as cult centres and linked to the distribution of metalwork and barrows. First, the rock carving locales in the Norrköping area are not comparable with those at Gärstad and Hästholmen farther to the west, as Selinge has pointed out. These are minor rock carving locales in terms of (a) the number of carved rocks and individual rock surfaces; (b) the numbers of motifs carved—only 63 and 144, respectively, a total including cupmarks (Selinge 1989: 150, 154); and (c) the types of motifs that occur. They are simply dwarfed by the sheer scale and variety of the rock carving locales in the Norrköping area in all these respects. Such places appear to be of equal significance only when marked on small-scale maps with symbols of the same size.

Second, while Early Bronze Age barrows do occur in the vicinity of Gärstad and Hästholmen, they are spatially separated from the carving locales in the Norrköping area, suggesting a different pattern altogether, in which burial of an ancestral elite is separated from the carved rocks. Here it is only in the Late Bronze Age that flat grave cemeteries occur in the same areas as the carved rocks.

Third, as Kaliff has argued, the notion that exchange was dominated by chiefly power in the western part of Östergötland during the Early Bronze Age is partly dependent on the presence of the unique, and recently discovered, Vistad settlement find. Other such sites might exist elsewhere and, during the Late Bronze Age at least, the most important centre of authority and power is in the eastern part of Östergötland, if we regard the (few) finds of possible Lausitz-style ceramic finds from the Ringeby cremation cemetery and the Pryssgården settlement as significant indicators of long-distance exchange contacts (Kaliff 1999: 70). Hauptman Wahlgren has cogently challenged all aspects of Larsson's interpretation of the Vistad settlement as representing the homestead of a chief controlling long-distance trade with connections to central Europe. She argues that the small amounts of so-called Lausitz pottery here and at Pryssgården and Ringeby was almost certainly produced locally and does not indicate contacts with central Europe and calls into question Larsson's interpretation of the Vistad post hole evidence (Hauptman Wahlgren 2002: 140–44).

Fourth, the amount of metalwork recorded from the whole of Östergötland is tiny and insignificant compared with that known from the south of Sweden, which seems to suggest that no area of the province was likely to be of great significance in terms of controlling the supply of bronzes. The conspicuous absence of bronze here relative to area seems to be the significant point, as both Malmer and Larsson have emphasized.

Fifth, how important was the Motala River as an inland channel of navigation leading west to Lake Vättern? Hauptman Wahlgren has recently argued that the emergence during the Early Bronze Age of the rapids at Fiskeby, several hundred metres long, would actively hinder its significance as a major channel of inland communication (ibid.: 27). She suggests instead that the Norrköping rock carving area marks a liminal passage through the landscape which must be crossed to begin a future journey. The rock carvings, and the rapids on the river, rather than marking an entry point *into* Östergötland, represent a threshold that must be crossed on the way *out* to another world (ibid.: 29, 40).

The work reviewed above naturally tells us rather little about the form and content of the Norrköping rock carvings, the rocks on which they occur, or anything about the location of these rocks in the landscape, apart from the general significance of water in general and the Motala River in particular. Since Nordén's (1925) work, there has been very little interpretive research in relation to the rocks themselves. The principal effort has always been directed towards inventory and documentation, together with some statistical analysis. Based on the new documentation of the rocks carried out by the Central Board of Antiquities in 1979–80, Selinge (1989) was able to provide a new general description and statistical analysis of the carving locales from Östergötland, showing the widespread distribution of cupmark localities, almost all of which are concentrated in the three central areas mentioned above and the extremely restricted distribution of the figurative carvings occurring only in the Norrköping area, Gärstad, and Hästholmen (ibid.: 148). As regards the Norrköping area, he notes their concentration on rocks of mica-schist and in an area with easily cultivated soils near the mouth of the Motala River. Selinge also notes significant differences between the types of motifs that occur to the north and south of the river. He regards the motifs, particularly the ships, as having a magical significance. They depict what was needed: ships, bronzes, herds of pigs, deer, and the like. He notes that agricultural scenes are absent. There are no ploughs or ards such as occur in Bohuslän on the west coast of Sweden, or any depictions suggesting the cultivation of crops. Cattle are only rarely depicted whereas horses are relatively common, suggesting the carvings represent cult scenes rather than narratives from daily life (ibid.: 153). Fish are also absent despite the fact that migrating salmon must have been common in the Motala River. That some ships are depicted as being drawn by horses, carried by people bearing trees or axes and decorated with symbols, again suggests to him that these are not normal, everyday navigational scenes or depictions of boats that actually existed, but have a quite different cult and magical significance.

Hauptman Wahlgren's excellent recent work (2002) is the first serious, detailed attempt to engage with, analyse, and interpret the Norrköping rock carvings since Nordén's (1925) study and is undoubtedly one of the most important and insightful studies of Scandinavian rock art produced to date. She emphasizes the paramount significance of water for an understanding of the carvings in three different ways: (1) the significance of the river and the rapids as mentioned above; cf. discussion of the significance of rapids in Tilley (1991); (2) the location of the carving locales in a marshy zone between dry land and running water (see discussion below); and (3) the general significance of water running over the rocks and the individual carvings connected with liminal rites of passage. Aspects of her specific interpretations will be considered in more detail in the discussion of individual rocks below. Here I only want to consider some more general issues.

As regards the imagery, Hauptman Wahlgren presents two lengthy statistical analyses and discussions. One chapter of her book is devoted to discussing the spatial distributions of individual types of motifs—boat figures, spirals, humans, and animals—with a review of previous interpretations of each in the context of Scandinavian rock art research. Another chapter considers combinations of different types of designs on individual rock carving surfaces. The inevitable problem with these types of analyses is that they are entirely dependent on the initial categorisation of both the motifs and what is supposed to constitute an individual rock carving surface. Within each category discussed—particularly as regards the boats (where there is enormous variation), but also in relation to the human and animal depictions, the frame/net, and other design types—differences and particularity become glossed and subsumed. It would seem to make a significant difference, for example, whether particular types of boats or other specific design classes are combined with domestic or wild animals, and in what particular manner, but such types of associations are not considered. The results of the analysis are therefore rather generalized and limited.

A third chapter discusses chronological issues and the meaning of the designs. She distinguishes between 'structural' compositions and 'transformational' compositions. The former include opposed design forms on different areas of a rock panel, such as groups of hafted axes orientated in different directions (ibid.: 193) or the opposed movement of groups of ships across the rock surfaces. The latter involve changing styles of human figures and their relationship with other symbols. Here she discusses in detail two selected panels, one from Ekenberg and one from Himmelstadlund. She also mentions two others from Herrebro in Borg parish and one from Leonardsberg in support of her interpretation of these specific panels as representing a transformational passage of the human figures from one social or ritual identity state to another, indicated by changes in size and form, and their relationship to other symbols, in particular, boats.

The landscape study of the rock carving locales, the general statistical analysis, and her detailed discussion of four specific panels from two locales (unfortunately the only ones considered in any detail in the book) all appear to be primarily based on a paper analysis rather than one involving their phenomenological experience and study in the field. Hence the form and character of the rocks on which these designs are carved and the manner in which both the images and the rocks interact with the body of an observer—the two key elements of the approach taken in this book—are little considered, apart from the possible significance of the presence of cracks in the rock on one of the Ekenberg panels (ibid.: 197, 216 ff.; and see discussion below).

The single most striking aspect of the rocks in the Norrköping area is the presence of deep glacial grooves on the rock surfaces and their clear structural relationship to the images on many carving surfaces. While their presence has frequently been noted in the written inventories conducted by the Central Board of Antiquities and in a few individual mentions of rocks by Nordén (1925) and Hauptman Wahlgren (2002), they have otherwise been completely ignored in all accounts. Nordén's (1925) and Burenhult's (1973) documentation of the rocks completely factor them out as blank white spaces between linear groups of images, the reason for whose strange linear alignment on white paper can only be guessed at by someone who has not visited the area. Hauptman Wahlgren shows two pictures of these rocks with grooves from Himmelstadlund and Leonardsberg (2002: 36–37), but her only comment about them is that they are areas in which water collects and runs off the rock surfaces.

The second part of this chapter will now consider the form and character of the rocks and their relationship to the images in detail.

THE SIGNIFICANCE OF STONE AND LANDSCAPE

The rock carvings are exclusively concentrated in localised outcrops of mica-schist, rich in andalusite and cordierite (Bergström and Kornfält 1973). Only cupmark sites occur in surrounding areas where granite outcrops. The mica-schist was thus recognized and marked out by the presence of the carvings as a special stone and its own particular qualities recognised.

The carved rocks occur today in a flat or only slightly undulating arable plain which stretches about 10 km north to south and 10–12 km west to east. This is bounded to the west by the freshwater Lake Glan, and to the east by Bråviken, an inlet of the Baltic Sea. To the north the plain is terminated by a fault line running from Svärtinge to Åby and beyond to the east, bordering the northern side of Bråviken. North of this fault line the landscape alters radically, being heavily wooded and covered with numerous smaller and larger lakes, granite hills and outcrops, and extensive boulder spreads. To the south of the river the low-lying arable areas are soon broken up by higher and more heavily wooded ridges and hills. The Motala River linking Lake Glan to the sea is situated more or less at the centre of the rock carving locales. To the north they run more or less parallel its course in a northwest to southeast band from the shores of Lake Glan to Himmelstadlund, the largest and most complex carving locale. To the south of the river the rock carvings run in the opposite direction, towards the river, from around Borg church in the southwest to the northeast near Fiskeby. Unlike the carvings north of the river, the band of carvings to the south does not terminate at any particularly extensive or significant carving locale (see Figures 4.1, 4.2).

Immediately to the north and south of the river, the plain is broken up by numerous low rock islands or more extensive rock pavement areas, virtually every one of which contains carvings scattered on one or more surfaces. These range in height from only a few metres or less to as much as 10 m above the surrounding land surface. Some may rise up quite dramatically, others are relatively low and flat topped. Each is unique in terms of its shape, dimension, and surface morphology. South of the river the archipelago of rock islands is usually less than 50 to 100 m in length and up to 50 m or so broad. At the northern end of the carving area, closer to the river, there are more extensive pavement areas, with exposed rocks around Borgs säteri. However, such large exposed rock pavements are more extensive north of the river. Here the most westerly series of rock carvings are effectively smaller or larger rock islands, but to the west of Leonardsberg, running towards Fiskeby, there are extensive rock pavements covering an area approximately 600 m long by 300 m broad on which carved panels are dispersed. To the east of the Fiskeby carving locales, again situated on rock 'islands', there are no carving locales, apart from a few cupmark sites, for a distance of 1.3 km, until Himmelstadlund, with its extensive exposed rock pavement areas, where the carvings are densely concentrated on 57 separate surfaces.

On the plain to the north of where the rock carvings are found, there are few rock outcrops or pavement areas until one reaches the fault line of the Svärtinge/ Åby ridge which rises up to 100 m or so above the plain. No rock carvings are found here apart from a few cupmark locales on the western edge of Bråviken. Similarly to the south, the absence of carving sites where the land becomes more hilly and broken up with ridges is quite striking. The most easterly of the carving locales with figurative carvings to the south of the river is at Egna Hem, unusual in both its isolation and location (see below). In general terms, the distribution of the carving locales is strongly associated with the river and its passage to the sea, connecting the inland with the coast, freshwater with saltwater. Lake Glan, from which the river flows, is itself huge. Measuring 12 by 8 km, it is itself a kind of inland sea, whereas paradoxically the long and narrow Bråviken salt inlet, only 4 km or less wide, fringed by reeds, has more the characteristics of a lake.

Besides having the greatest number of carvings and carving surfaces, Himmelstadlund stands out from all the other rock carving locales in a number of important respects. First of all, it is relatively isolated in relation to the distribution of other rock carving sites both north and south of the river. It is more or less continuous, with only a few hundred metres (and in many cases considerably less) separating one carved rock island or pavement area with carved panels from another. On the riverbank immediately to its south and beyond, there are no rock carving locales. To the west there are none until Fiskeby, over 1 km distant. To the north there is only one cupmark site 600 m away, and only three others to the east before Bråviken and the coast. Second, while in general terms all the carving locales are near the river, Himmelstadlund is conspicuously invisible from most. Moreover, it is one of the few places from which the river is actually visible. Third, it is the closest major site to the sea with figurative carvings, and it occurs almost equidistant between two important sets of rapids—upstream at Fiskeby and downstream in central Norrköping. The rapids at Fiskeby mark the ends of the bands of rock carvings both to the south of the river and to the north—except for the Himmelstadlund site itself, which is set apart from both. Its extensive exposed pavement areas are at the same time rock islands. It thus combines rock 'island' and rock pavement characteristics.

The mica-schist on which the rock carvings are found is a very heavily metamorphosed rock of sedimentary origin. Locally it varies considerably in character. In areas without lichen development, where the rock appears as a uniform matt, dull grey, the rocks are significantly different in character. By the shores of Lake Glan and along the cycle track that runs through the Himmelstadlund carving surfaces, the rocks are revealed as bluish grey in colour. Throughout the area, rock exposures are found with irregularly shaped areas of what resembles bronze metallic staining on their surfaces. This glitters markedly in the sunlight, almost as if molten metal has been spilled over the rock or is oozing out of it. When freshly carved, the images must have seemed to give forth a metallic sheen. So carving images of swords, axes, and spearheads in this rock must have had a particular symbolic power and resonance.

Compared with granite, the rock is relatively soft and very dense. In section it resembles a sedimentary shale, which we know has been metamorphosed into its present form. It has a marked tendency to split laterally along bedding planes. Besides the metallic sheen found in some areas, the numerous mica inclusions found everywhere also cause the rock to glitter in the sunlight. Compared with the coarse pink granite that also outcrops in surrounding areas, the mica-schist feels incredibly smooth.

These rocks have another very special quality—glacial grooves crossing the rock surface. These are found everywhere that the mica-schist outcrops and is exposed. They were formed by frozen blocks of stone in the base of the moving ice sheets gouging out parallel furrows in the bedrock. Immediately to the west and south of Norrköping, the ice moved from the northwest to the southeast, and so the grooves have their long axis consistently orientated in this direction (Bergström and Kornfält 1973: 31, fig. 12b). Despite the ubiquitous presence of the grooves on the mica-schist, their form and character vary markedly between the different rock islands and pavement areas and between the north and south sides of the river. It is noteworthy that such grooves do not occur in the granite.

North of the river, mica-schist outcrops are most extensive and massive on a rock island southwest of Leonardsberg, only 250 m distant from the Motala River near where it flows out of Lake Glan. This rock rises up, quite steeply, to 10 m above the level of the surrounding land. Today it is surrounded by marshy land except on the eastern side. Here the grooves have an almost perfectly symmetrical profile and measure up to 0.5 m deep and 1 m broad. The longest are 25 m or more in length. They cover extensive parts of this island in a series of ten parallel troughs from the northwest side and up to the almost horizontal flat top of the rock (Figure 4.4). Interestingly, this is one of the very few rock islands north of the river on which no carvings have been found. Elsewhere there is a general tendency for the grooves to become larger, longer, and more pronounced and symmetrical in profile as one moves east through the rock carving area towards the sea. They are scarcely developed on rocks near the river mouth running out of Lake Glan. At Leonardsberg rock 28 (see below), they are short and rather narrow and asymmetrical in profile, having only a base and one well-defined upper side, being about 8 m long and 0.5 m or less broad (Figure 4.5). To the north, at Ekenberg, they are shallow, short (2–3 m long), and discontinuous. Across the extensive pavement area between Leonardsberg and Fiskeby, they are more symmetrical in profile, up to 10 m or more long, and 1 m broad but generally shallow. They are most fully developed at the northwest end of Himmelstadlund, where five parallel grooves, four of which are symmetrical, cross the rock surface for a distance of up to 20 m, with a width of up to 1.5 m (see description below). Here they are distinctly graded in size, with the widest highest up the rock surface near to its top. Elsewhere at Himmelstadlund, to the east, they are much more weakly developed, often asymmetrical and discontinuous, resembling those found at Ekenberg. South of the river the grooves are generally less numerous and weakly developed, being in most cases shallow and discontinuous and mostly asymmetrical in form, with a flat base and only one pronounced side. Particularly impressive asymmetrical grooves are found at Borg (Herrebro) rock 51 and at Skälv rock 31 (see discussions below). Extensive, long, parallel series of well-formed symmetrical grooves as found at Himmelstadlund are absent. There is another important difference in the character of the grooves that should be noted:

FIGURE 4.4. Huge glacial grooves crossing the rock island near the Motala River at Leonardsberg.

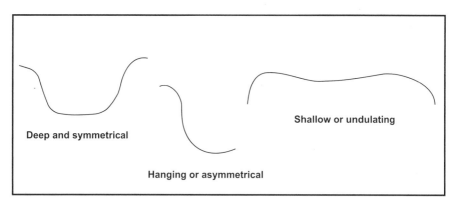

FIGURE 4.5. Profiles of the main types of grooves found on the mica-schist rocks in the Norrköping area.

their relationship to the river. North of the river, on most rocks they run parallel to the course of the river, which mostly flows through the area in which the rock carvings occur, except where it bends around the rapids at Fiskeby, northwest to southeast. South of the river this is not the case, and the long axis of the grooves runs at right angles to the river rather than following its flow.

In choosing to decorate these rocks, there was clearly a recognition of four very special qualities:

1. The smoothness of the stone.
2. The manner in which the mica sparkles in the sun and moonlight and glistens in the rain.
3. The molten metallic qualities of the mineral staining and inclusions.
4. The presence of the grooves or furrows crossing the rocks.

Just as in the Simrishamn area of southeast Skåne there was a recognition of the special but markedly different qualities of the Cambrian sandstone (see discussion in Tilley 2004), in this area of Östergötland the presence of the mica-schist to the west of Norrköping in itself provides at least a partial explanation for the extraordinarily dense concentration of carvings.

The bands of rock carving locales in the landscape both significantly terminate around the upper rapids at Fiskeby. For a while, during the earlier Bronze Age, the only place freely accessible by boat from the sea along the river course would have been the major carving locale at Himmelstadlund. Until the lower rapids formed, this was near the place where freshwater met seawater. Most of the rocks with carvings are found in what Hauptman Wahlgren (2002: 38) has termed a transitional zone between open water and dry land. The rocks were well defined in relation to the boggy areas and, she argues, difficult to access. Passage out to the rocks could easily be restricted through controlling passage along platforms built out to the rocks from dry land. Many carvings are orientated towards boggy areas where, Hauptman Wahlgren argues, it is unlikely large numbers of people could congregate. However, this is arguably an agrarian or a modern perspective on the land. Hunter-fisher-gatherers have few problems negotiating marshy areas, which provide such bountiful resources of fish and fowl and plant foods. The rocks certainly provided important orientation points through the landscape, each with its own unique character and associations. The visual setting of the rocks in relation to others elements—the river, the lake, the marshes, the rapids, and their sounds and smells—is a significant factor in their meaning. The rocks in the landscape are particularised as significant places in three basic ways:

1. In relation to their immediate surroundings, whether this be open water, marsh, or dry land.

2. In relation to the individual character of the stone of which they are composed—that is, they have their own particular, inherent sensuous and morphological qualities.

3. In relation to the structuring of the carvings themselves—that is, the specific content, qualities, scale, and orientation of the motifs.

In the following section I discuss in detail a sample of six carving locales south of the river, and six to the north, and then examine the most important of the carved rocks, those at Himmelstadlund.

CARVING LOCALES SOUTH OF THE RIVER

Borg 51 (Herrebro)
(Documentation: Nordén 1925: Hb 8–14; Burenhult 1973: Herrebro 7A–C; Lindeblad and Nielsen 1993)

Borg 51 is a substantial rock outcrop which during the Early Bronze Age formed the tip of a peninsula jutting out into a shallow freshwater lake with marshy shores draining north into the Motala River. The rock is orientated approximately northwest to southeast and would have been surrounded by water or boggy land except at the southeast end. The carvings are found at the higher, northwest end of the remaining rock, approximately 40 m long and 20 m broad, part of it having been removed for motorway construction. In new documentation, 163 rock carvings have been found on 23 different areas (Lindeblad and Nielsen 1993: 18). Five of these have now been removed in the course of road building. The remaining carvings are found on the southwest-inclined faces of the rock, along the top of the rock, and on the northeast upper slopes (Figures 4.6, 4.7). The rock dips away gently at its northern end and along its southwest face, which is uneven, hollowed, and fractured in the middle. By contrast, the northeast side rises up steeply and abruptly to about 3 m above the surrounding ground surface. The rock surface is smooth and crossed by two strikingly powerful asymmetrical, parallel grooves, the uppermost being so

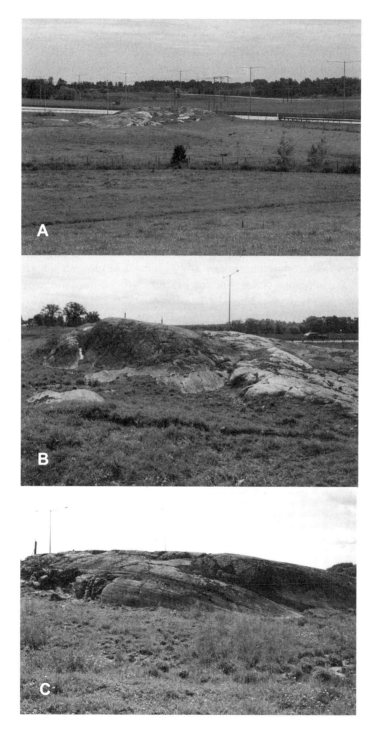

FIGURE 4.6. The rock at Borg 51 (Herrebro) *A*: General view from the northwest. *B*: The southwest face of the rock. *C*: The northeast side of the rock.

broad as to form a hanging shoulder with a well-defined upper side. The grooved structure of the rock together with glacial striation lines give the rock here a sense of directionality and kinetic force lacking elsewhere, and it is here on surface 13 where the most dramatic figurative carvings occur. These consist of a row of seven unusual human figures, at least three of which have horned headdresses and upraised arms, below which is a group of seven boats, all of different forms and dimensions. Circle rings frame the boats, and there are eleven cupmarks. The human figures occur uppermost on the hanging side of the groove, and the boats run below them along its base (Figure 4.8A). All the boats are moving parallel with the groove, four to the right and two to the left, or northwest and southeast. While the boats are seen in profile, at least four of the human figures directly face an observer and are therefore seen in an intimate perspective. Two of the humans, those farthest to the right, are significantly different in form from the others to the left. This might suggest a narrative of human transformation in relation to the movements of the boats below (Hauptman Wahlgren 2002: 220).

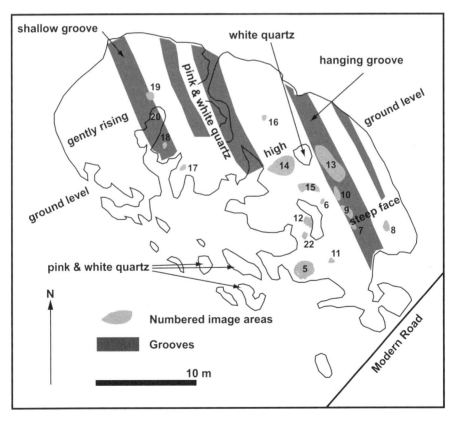

FIGURE 4.7. Carving surfaces in relation to grooves and other features of the surface of Borg 51.

To see all these carvings, they must be viewed from the northeast, standing on the rock itself. Besides their unique form, what gives the human carvings a particular power and significance is that they are positioned just below a pure white quartz inclusion on the very top of the rock (Figure 4.9). This is roughly square shaped, about 1 by 1.5 m in diameter and very fractured. In sunlight it glistens and looks wet, like ice melting. It cannot be seen from off the rock, either from the southwest or the northeast, and constitutes a visual surprise, as it can only be seen in close proximity as one moves up and over the rock surface towards it, a wondrous sight empowering the carvings in its vicinity. Farther southeast along the northwest side of the rock and placed parallel with the line of the groove, there are a number of other small carved surfaces (Figure 4.7:6–10) on which boats and shoe-soles occur.

By contrast, the southwest side of the rock is fractured and irregular in form and rises up much more gradually from the surrounding land. Cracks and hollows split it up into a number of irregularly shaped areas, and there is little sense here of any regularity of bodily movement or overall directionality as one moves between the panels. At the northeast end there are weaker, shallower, and less well-defined grooves and a large pink quartz vein running between them, varying between 1 and 3 m in width. Rock carvings are few in this area, apart from a small unelaborated single-line boat, some cupmarks, two shoe-soles, and a horse (Figure 4.7:17–20). These parallel the lines of the rock grooves.

The largest carving surface on the southwest face of the rock (Figures 4.7:5, 4.8B) is a sloping panel with seven animals, twelve boats, one shoe-sole, a number of cupmarks, and a circle. This surface is distinctive in the massing of boat designs and the presence of the animals. It has slight groove development towards the top, and the animals and boats run parallel to the orientation of the groove, in it, above it, and below it from northwest to southeast. Virtually all are depicted as moving to the right (or the southeast) across the sloping rock surface. The shoe-sole, by contrast, points down the rock to the ground beneath. The designs constitute a single visual field and are placed so as to be seen from below and off the rock surface.

Above panel 5 are panels 11, 12, and 22. Panel 12 depicts a ship and another undeterminable figure. Panel 22 consists of a boat running parallel with the slope and a shoe-sole of ambiguous form pointing up and down the slope. Panel 11 consists of a shoe-sole pointing along the rock to the northwest, to an area below panels 12, 14, and 15. Panel 6 also consists of a single shoe-sole pointing along the top of the rock, towards panels 14 and 15. These two shoe-soles thus point towards the lower and upper extent of panels 14 and 15. These two panels are on the upper southwest side of the rock surface, almost at the top, separated by about 2 m and situated next to the white quartz inclusion. Both include shoe-soles pointing down the rock, those in panel 14 towards panel 5, boats, and cupmarks. Panel 14 is the only panel to include a boat moving down the rock slope. Panel 15 (Figure 4.8C) has a frame/net motif with six or seven internal divisions, matching the number of

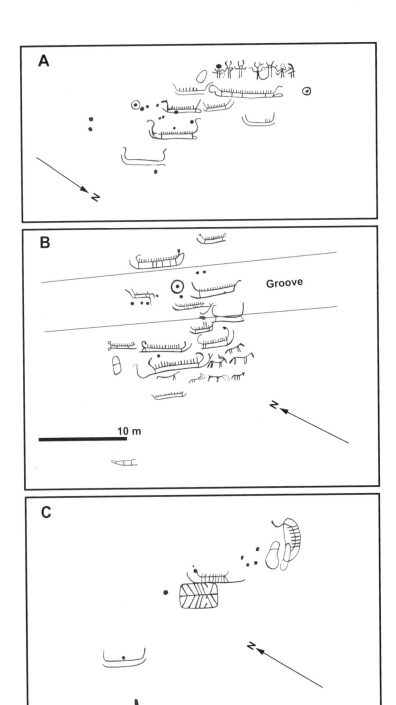

FIGURE 4.8. Motifs from selected areas of Borg 51. *A*: panel 13; *B*: panel 5; *C*: panel 15. For locations, see Figure 4.7. *Documentation after Lindebladh and Nielsen 1993.*

FIGURE 4.9. Quartz inclusion at the top of Borg 51 with groove below (left) in which panel 13 (Figure 4.8A) is found.

(invisible from here) human figures found in panel 13, just below it on the north-west side of the rock. The frame/net design and the presence of the white quartz inclusion next to it mark out the top of the rock as very special. They both, in very different ways, constitute visual traps which mesmerise and transfix the eye in their strangeness and juxtaposition.

None of the panels with carvings along the northwest side of the rock are visible from the southwest side. While all the rock areas with designs are intervisible along the southwest side of the rock, in order to see and experience the designs themselves an observer has to move up and over and across the rock. In the course of movement along and around the rock, one set of designs comes into focus while the previous one falls out of focus, becoming background rather than foreground— a constantly changing visual kaleidoscope. By contrast, viewing the carvings on the northwest side of the rock requires only a horizontal, linear movement passing along and being guided by the directionality of the grooves. The panels on the southwest side require reading in a vertical relationship passing up and down the rock surface. The panels on the two sides of the rock thus demand very different kinds of bodily interaction: in one case moving along the rock in a structured man-ner, and in the other moving up and down where the directionality of movement between carved panels is much more free and less obvious. The orientation of some of the shoe-soles does seem to provide clues with regard to directionality and move-ment here between different carved panels, both along and up and down the rock surfaces.

While boats occur in all areas of the rock surface, there is a clear physical and visual separation between the animal and human depictions and the frame design at the top. Interestingly, the greatest concentration of cupmarks on the rock mark out and distinguish by far the most complex and important panels: 5, 15, and 13.

Borg 54 (Herrebro)
(Documentation: Nordén 1925: Hb 3)

This rock is situated about 250 m south–southeast of Borg 51. It is a small exposed tongue of mica-schist but lacks any visible grooved structure. Immediately to the northwest of the schist there is an exposed granite outcrop and another to the southeast. Neither bears any carvings, and the contrast between the pink-hued granite with its rough dull surface and the shiny schist is quite striking. In the Bronze Age the rock was situated on the edge of a shallow lake or marshy area to the south and west. The main group of carvings, covering an area of 4 by 2 m, occur along the top and halfway down a slanting southwest slope. They are all designed to be seen from the southwest, off and below the rock, and constitute a single visual field requiring no bodily movement to see the different designs. Their spatial arrangement is unusual in that the figures point up the rock surface in the lower sloping area but run along it on the top. All are very deeply carved. The carving surface consists of six boats, ten animals, 43 cupmarks, an axe, and some unidentifiable figures (Figure 4.10). Most of the boats run along the top of the rock in a northwest–southeast direction, while the animals occur on a slanting slope running up the rock from the southwest to the northeast. In the centre the two largest

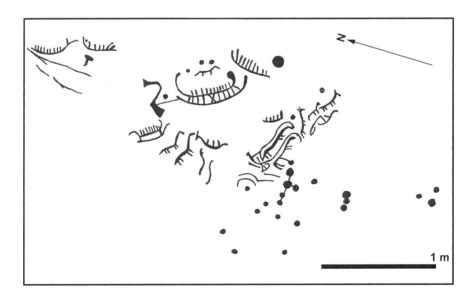

FIGURE 4.10. The motifs on rock Borg 54 (Herrebro). *Documentation after Nordén 1925.*

animals, horses, pull a human figure in a wagon, with four or five others possibly being herded in front, a probable narrative scene. Below the two horses there are a series of large and deeply cut cupmarks, some of which are conjoined or joined with grooves. The large axe is conjoined with the largest and most elaborate boat which has internal hull decoration and elaborated prows. There are two planes of spatial movement: the ships moving along the top of the rock, either right or left, and most of the animals moving diagonally up it from left to right.

Borg 53 (Herrebro)
(Documentation: Nordén 1925: Hb 1 and 2; Burenhult 1973: Herrebro 1)

Borg 53 is situated about 50 m east of Borg 54. The long axis is orientated northwest–southeast, and it dips away to the north and south. The figures form two distinct groups. The upper group is orientated along the flat top of the rock, along which occur a series of shallow and narrow grooves about 30 cm in diameter and up to 10 cm deep. The designs consist of a series of five circle cross and circular figures, three axes, one dagger, a complex frame design, and cupmarks. Some of these are carved along the bottom of the grooves; others are on slight ridges of higher rock in between. The lower group is orientated across the dipping southern side of the rock, consisting of seven boats, most of which have elaborated hulls and animal-head prows, two horses, and at least two axes (Figure 4.11). This group constitutes a single visual field and is designed to be seen from off the rock to the southwest. The upper group of designs can only be seen as one walks onto and across the rock between them, with the frame, dagger, and axe designs occupying the grooved top surface of the rock at the southeast end. This requires a more engaged and intimate relationship in which one encounters the designs and looks directly down at them. Those on the dipping slope of the rock require only a more distant and horizontal gaze. The frame figure is particularly complex, while the dagger is the only certain one documented south of the Motala River. All of these designs are deeply carved and consistently orientated. Only one ship appears upside down from the perspective of all the others.

Borg 52 (Herrebro)
(Documentation: Nordén 1925: Hb 7; Burenhult 1973: Herrebro 8A–C)

Borg 52 is a substantial rock outcrop with its long axis orientated northwest–southeast. The carvings, located towards the northern end of the rock, cover an area about 26 m long and 7 m wide. They occur along the flat top of the rock and on the northern incline that dips steeply down to the surrounding ground level. Both are crossed by a discontinuous series of shallow grooves that are either ill defined, absent, or only weakly developed. All the carvings are orientated along the axis of the grooves, northwest–southeast, and occur along the flat bases of the grooves and the slight ridges of higher rock in between them. They are not intervisible, and to see them

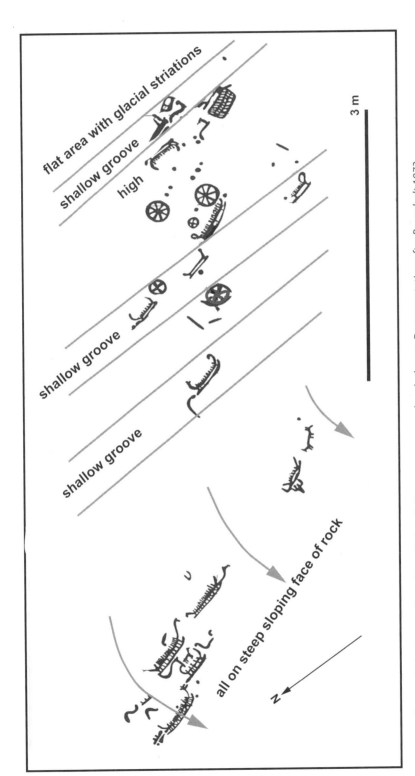

flat area with glacial striations

shallow groove

high

shallow groove

shallow groove

3 m

all on steep sloping face of rock

N

FIGURE 4.11. The motifs on Borg 53 in relation to grooves and rock slopes. *Documentation after Burenhult 1973.*

requires walking up and over the carving surface. This carving surface is dominated by boat designs. There are around 50 ships. The largest and most elaborate of these occupies the bottom of the broadest and most strongly defined groove running across the rock. Following the lines of the grooves, the boats have a consistent orientation. The majority of these are meant to be seen from the northeast side; a few examples require viewing from the southwest side. Three pairs of shoe-soles at the northern steeply inclined end of the rock point steeply down and off it towards the northwest, where Borg 51 can be seen. Movement across this rock was probably from the southeast towards the shoe-soles at the northwest end, as most of the boats are consistently orientated so as to be seen from this direction. A series of three concentric rings mark a high point on the rock. Moving between these and the shoe-soles requires walking across the corrugated surface of the rock in a movement that is obliquely choreographed across the grooves, and this journey ends when the shoe-soles, pointing down, indicate movement off the rock and beyond. The rings are situated on a flat shoulder of the rock. They cannot be seen from the ground below; encountering them requires traversing the steep rock surface from the eastern side—an unexpected encounter. From the spirals, most of the designs on the rock surface can be seen as far as point A (see Figure 4.12). Beyond, the rest are concealed by the grooves and the dipping and rising of the rock surface. From point A, one has a wide visual field down the slope of the rock, but the shoe-soles are not visible because just above them the rock surface dips steeply away to the northwest. Moving down the rock and encountering them brings another visual surprise. Situated below them are two axes with their blades similarly pointing down and off the rock and a much smaller and simpler circle ring. A basic symmetry is readily apparent in the spatial relationships of the axes and pairs of shoe-soles here. The complex circle rings on this rock are situated on a flat, high point towards the southeast end in a similar fashion to the complex frame design on Borg 53. Cupmarks are scattered across the higher and flatter areas of the rock surface, while the boats are moving from right to left or left to right, parallel with the lines of the grooves. The most elaborate with internally decorated hulls occur in the centre of the carved area. There is one small depiction of a horse; otherwise animals are absent.

Borg 31(Skälv)
(Documentation: Nordén 1925: SK 9–12; Burenhult 1973: Skälv 1–2)

Two main panels of carvings separated by a distance of 15 m occur along the top and upper sloping surface of a prominent rock outcrop, which is about 100 m long, orientated northwest–southeast, and 30 m above the present-day sea level. The panel to the north occurs in an area with extremely well-developed and defined grooves running across the rock surface. All the carvings are concentrated along the largest, deepest, and most prominent grooved surface on the rock, which is dramatic and powerful in itself. They occur along the base and upper side of the groove facing south. They are orientated along the groove and designed to be seen from below,

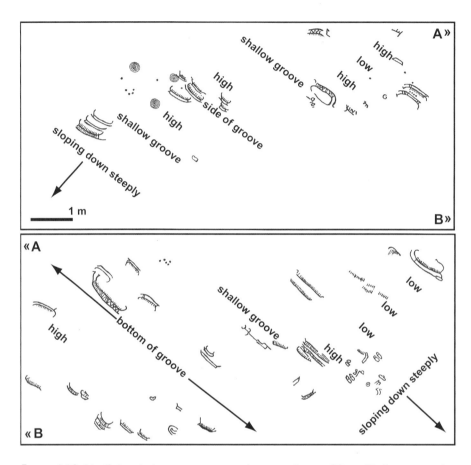

FIGURE 4.12. Motifs in relation to grooves on the central part of Borg 52. *Documentation after Nordén 1925.*

standing on the lower part of the rock surface which is also conspicuously grooved. The particular groove along which they occur is markedly 'hanging' or asymmetrical in profile, with a relatively shallow outward ridge and a much higher inwards ridge to the north which is approximately 1 m high, the base of the groove being about 50 cm wide. It is unusually flat bottomed and strikingly resembles a canoe seen in profile (Figure 4.13). The groove gradually rises along its length from the northwest to the southeast. There is another, narrower and less well-defined groove immediately above it on which carvings are absent, and this contains no carvings, undoubtedly because the rock surface here is markedly irregular by comparison with the smoothed surface of the groove below. From a viewpoint standing south and below the groove along which the carvings occur, they are almost at eye level and constitute a continuous visual field about 7 m long, along which the eye passes from one end to the other. The structure of the depictions encourages linear movement along and below them. On this surface there are at least eighteen boats, which move from right to left or southeast to northwest. All are markedly different in form and size. Together with these, there appear to be at least two animals, a circle cross, two humans facing towards an observer, and a left shoe-sole pointing up the rock.

The second area with carvings occurs, by contrast, in an area of the rock that is not so distinctly grooved. The carvings occur along the top and upper sloping surface of a slight ridge in the rock surface, with the flat base of a groove to their south—that is, along the side of a groove. The infilled circular design is at the very

FIGURE 4.13. *Left*: The hanging groove at Borg 31 (Skälv) along which the motifs were carved. Iron posts were erected to protect the carvings. *Right*: The motifs running along the groove. *Documentation after Burenhult 1973.*

214   CHRISTOPHER TILLEY — BODY AND IMAGE

top of the rock, and a pair of shoe-soles are positioned where the rock begins to dip down. They point down and off the rock to the south. Again the boats appear to be moving to the left.

St Johannes 14 (Egna Hem)
(Documentation: Nordén 1925: Eghm 1–2; Burenhult 1973: Egna Hem)

This rock is peculiarly isolated from all others with figurative carvings. It is situated 7.5 km east of the main concentration in Borg parish, south of the Motala River. During the Bronze Age it was located only about 500 m from the coast to the east. Closer to the coast to the northwest and the southeast there are some other rocks with cupmarks. This is a prominent domed rock, a local high point with wide, sweeping, and distant views. The land drops away very steeply to the north. The rock has virtually no groove structure. There are slight northwest–southeast grooves running up parts of the northwest side of the rock, but these bear little relationship to the location of the image fields. The rock surface is smooth on the northern and eastern sides, where the motifs are concentrated, markedly more rough and broken towards the top. On the very summit of the rock is a white quartz inclusion about 0.5 m in diameter. Like that at Borg 51, this is only visible when walking up and over the top of the rock. Here it is 3–4 m from the nearest carvings. On a steep eastern slope of the rock there is a smooth rock slide about 2.5 m long and 0.5 m wide, a unique feature for the Norrköping area.

All the carvings are located on sloping surfaces around the northern and eastern ends of the rock and cover an extensive area 20 m long and 6 m wide. The surface is pecked with many cupmarks (180). Also depicted here are twelve boats, fourteen shoe-soles, and six circle crosses. In addition to these, there are two unique designs: a large oval figure 2 m long and 1 m wide, and a giant horse over 2 m in length. These are the two most dominant and powerful visual images (Figure 4.14). As they are 6 m apart, they must be viewed individually rather than together. Their physical and visual separation is obviously important. Shoe-soles ring the oval design on the northern and eastern sides and are also closely associated with the horse, as is a circle cross with cupmarks in each of its four quarters. Most shoe-soles are paired and point down and off the rock, as is usual elsewhere. The boats are concentrated to the northwest end of the carved area of the rock and below the horse figure. There is a complete lack of consistent orientation. Seen from below, some appear upside down; others are positioned down rather than across the rock slope.

As the designs cover such an extensive area, an observer must walk around, up and down, and across the rock in order to view them. There is no sense of sequence or order to the designs, and the overall effect is disorientating. Walking across the rock inevitably means that one looks directly down on the designs. However, the horse and the oval figure are so large that to see them one must stand some distance away.

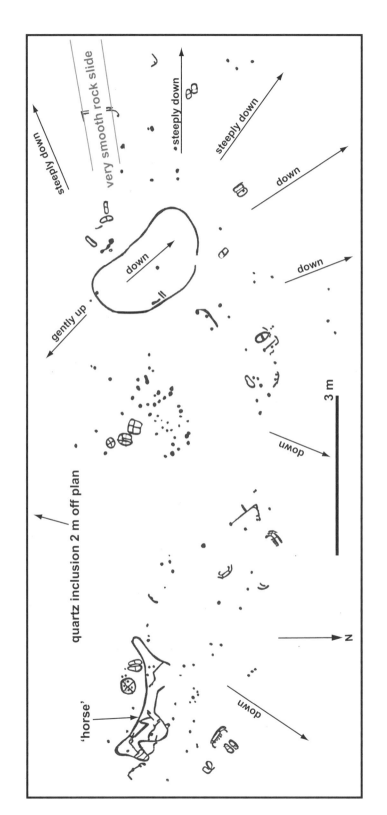

FIGURE 4.14. Motifs on the central area of the St Johannes 14 (Egna Hem) rock carving. *Documentation after Burenhult 1973.*

CARVING LOCALES NORTH OF THE RIVER

Ö Eneby 45 (Karlsberget)
(Documentation: Nordén 1925: LM49)

The rock carvings at Karlsberget occur at the extreme northwest end of the distribution of figurative carvings north of the Motala River. This is a distinctive domed rock rising directly out of the marshes at the eastern end of Lake Glan (Figure 4.15). The carvings are situated just above water level. Nordén (1925: 64) reports that at times of high water, the carvings are washed by the lake's waves, the lowest lying only 0.17 m above the present-day high water level. Their current situation—surrounded by marsh with variable periods of more open water—allows one to directly envisage the original situation of many other carving sites elsewhere before the effects of modern drainage. Now approached along an artificial causeway, this rock would originally have been a small island in the marsh. The carvings, consisting of nine small boats, a wheel cross, four lines, three cupmarks, and a shoe-sole, occur along the southwest-sloping face of the rock. The boats are simple and unelaborated. A group of six to the southeast are orientated across the slope and are moving right or downstream. Another group of four to the northwest appear to be moving to the left or upstream. The single shoe-sole is a right foot orientated northwest to southeast, pointing in the direction of other carving surfaces. The carvings constitute a single visual field when seen from below, or to the southwest, from the edge of the fen.

FIGURE 4.15. Ö Eneby 45 (Karlsberget). The carvings are situated low down on the rock surface to the right of the photograph.

Above the carvings the rock rises up abruptly. Its upper surface is markedly more cracked and rougher than the smooth area where the carvings occur. Here there are distinctive snake-like bands of white and pink quartz about 15 cm in diameter which meander across the rock surface, giving it a distinctive character.

Ö Eneby 44
(Documentation: Nordén 1925: LM48)

The carvings are situated on the almost flat surface of the top at the northwest end of a prominent (northwest–southeast) rock outcrop jutting out towards Lake Glan. Like rock 45, this rock lacks distinctive glacial grooves except for small areas of the southwest face, which are left uncarved. From the top of the rock one looks down and across at rock 45, with extensive views across Lake Glan and down the Motala River. Five boats cross the rock surface; all move towards the right (or downstream). These occur in two distinctive groups, one with pecked-out hulls, the other with internally decorated hulls. Two circle crosses are positioned above the boat with the most elaborate internal hull decoration. Other designs here include two parallel lines and an oval form. The carvings constitute a single visual field in which an observer must look directly down on the carvings when facing in the direction of the river, having clambered up the rock from below. Originally, like rock 45, this would have been an island surrounded by fen.

Ö Eneby 27 (Leonardsberg)
(Documentation: Nordén: 1925: LB1; Burenhult 1973: Leonardsberg 1)

The carvings here are situated at the northwest end of an extensive group of carved surfaces and occur on the most distinctive rock in this area, which rises up abruptly about 3 m above the surrounding area. Even today, surrounding areas of the rock on all sides are marshy even in dry weather, and originally, again, it would have been a distinctive rock island in a riverside fen area. The lower southwest face of the rock, where all the carvings occur, is dramatically and distinctly grooved (Figure 4.16). These grooves, asymmetrical in form, run northwest to southeast across the rock face, abruptly rising up from the surrounding ground level and running across the rock to gradually fade out towards the southeast end. The domed top of the rock, where the grooves are either absent or only faintly defined, is undecorated. The carvings run along the base and the higher northeast side of five parallel grooves. Seen from below and off the rock to the southwest, they constitute one visual field about 7 m long and 3 m wide (Figure 4.17). All the carvings are orientated so as to be seen from below and from this direction (southwest). One must look up and towards them. This complex carving surface, with around 120 motifs, is dominated by depictions of boats (c. 36) and humans (c. 20), together with seven animals (including two deer and three probable horses), a number of oval figures, lines, and cupmarks. Most of the cupmarks cluster at the lower northwest end of the carving surface, with the boats, animals, and human figures being central. Only one of the boats appears upside down, but this seems to be carried by two humans in a procession moving from right to left along the second lowest groove.

The deepest and most pronounced groove is also the lowest on the rock at the bottom northwest end, which is where a series of cupmarks and three boats are depicted. These are all moving to the left or upstream (Burenhult depicts only one boat, that farthest to the right). The second groove contains one large deer facing left and a procession of eight or nine humans of markedly different sizes, leading Nordén to suggest that men, women, and children are depicted here in procession (Nordén 1925: 58). Two figures, farthest to the right, appear to be carrying an inverted boat. The directionality of these figures seems to be to the left (or upstream in relation to the river). Beyond them, to the right, another group of five humans are shown on either side of another small boat. The third groove portrays another processional scene: seven humans appear to be moving to the right in the same direction as the animals and boats also depicted along the groove. The fourth groove also depicts animals moving right and possibly another human boat-carrier. The top groove consists entirely of boats moving to both the left and the right. The narrative scenes here can perhaps be interpreted as processions of humans, together with animals, carrying or dragging boats over the land. What is striking here is the concentration of the human figures low down in the grooves to the northwest (left) of the carved panel. The higher areas of the rock where the grooves shallow out are occupied entirely by boats unaccompanied by humans. Human and animal activity occurs at the lowest, most

FIGURE 4.16. Ö Eneby 27 (Leonardsberg) showing the grooves crossing the rock along which the carvings are situated.

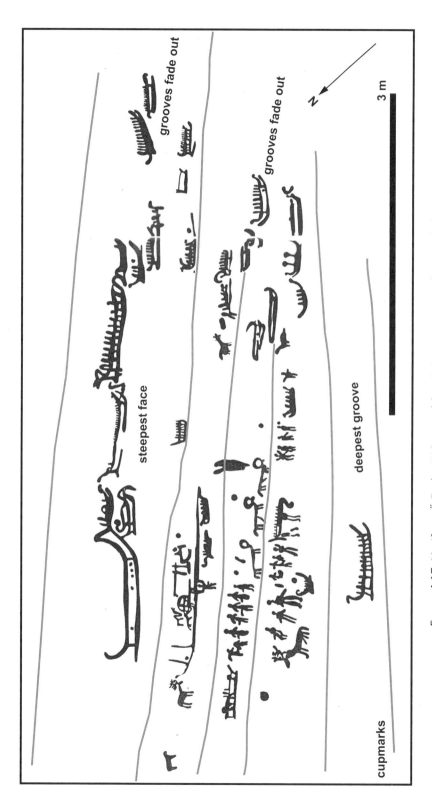

FIGURE 4.17. Motifs on Ö Eneby 27 (Leonardsberg). *Documentation after Burenhult 1973.*

deeply grooved and steepest part of the decorated area of the rock. This might be related to the effort required to pull the boats up and out of the water.

To the east, north, and south of this rock there are a series of other carved panels, the nearest about 100 m distant, but here the rocks have an entirely different character. They form extensive, more or less flat pavement areas. These are crossed by grooves which in places are well defined, in others barely discernible. None are so dramatic and prominent as the hanging grooves on Leonardsberg 27.

Ö Eneby 23 (Ekenberg)
(Documentation: Nordén 1925: FE: 1–10; Burenhult 1973: Ekenberg 1–9)

This is one of the largest of a number of low 'rock islands' situated a short distance to the northeast of the main cluster of carving surfaces at Leonardsberg. In the Bronze Age the island was situated on the edge of a watery fen that extended to the west and south and to Lake Glan. To the east and the north, the land was mostly dry and accessible on foot. This large exposed rock pavement rises gently out of the ancient fen to a high point at the northeast, a few metres above the surrounding fields. Parts of the rock are covered in a thin layer of turf, while large areas are bare rock. The majority of the carvings are situated low down on the rock surface towards the southwest and southern edge. In contrast to most of the exposure, the lower portion of the southwest part of the pavement has a markedly undulating surface. This pronounced feature, with shallow crests and dips, quickly diminishes and fades into a gentle but continuously sloping and undifferentiated surface that extends to the highest point.

We can describe the undulating lower part of the rock surface as being crossed by a number of shallow, wave-like grooves running parallel to each other along a northwest–southeast orientation. The grooves are less than 10 cm deep, with mainly flat bottoms about 20 cm wide. Although for the most part always recognisable , the grooves are not prominent or particularly well defined. They are discontinuous and have the tendency to fade in and out of definition along their linear course or axis. The arrangements of the carvings follow and respect the northwest–southeast axis of the grooves, and some of the largest and most prominent motifs, especially some of the swords and the circular designs, occupy the flat bottoms of the grooves where these are most clearly defined. The cracks on this part of the rock are minor and insignificant and do not constitute meaningful breaks or divisions between the image fields. Indeed, where the cracks are at their largest at the northwest end of this main area, the boats are consistently carved across them, ignoring their presence. That said, in general, the rock surfaces that have been chosen for carving are those that are the smoothest.

On the lowest part of the rock, the carvings extend across a surface some 17 m long by 5 m wide (Figure 4.18). Overall, three distinct sections or panels running northwest–southeast can be described, and these are separated by wave-like linear areas, slightly raised, with a rougher surface. This is especially the case between the

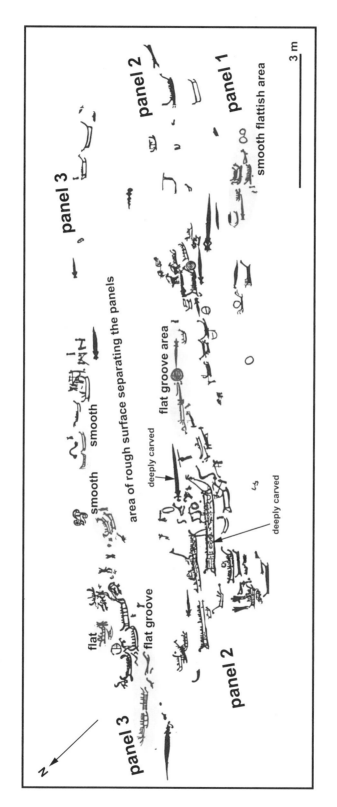

FIGURE 4.18. The motifs on Ekenberg 1. *Documentation after Burenhult 1973.*

panel 2

panel 1

smooth flattish area

panel 3

area of rough surface separating the panels

smooth   smooth

smooth

flat groove area

deeply carved

deeply carved

flat

flat groove

panel 2

panel 3

N

3 m

two upper panels. All the motifs are consistently orientated so as to be seen from a standing position lower down, from below, towards the southwestern edge of the rock. None of the images appear upside down or inverted from this general viewing position. Standing below and in the middle of the carving surface, one's eye can run across the images from the northwest to the southeast and back again. The images fill the field of vision and stretch out before the viewer like a panorama that invites and encourages a physical engagement with the scene and in so doing a participation in the linear composition and arrangement. The reading of individual motifs provides an overwhelming directionality from left to right or northwest to southeast. Although we can take in the panoramic scene from a single viewpoint, to read the component parts in detail one must move forward and close in, tracking across, in, and over the images as they are laid out below one's feet. Hauptman Wahlgren (2002: 194–95) has pointed out that relatively few of the carvings are orientated to the left, and usually these are set in opposition to images moving right. The spectacular display of carefully drawn and deeply carved sword images on this rock is exceptional and undoubtedly highly significant (Figure 4.19). Of the swords depicted, only three point left while eleven point right. Typologically, all the swords are of Early Bronze Age date. Their position in the bottom of the grooves and among the ships may imply a watery connection, either in terms of their origin, social status, or symbolic deposition and sacrifice. These swords are not part of any narrative scene and seem entirely different from those objects carried on the bodies of the humans depicted. The dense concentration of boats is equally spectacular. Only ten boats

FIGURE 4.19. Detail of sword motifs, Ekenberg 1.

face left, while three times that number are depicted moving to the right (i.e., downstream in relation to the flow of the Motala River), including all the largest and most elaborate boats with their complex hull decoration.

Standing below this panoramic scene, the uppermost panel of images is viewed more or less at eye level. Those in the middle panel (panel 2—the most complex) are seen at an oblique angle, and those in the lower panel are essentially looked down upon. The lowest panel, panel 1 (see Figure 4.18), is the smallest and consists of four unfilled circles, seven boats, and two swords. The boats at the left end move right, in the same direction as the swords point. The three boats at the right end move to the left. The open circles are located low down at either end of the scene. A basic symmetry is suggested, and compared with the other panels, the carvings in this panel are relatively uncomplicated.

Panel 2 is the most extensive panel on the rock and contains the largest and most elaborate boats. These are depicted at the northwest end of the panel, the two biggest being a massive 2 m long (Figure. 4.20). The decorated boats and the numerous life-size swords are unquestionably the most visually dominant motifs. The images are most densely concentrated at the northwest end and thin out in the middle, where a concentric circle motif occurs in the base of the flat-bottomed groove. This is strikingly framed with two opposed swords. Might this central image represent the act of watery deposition? It certainly halts the directional flow of movement right to left by virtue of its perfect symmetry and symbolic form. After this arresting image, the panel continues to the right with an increasing concentration of

FIGURE 4.20. Detail of boat motifs, Ekenberg 1.

images consisting mainly of boats, although these are less elaborate and simpler than those to the left of the panel. The swords in this panel, because they are life-size, or over-dimensioned, appear huge, and most are deeply carved. Two swords are over 1 m in length.

In close association with the huge, elaborately decorated boats are the two largest and dominant images of humans occurring anywhere on the rock. Their massive, boxy, and bulky forms stand in contrast with all other depictions of human beings (Figure 4.20). They have no arms; their shoulders are broad, and their torsos are tapered from top to bottom. These figures also appear to stand as if to face or confront the observer (cf. Hauptman Wahlgren who has them moving to the right). The contrast in size and form between these (super) human figures and all the others carved on this part of the rock is quite striking. They occur with other human figures immediately above a boat with an elaborately decorated hull and appear to be emerging out of the boat. There are at least twelve other humans depicted, four of which are shown in boats with elaborate hull decoration moving right. Three are spear-carriers—two with spears pointing right and one to the left. The directionality of the other human figures is uncertain, and all, apart from two of the spear-carriers, are small. At least eight small animals occur. Two are probably deer moving to the right; the rest are diminutive in size, and all but two move to the right. In an obvious contrast to the disposition of all the other images, one single shoe-sole points down the rock slope.

Like panel 2, the uppermost panel, panel 3 (Figure 4.18), similarly has the densest concentration of images at the northwest end, including one of the largest swords. This sword unusually points to the left, in striking contrast to virtually all the other swords on the rock which point to the right. (Only one of the swords framing the concentric circle motif in panel 2 also points to the left.) Apart from this dominant sword, one of the most striking images is that of a boat being pulled to the right by two horses. This panel also has a much larger and more clearly defined group of human images than those depicted in panel 2. At least eighteen can be identified. At the northwest end there are five figures with raised and outstretched arms who appear to be turning or facing left in opposition to the rightward movement of the boats and horses. This scene might be interpreted as one in which the humans turn towards the boats and horses, encouraging them to move forward and across the rock. The significance of the other group of eleven human figures on the left-hand side of the panel is much more ambiguous. Six are grouped above a large right-pointing sword, and four others are associated with a boat from which one person may be fishing.

How are these panels to be understood? One possibility is that the upper two panels in particular could be read together, with the two large human figures and elaborate boats at the northwest end of panel 2 representing the final part of a spatial narrative. The main motifs and themes depicted are those of boats, swords, animals, humans, directionality, movement up- and downriver (right = downstream and left = upstream), and arrival. This allusion to movement represents journeying and the flow and directionality of people, exchange, and knowledge. The large (super) human figures and boats, in such a context, represent social transformations in wealth, power, and prestige. The dominant directionality is outwards and transgressive, marking the internal power of these communities to distinguish themselves as different from others. The two large, static (super) human figures, together with their extraordinary boats, could represent an expression and assertion of the achievement of (or aspiration to) high social status within a wider geo-social world. The inscribing of the smooth grooves, which themselves represent movement across the landscape out of the fen and onto dry land, is a means of imposing and fixing a powerful narrative depicting the sociopolitical relations of mobile communities.

The panels described above are not the only images carved on this rock island. Some 23 m to the southeast are another set of carvings (E:7). They are located towards the southeastern end of the rock exposure. Although both groupings (E:1 and E:7) are intervisible, it is not possible to read one from the other, and therefore they should be regarded as separate, requiring movement between the two. Unlike E:1, the rock surface of E:7 is virtually smooth, with only slight undulations or indications of the wavy grooving pattern encountered elsewhere. The most obvious undulation is at the top of the rock surface, where a wide and very shallow, flat-bottomed groove is occupied by the depiction of an elaborate procession of human figures.

The whole rock surface on which the carvings are found measures some 4 m across and 5 m high from the bottom to the top. Again, the carvings can described as constituting three panels. The uppermost occupies the shallow groove base, while the two lower panels are divided by an unusually prominent crack that is respected (see Figure 4.21). The three panels constitute a single visual field to be viewed from below to the southwest, although to see clearly the highest and most elaborate panel, one has to move up and across the rock. When viewed from below, all the images are upright except for three boats: two in the top panel and one in the lower left panel. There is also one image in the lower right panel that shows two boats set vertically and against the usual horizontal axis of the composite scenes depicted.

The most elaborate boats occur in the top panel, and in comparison with the others, these are by far the most complex (Figure 4.22A) These boats, however, are not fabulously decorated like those in E:1. The lower two 'upside-down' boats are obviously striking because of their inversion. The top two move to the left (upstream), the bottom boat to the right (downstream). Part of a fourth boat appears to the left of the procession of seventeen deeply carved human figures. From the depiction of scabbards trailing behind the figures, it appears that the procession is moving from the right to the left. This procession includes a lassoed figure twice the size of the others being pulled along. This extraordinary image disrupts the repetitive pattern of the other figures. At the top of the panel is a small, isolated, single human figure with a markedly different body form. Compared with the others, it is slim with a small head. In the lower part of the panel are two more figures, the lowest of which bears aloft on outstretched arms a circular motif, possibly a

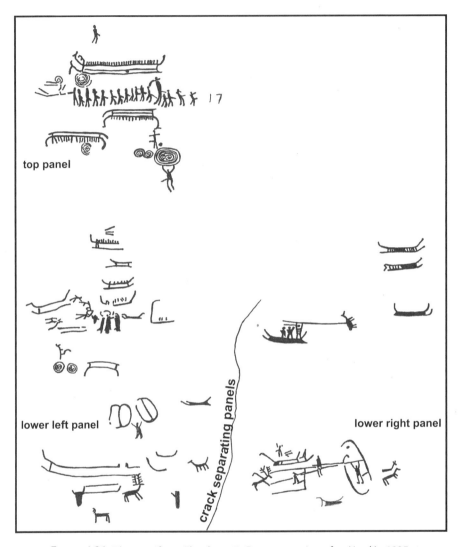

FIGURE 4.21. The motifs on Ekenberg 7. *Documentation after Nordén 1925.*

shield, containing a double spiral. Within the general grouping are two slightly ambiguous concentric circles or spiral disks, a small spiral motif, and a double-spiral design adjacent to the figure holding the 'captured' double-spiral depicted on the possible shield. The massing of these circular or spiral designs, together with the concentration of boats—some inverted—suggests the possibility that these images are meant to represent whirlpools. Whirlpools are themselves metaphors for transformation and change. Locally they occur when water has to negotiate a fall in the land, and they are experienced when the current is strong and danger-ous after the melting of the winter snow. Almgren long ago suggested that the pro-

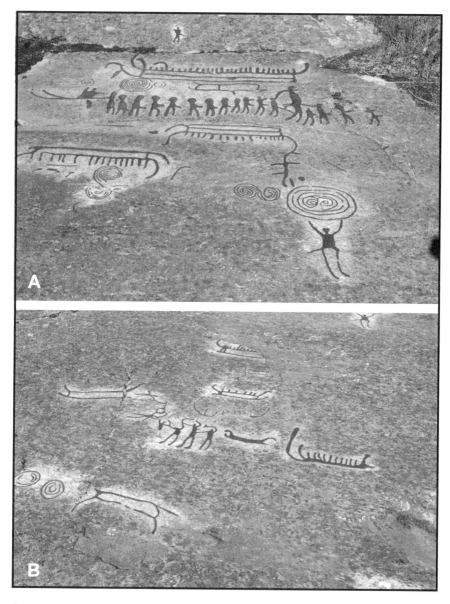

FIGURE 4.22. *A*: Detail of the top panel of Ekenberg 7. *B*: Detail of the bottom left panel of Ekenberg 7.

cession scene represented a deity being led forward (Almgren 1927: 129–31). Other suggestions have been that the lassoed figure represents a human offering: a ritual hanging or sacrifice. Hauptman Wahlgren (2002: 197, 217) suggests a number of important possible alternative interpretations. Unlike Almgren, who separated out the processional scene from the rest of the panel, she suggests we should consider a reading of the whole. She argues that if we read the human images from the top to the bottom of the panel, we can see a representation of the transformation in human status: a depiction of a rite of passage. She associates the spirals with the power of the sun and whirlpools in the water. The mythological rite of passage involves passing through the water into the sun, and the structural relationship between the boats and circle figures possibly symbolise the world's horizontal and vertical boundaries (ibid.: 217). The rite of passage takes place in four stages. It begins with an isolated, immature human at the very top of the panel. Below are the boats, which mark both ritual boundaries and bridges to another world that are crossed. In the second stage, among the boats a procession takes place, with one human figure marked out as larger than the others in order to emphasize a transformational change of status. Then there is a third figure below, with a phallus or scabbard now shown on the left-hand side of the body in opposition to those depicted in the processional scene. Finally, there is the human bearing the circular motif (usually interpreted as either a sun or shield) containing concentric circles and a double spiral. This human figure is utterly different from those shown in the processional scene, with its upraised arms, long legs, and no shield or phallus. Hauptman Wahlgren suggests the figure is a dancer (ibid.: 218) and that the rite of passage being shown represents a life's journey through different stages or from life to death. From another temporal perspective, it can be suggested that what we also see is the passing of the seasons and particularly the move into and out of winter, when the rivers and lakes are iced over and boats become redundant. At such times the boats need to be extracted from the water and turned upside down. The ease of movement across the water is halted and life assumes a different rhythm. The nights are long and days are very short. The life-world of communities becomes totally differentiated, ending only by the disappearance of the snows and the meltwater flooding of the rivers and adjacent lands. The depiction of a procession, possible sacrifice, spiralling forms, boats (some upturned), and celebratory dancing could be interpreted as the precursor to the travelling and hunting shown on the panels below.

The lower left panel consists of boats moving both right and left, five distinct human figures, and three animals. Two concentric circle motifs occur to the left and close by the only upside-down boat (Figure 4.22B). As in the top panel, one human figure bears aloft a circular design, but here the object or objects appear to be two disproportionately large probable circle crosses (Figure 4.21). In the upper part of the panel, along with seven boats, there appears to be a possible scene showing animal–human transformation. Two conjoined human figures on the right seemingly transform themselves into an animal with human physical attributes (see Figure 4.22B). At the bottom of the panel there are two figures hunting, one with arms outstretched and the other holding an impressive spear aloft and about to kill an equally impressive large stag. Two other animals are passively depicted in the vicinity.

The lower right panel shows mainly boats, the majority of which are moving to the left. Several of them have their hulls entirely pecked out in a contrasting style to the others on the rock. Five animals are shown moving across the surface from left to right, one appearing to be chased by two human figures, one of whom is carrying a spear. In obvious contrast, a sixth animal is depicted not travelling across the rock but laid out up and down the surface. This animal is dead, speared by three humans in a boat. To the bottom of the panel, two more stylised boats are portrayed at right angles to the general horizontal movement. The curvaceous hull forms embrace a human figure within, who seems to be holding a giant spear pointing left. It is as if the boats are being used out of their natural element as a hide on dry land. Perhaps the most striking image of all in this panel is the largest boat in the group, with an elaborate stag antler prow containing another human figure. Another figure holding a spear conjoins these two images. There is a visual interlocking of weapons, and it appears that, rather than hunting animals, these figures are fighting each other. One spearpoint penetrates the boat of the other. The animals nearby are shown disengaged and moving away from the scene, uninvolved in the drama being depicted.

On this rock surface, at one level unified, we seem to have three very different scenes. The top involves the procession of humans, inverted boats, and human transformations and even the possible transformation out of winter into the light and plenty of the new year. The lower left panel involves possibly the depiction of the extraordinary transformation of humans into animals and the equally magical relationship between animals and people in the act of hunting. It also shows the continuing theme of boats and whirlpools. The lower right panel again shows the interrelationship between humans and animals and boats; in one scene a boat is shown with an animal head. Boats become animals and embody the same spirit.

Here on both carving areas (E:1 and E:7), a great chain of interdependence is shown in which an entire world is connected geographically, socially, and across time. The world is shown as it is known, not how it is seen. Boats, humans, animals, and swords are depicted not according to a consistent scale, but according to a scale that enables their meaning and context to be shown. The abstract forms of circles and spirals have no obvious literal reference or natural scale and therefore can exist in any or many dimensions. Boats move repetitively up and down known routes of communication, and this is expressed by carving on the worn ice-polished grooves of the rock that seem to emerge from out of the fen. The largest figures and the grandest boats occupy the grandest groove, as do the most spectacular swords. We see the boats from the keel up—not as they would be seen in the water. We experience the swords in a different plane—on a different scale and carved more deeply than anything else. It is through the use of a variety of pictorial devices that the conceptual distinctions between the objects (and subjects) are illustrated. The status of weaponry, or the idea of weaponry, is also evident in the disproportionate size of spears relative to the human figures carrying them and the animals they kill. For the most part, animals and humans are depicted similarly, as if belonging to same world, and this comparative treatment suggests a commonality which ultimately allows for the possibilities of transfiguration seen at E:7, where humans can become animals and, no doubt, vice versa. As already discussed, the two special figures carved in the middle panel of E:1 are the exception, their (super) humanness complete and secure and perhaps depicting an emerging or established social elite or political class. These are not real people but, like the swords and special boats, metaphors of power and status.

We have described the two main rock carving areas (there are a few other, small panels above E:1) on this low rock island as distinct but related. Their commonality is expressed by many similar and shared iconographic components as well as by a powerful sense of public and private theatre displaying social experiences and knowledge. The carvings depict a life-world showing traditional activities, the use and experience of rituals, and the acquisition of knowledge and material culture from both within and without. Change and interdependence are depicted at many levels of resolution.

Ö Eneby 8 (Fiskeby)
(Documentation: Nordenskjöld: 1871; Nordén 1925: FM18)

This domed rock outcrop is a local high point; the surrounding land gently drops away from it on all sides. It is situated only 100 m north of the river at a point where it bends sharply to flow east, just beyond the uppermost rapids, 200 m southeast of the carvings. The waters are now regulated, but in the past, the sound of the fast flowing and violent water would have been audible at the rock, which is also situated just 1 km to the southwest of the extensive Pryssgården settlement area.

The carved rock consists of two distinct planes. The upper plane is inclined upwards to the northwest. Below this, the remainder of the rock surface is flat and somewhat hollowed (Figure 4.23). There are no grooves on the rock surface, and cracks are few, narrow, and generally indistinct, thus offering no basis for a subdivision of the carving surface into panels. Some cracks have been carved over, and one has been used as a base line for a boat carving. The upward sloping part of the rock resembles a wave or waterfall and is crossed by sinuous quartz veins which are lacking in the flat low area. Here water runs down the surface to collect in the flat area with depressions below. So there is a distinct surface of the rock over which water runs and an area with still water below where it collects. Given the proximity of this rock to the rapids on the Motala River, this natural division of the rock surface has particular metaphorical significance.

The upper carving field is orientated so as to be seen from the southeast, standing on the rock below. The carvings constitute a single visual field over and along which the eye passes. Centrally positioned and visually dominant are two large human figures, armless, with boxy torsos and almost identical to those found on Ekenberg panel 1 (discussed above). They are utterly different from the much more naturalistic depictions of people found elsewhere on the rock. Above and below them and on either side, there are pairs of shoe-soles and a right shoe-sole all pointing down the rock. Another pair of shoe-soles occurs to the right. The remaining images depict animals, humans, and boats. Many of the human figures bear spears

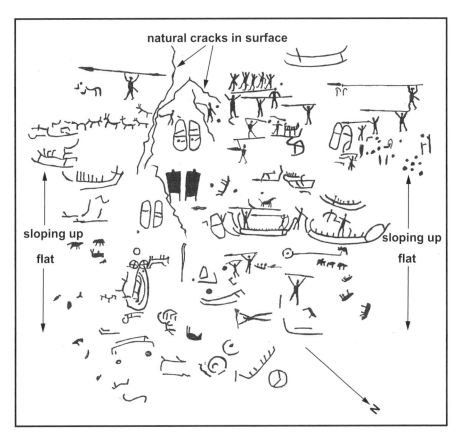

Figure 4.23. Motifs on Ö Eneby 8 (Fiskeby). Modified with additions to Nordenskjöld's 1871. *Documentation reproduced in Nordén 1925.*

and are moving to the left (Figure 4.24), as are the boats (downstream in relation to the river). There is an obvious emphasis here on pairing and symmetry: two paired boats on the right-hand part of the rock, the pair of large humans, pairs of shoe-soles, pairs of spear-bearers. On the left-hand part of the rock, two groups of four animals face each other below a prominent spear-bearer. The numerous naturalistic human depictions (23), when compared with those found elsewhere, appear to be particularly animated, bearing spears, swords, a bow, and other objects held aloft or with upraised arms. These are seen in profile. By contrast, the two humans with large bodies but no arms and standing directly facing an observer seem peculiarly static and lifeless. They appear to be inactive compared with the figures bearing large spears who seemingly are engaged in acts of strength, dominance, and power.

The lower carving field is very different. Wherever one stands, some carvings appear upside down or are otherwise shown at a difficult viewing angle. Some must be seen from off the rock to the northeast. Others must be seen standing above the upper carving field to the southwest. As some of the designs cross the rock lateral-ly, these must be viewed from the west or east sides or right and left of the carved surface. To see these designs in their correct visual perspective thus requires a much more active process of moving around and across the rock, at multiple viewing angles. The images here are much more fragmented, divergent in both orientation and content. The contrast between the upper part of the rock, which can be viewed statically, and the lower visual field, requiring constant movement up, down, and across the rock, is quite striking and is interesting in terms of a distinction we have already alluded to: water flowing directionally down the upper part of the rock and collecting below. If the rock metaphorically represents a waterfall, this is a distinc-tion between the directional flow of water over rapids and its swirling motion below. In effect, the images on the flat surface of the rock 'swirl' around, with a lack of overall directionality, fragmented and pictorially incoherent. Here there are sim-ple depictions of boats in which directionality of movement is uncertain, depictions of pigs moving at different angles and directions across the rock, four human spear-bearers, one of which crosses the rock laterally, and two horses pulling a wagon.

Standing on the top of the rock above all the images, there is a powerful distinc-tion between the packing and density of those on the slope over which the eye runs (seen upside down from this angle) and the dispersed character of the images on the flat surface below. The sloping rock has a strong dynamism in terms of the 'speed' and 'flow' of images, which becomes dissipated in the flat area below. Metaphorical-ly, it is possible that the upper area of the rock depicts acts of human power and defi-

Figure 4.24. Detail of spear-bearer on Ö Eneby 8 (Fiskeby).

ance in relation to the malevolent forces of nature—humans and boats crossing the flow of the river rapids—whereas the panel below depicts the maelstrom of existence below the rapids, showing the loss of valuable chariots, boats, animals, and people.

Ö Eneby 1 (Himmelstadlund)
(Documentation: Nordén 1925: H1-53; Burenhult 1973: Himmelstadlund 1A-8B)

Himmelstadlund is by far the most complex rock carving locale in the area; it has both the greatest number of carving surfaces and the highest frequency of designs, with 1,670 surfaces recorded, or 27 percent of the total number documented north of the river (Hauptman Wahlgren 2002: appendix I). It consists of a series of domed rocks and pavement areas exposed over an area about 270 m long and up to 70 m wide. The rocks are situated only 100 m north of the river and run parallel to it from northwest to southeast, 1.3 km to the east of the rapids at Fiskeby and 1.6 km to the west of those now situated in the centre of Norrköping. As noted above, this is one of the few carving sites in the area from which the river is visible. It is situated at the far eastern and coastal end of the major locales with figurative carvings, both north and south of the river, and during the Bronze Age was situated only 1.5 km from the coast. The carved rocks during that time were effectively islands bounded by the river to the southeast, which is likely to have seasonally flooded alongside them, and marshy areas to the northwest and east. They rise up from the surrounding land at the northwest end to their highest point in the centre of the carving area. There are three main pavement areas, with carvings along the northwest–southeast long axis of the rocks separated by distances of 50 to 60 m. Glacial grooves at the northwest end are the most well developed, symmetrical in profile, and prominent in the entire distribution of carvings. Elsewhere in the central and eastern parts of the rock outcrops, they are far less dramatic and distinct, although relatively small areas with grooving occur in most areas. In the following account we discuss the major rocks with carvings at the northwest end and in central areas where the images are both most numerous and complex (see Figure 4.25).

Rock 1A

Rock 1A (Figures 4.26, 4.27) is the most northwesterly of the rock outcrops at Himmelstadlund and has the most complex carvings. It is about 25 m long and 20 m wide; it rises up from the northwest, with its highest point in the middle at the southeast end. The rock dips gently down along its northeast and southwest faces. Running across the rock surface there are five parallel grooves on the northeast half, varying in depth, width, and definition. On the southwest half there is one groove separating two broad, convex faces. The vast majority of the carvings are massed along the five parallel grooves on the northeast side, below the middle and the highest point of the rock. The grooves are distinctly graded in size. The lowest (groove 1) is 15 cm wide and about 5 cm deep. Groove 2 is 40 cm wide and about 10 to 15

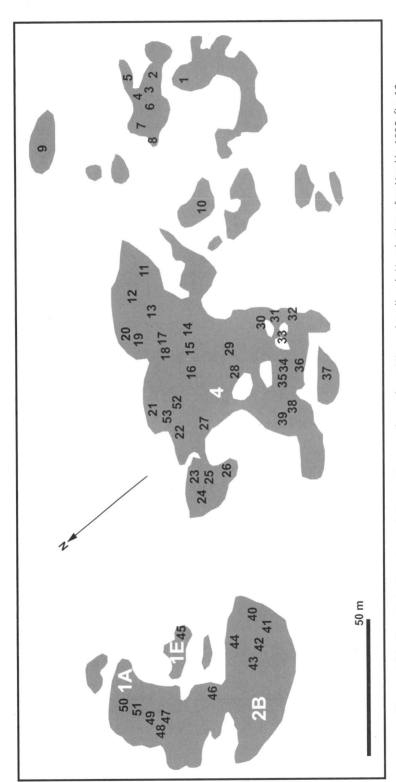

Figure 4.25. Plan of the locations of the carvings on the rocks at Himmelstadlund. *Numbering after Nordén 1925: fig. 19.*

50 m

cm deep; grooves 3 and 4 are wider again, about 75 cm wide, while groove 5 is 160 cm wide. The carvings occur along the flat bases of the grooves and along their sides in five long, parallel, linear series. The size of the carvings is clearly intimately related to the size of the grooves along which they occur. Groove 1, asymmetrical in form, is very narrow and is the only one not to have a well-defined northeast side. The rock rolls over here earthwards. Groove 2 is most striking in terms of the constriction of its two sides, making it appear very deep. By comparison, groove 3, being broader, appears to be shallower (Figure 4.26). Groove 4 is only well defined along its northeast side and contains few carvings. Groove 5 is the widest and highest, and here the carvings spread out across the flat base. The very top of the rock lacks both grooves and carvings. Groove 6 on the southwest side of the rock is broad and shallow, with carvings on the higher northeast face. All the grooves are deepest and most pronounced at the northwest, lower end of the rock, becoming somewhat shallower as it rises to the southeast.

At the lower northwest end, the rock appears in its most dramatic and monumental form, heaving up out of the surrounding land, the sculptural grooves stretching away into the distance.

Standing on the southwest edge of the rock, the only visible carvings run along the rising face of groove 6. These constitute a single visual field and are orientated to be seen from below and the southwest. The carvings here are simple. Two boats in the lower part of the rock run across it, facing right. Two upper boats face left. Shoe-

Figure 4.26. Some of the carvings running along grooves 2 (right) and 3 (left) on rock 1A at Himmelstadlund looking towards the northwest. For location, see Figures 4.25 and 4.27.

soles point down the rock. It is only when moving up the rock to the lower of the two boats that the carvings in groove 5 become visible. Those in grooves 1–4 are still hidden. Standing on the highest point of the rock, most of the carvings along grooves 2, 3, and 4 are visible, but those in groove 1 are hidden. The carvings here only become visible from groove 5, when one has passed the highest point of the rock.

From the northeast edge of the rock, the carvings along grooves 1–5 (hereafter G1–G5) are visible together with the river beyond in the distance. The carvings in G6 (the boats appearing upside down from here) are only visible from G5 as one moves up the rock slope. Walking across the rock surface here from the northeast to the southwest sides is markedly different from elsewhere at Himmelstadlund where the grooved structure of the rocks is less pronounced and much more fragmented. G1–G3 are so narrow that one tends to step over them from one side to another. Whereas G4 is ill defined and has few carvings, G5 is so wide that one must walk across it and the carvings it contains. Bodily movement entails walking over three groups of carvings and walking among the others—crossing and then 'entering' the parallel design fields.

Standing at the lower northwest ends or the higher southeast ends of each of the parallel grooves, one can see the designs stretching away along them, becoming less and less distinct in the distance (see Figure 4.26). Along G1, G4, and G5, all groupings of carvings are visible. By contrast, in G2 and G3 carvings at the ends are concealed. Viewing the designs on this rock requires interaction with those in each groove, passing along and up it from the lower northwest end or down the groove from the higher southeast end. Linear movement along the rock is required by the structuring of the design fields in the parallel grooves. Moving along the grooves, designs are continually being backgrounded and foregrounded, coming into focus and at the centre of one's visual field and then falling away at the periphery. One cannot simply view the designs standing still and see them properly from any single point. Their disposition actively choreographs and demands linear movements of the body. This is part of what gives these motifs their visual power, but the overall effect is markedly different from groove to groove.

In G1 the design structure is simple, consisting of 21 boats and two animals. These are all small and are carved along the base of the groove, their size clearly being determined by the groove dimensions. They face or move to the right and must be seen from off the rock on the northeast side. The directionality of these designs is thus down the groove and in the direction in which the rainwater runs off the rock (upstream in terms of the river flow; the river is visible when one looks up).

At the right or northwest end of G1, the designs in G2 are upside down. To see them requires stepping over the groove and turning round to face them with one's back to the river. Here there is a scene of a herd of seven animals facing or moving right up the slope (upstream), together with five human figures. At the end, two or three boats and two animals move to the left (downstream). These are carved along the southwest side of the groove. Below there is one much larger human figure, probably a spear-bearer, carved in the base of the groove facing left.

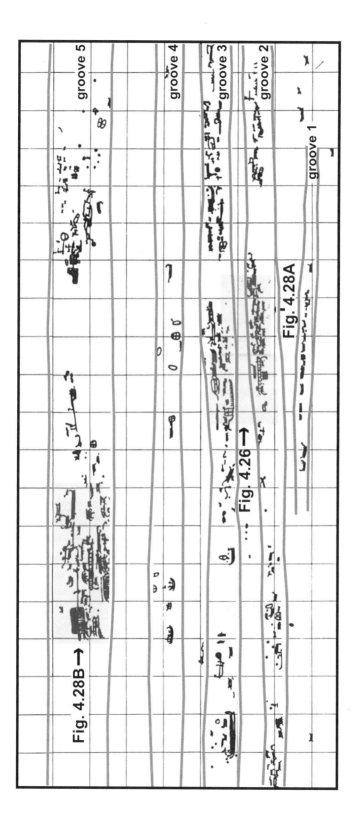

Figure 4.27. The motifs on rock 1A, Himmelstadlund, shown in relation to the grooves on the rock surface. Positions of other figures are annotated. The grid is in 1-m squares. *Motif documentation after Burenhult 1973.*

With the exception of four small boats, the next group of images along the groove must be seen from the opposite side, stepping over it and turning round The imagery is dominated by boar, some of which are very large, together with two possible horses at either end, all facing right, and four swords and daggers all carved in the bottom of the groove and pointing both to the left and right (Figure 4.28A). The next image is of a large boat moving right. To view this right side up requires stepping over the groove and turning round. Beyond is a right shoe-sole pointing up and along the groove in the direction of movement, to the right, together with three small boats. Passing farther along the groove there is a human pole-bearer and three further small boats. The next two boats appear upside down, and to see them in correct visual perspective requires crossing over the groove again. Here a human figure, unusually carved in the bottom of the groove but depicted sideways on, facing to the right, seems to act as a visual prompt to cross the groove. To see the next boat requires moving along the groove. The next image is of another small human lacking arms that similarly acts as a prompt to cross the groove again to see the four boats with which it is associated right side up. The next boat appears upside down. Here a right shoe-sole points across the groove, prompting movement over it. From this side, other boats farther along the groove appear upside down. A further pair of shoe-soles prompts movement over the groove again to turn round and see the imagery in its correct visual perspective. Cupmarks then mark where an observer must cross the groove again to see an upside-down boat. Farther along, another human carved in the base of the groove acts as a visual prompt to cross it to see the final set of images, a large group of boats, from the southwest side.

A unique and remarkably choreographed sequence of bodily movements is required to see the carvings on this rock, involving walking along a groove, turning to the left or right, stepping over it, and then turning round once more to face the images, a directed staccato spatial dance in which one crisscrosses from one end of the groove to the other. In addition to the movement of the observer, the images themselves switch relational directionality to point (or move) to the right or the left. At the beginning of the sequence, the images move left (up the groove), then predominantly right (down), then in both directions where the images are fewer and more scattered, and finally to the left.

To see the designs in groove 3 in correct visual perspective requires a similar spatial dance crisscrossing the groove from one side to another, guided in some cases by the directionality of shoe-soles but usually by the orientation of the designs. The lower northwest end of this groove is dominated by images of domestic pigs, huge wild boar, and humans who appear to be herding them together with the two largest swords on the rock and a boat-carrier. The dominant and primary directionality is up the rock to the left (downstream in terms of the river flow).

Groove 4 contains only a few scattered images, primarily of boats running along its course and shoe-soles, single or in pairs, which traverse it and point towards groove 3. Absent are the swords and narrative scenes involving humans and animals so characteristic of grooves 2 and 3. Groove 5 is by far the widest on

Figure 4.28. *A:* Detail of motifs along groove 1, rock 1A, Himmelstadlund.
B: Detail of motifs along groove 5, rock 1A, Himmelstadlund.

the rock and the highest. The designs are all carved along the base of the groove in two panels, each with prominent net or trap motifs. The panel lower down the rock to the northwest has many animal depictions all meant to be seen from the southern side, having passed over groove 4. A few boats appear upside down from this perspective. Pairs of shoe-soles point up and down across the groove. Others point along it towards the second and more complex panel. This consists primarily of boats and contains the largest and most elaborate boat depictions on the rock (Figure 4.28B). To see these in correct visual perspective requires walking across the groove and viewing the boats from either side. Three humans are depicted, and these are intended to be seen from the highest point of the rock above the groove on the northern side. Two of these bear a pole attached to a large frame/net or trap motif. These frame/net motifs, the largest and most elaborate in the entire Norrköping rock carving area, are visually dominant and effectively entrap, or entice, the eye. In part this is because their internal divisions are both complex and irregular, with herringbone, cross, and diamond patterns.

Groove 6 occurs lower down the rock, to the north of groove 5. Here there is a distinct lack of visual intensity and complexity compared with other parts of the rock. The designs consist of boats and shoe-soles. All the boats must be seen from below the panel to the southwest. These run across the rock to the right and left. By contrast, a series of eleven shoe-soles point down and off the rock in various directions.

Rock 1E

Rock 1E is exposed about midway between the two major carved rocks at the northwest end of Himmelstadlund, rock 1A and rock 2B (see Figure 4.25). It is a long, linear, almost perfectly flat rock exposure, lacking any grooves but with glacial striation lines. Here there are a series of boat images, some moving upriver and some moving downriver. All but one are meant to be seen from the south and looked down upon, constituting a single visual field. Apart from the boats, there are pairs of shoe-soles orientated across the rock to the south and rock 2B, directing movement in that direction and towards the single boat on the northern face of that rock visible from here. One of these pairs of shoe-soles is unusually transposed across a boat.

Rock 2B

Rock 2B is situated nearest to the river and downslope about 40 m south of rock 1A. Overall the rock exposure is 26 by 24 m. The rock is quite irregular in form, with a steep incline facing the river to the south and a slighter face dipping to the north. On this northern face there is a large, isolated, single-line boat visible from the top of rock 1A. The majority of the other carvings are located on a smooth, flat area of the southern face of the rock just below its top. The lower area has a much more irregular surface, which is not carved. Unlike rock 1A, this rock lacks any distinctive or well-defined grooves.

Another contrast is that all the carvings are consistent in their orientation to an observer and are meant to be seen downslope from below, standing on the rock itself. There is a break in the slope of the rock, with a more or less horizontal ledge marking a more or less horizontal division in the rock face; the upper part contains all the carvings.

Standing in the middle of this ledge, all the carvings can be seen except for some circle crosses at the top of the rock at the eastern end, which are just on the periphery of the visual field. The upper carvings are seen in a horizontal field of vision, while those below are looked down upon. Again, this is a significant difference from rock 1A, which requires constant movement over and across the rock in order to see all the carvings and view them in correct visual perspective.

There are only a few human figures and animals on this rock. Otherwise the images are dominated by large and elaborate boats and hafted axes to the right of the panel. All the blades of these axes face down the rock in the direction of the river. They occur in two distinct, opposed, symmetrically organized groups, one to the right with blades depicted hafted to the right, the other to the left with blades hafted to the left. Narrative scenes and swords are conspicuously absent. Some shoe-soles face down and off the rock. One at the eastern end faces up. The majority of the boats are depicted moving to the left, or inland and upriver.

Rock 4

Rock 4 is the highest rock at Himmelstadlund; it is situated in the centre of the carving area and is the largest. This rock exposure is an elongated, flat-topped dome with sloping faces to the south running down towards the river and to the north running away from it. The western and eastern ends dip away gently. The majority of the carvings are located on the northern and southern slopes. The whole rock is covered with striation lines, and in some areas there are grooves present, but the latter are broken, relatively short in length, and comparatively shallow. They are not continuous and dramatically developed as on rock 1A. The grooves are only pronounced and well developed on the northwestern sloping corner of the rock facing the river, and it is here that the densest concentration of carvings occurs. These consist almost entirely of boat designs running parallel along the grooves, some facing right and moving downriver, others facing left and moving upriver. Apart from over 80 boats, there are a couple of swords, some animals dispersed among the boats, and one narrative scene depicting a human and five animals all moving right, led by a dog. Virtually all these designs are consistently orientated to be seen from the south. They constitute a single visual field, and in terms of bodily posture they demand that an observer look obliquely down and to the left and right when standing on the rock below the carving field.

In the southeast corner of the rock there are further well-defined, narrow grooves with a series of very small animal and boat designs running along them. These constitute another single visual field, again designed to be viewed from the south.

Above the main group of carvings, in the northwest part of the rock, about 2 m up from the images that occur at the eastern end of the panel, there is a track of at least 25 bear footprints that run across and then obliquely down the rock for a distance of 20 m, from the southeast to the northwest. They thus parallel the direction of the grooves found in the Himmelstadlund carving area and elsewhere. However, these footprints are not themselves orientated in a horizontal field or located in an area of the rock surface that has any discernible groove structure. There is an enormous contrast between the strict and rigid organisation of the boats and animals and swords running along the grooves in the northwest corner of the rock and the much less constrained placing of the sinuous course of the bear footprints, even though both follow a general northwest–southeast line of orientation. At the southeast end these footprints occupy one of the highest parts of the rock. The bear being depicted in such a manner is moving inland. The bear footprints terminate 1 m above the narrative scene depicting a human figure, five animals, and a dog, moving right or towards the coast.

At the tenth bear footprint, travelling northwest, a remarkable visual transformation occurs (Figure 4.29). Two further bear footprints are placed next to each other, but orientated south to face towards the river. Rather than being one behind the other, suggesting an animal moving forwards on four legs, the placement of these footprints suggests that the bear is now standing up on its hind legs, viewing the scene: seeing, knowing, and thinking, an animal–human transformation (Hauptman Wahlgren 2002: 202). Just below these two footprints are a pair of shoe-soles pointing in the same direction and hafted axes with their blades facing in the same direction. The relationship between the shoe-soles and the bear footprints itself implies the animal–human transformation. From this point of transformation, the bear footprints continue in a northwest direction but become significantly more widely spaced (distances between the prints change from 30–50 cm to 60 cm–2 m). The ritual and symbolic importance of the bear in relation to Saami shamanistic practices, and in Nordic and Eurasian mythology more generally, has been extensively documented (e.g., Bäckman and Hultkrantz 1978; Edsman 1965).

About 6 m above the line of bear footprints at the approximate centre and top of the rock, a dramatic boar-hunting scene occupies the base and side of a short groove facing the river. The boar, confronted by two spear-bearers, is huge, its size emphasized by the much smaller animals shown near to it. This scene is designed to be seen from the south (Figure 4.30).

From the pig-hunting scene, the rock exposure begins to slope down steeply away from the river. The rock here is relatively smooth, with little or no discernible groove structure, and is covered by various distinct and scattered design panels separated from each other by distances of 4 to 8 m. The carvings here are dominated by images of boats. Some are huge, up to 3 m in length. All are meant to be seen from the north, and although different panels are intervisible, they constitute individual fields. Depictions of humans are rare and usually occur in the boats. On one of the lowest panels, a complex net/trap design is associated with the boats, together with animals and a spear-bearer. There are no obvious narrative scenes. Occasional pairs of shoe-soles traverse the rock and point down and off it. Here there is no obvious pattern of encounter or movement between the various carved panels. To see them requires moving up and down and across the rock, and patterns of movement and encounter could be infinitely varied from one occasion to another. This would enable the construction of numerous potential sequences from the same set of fixed design fields, so that radically different stories could be told from the manner in which they were seen—in effect, making the relationship among these different

Figure 4.29. The transforming bear footprints on rock 4, Himmelstadlund.

Figure 4.30. Boar-hunting scene, rock 4, Himmelstadlund. For location, see Figure 4.25.

panels mobile rather than fixed. For example, different panels might be seen on different occasions or in a different sequence or order.

ROCKS, IMAGES, AND THE BODY

Based on the discussions of individual rocks and carving surfaces presented above, we can distinguish four different kinds of relationship and bodily encounter between fields of images and an observer:

1. A relationship that remains relatively distanced and passive. The observer stands below or besides the images, which can be viewed within a single visual field. They can be experienced all at once on an extensive panel. All that is required to experience them is a gradual turning of the head from one end of the carved panel to another. They successively slip into and out of visual focus, or become foregrounded or backgrounded. This requires no bodily movement or direct physical interaction. According to the character of the rocks, one may have to look up at the images, in which case they become dominant, or look down on them (observer dominant), or look horizontally across towards them at eye level or from side to side.

2. A situation in which direct participation is required, moving from one set of images to another on the same rock surface in order to view them and bring them into focus. Here the observer may have to move into and walk over the fields of images in order to move from one to another. This directly involves the contact of one's feet with the images and movement of the body between different fields, or areas, with visual images on the rock surface or between different rocks. As if on a stage, the observer enters the scenes and becomes an actor in their stories. Such internal participation with the images may be relatively unstructured in terms of moving at will between different image fields, without visual clues as to how to move. Or it may be a much more ordered, 'scripted', or constrained process, where one moves sequentially between one group of images and the next, up and down or along the rock.

3. In many cases the linear structuring of the images along the lines of the glacial grooves requires directional movement to the right or the left and up and down and along the rocks in order to see the different sets of designs, but the observer walks along and outside the image field without entering or walking over it. He or she remains outside, rather than inside, the image field.

4. An interaction with the images involving continuous staccato movement back and forth and over the image fields, stepping or crossing over them and turning the body through 180 degrees. Such movement is usually determined by a combination of how the images are linearly structured and whether the images themselves appear upside down or right side up. This kind of interaction reaches its extreme form at the northwest end of Himmelstadlund.

Table 4.2 lists these types of bodily engagement in relation to the rocks discussed in detail above. Some require only a passive or relatively distanced engagement. Others require direct participation and linear movement, moving along and/or around the image fields. The rocks at Himmelstadlund are the only ones in which all four forms of bodily participation are required, again marking this place out as very special and different from all the others.

TABLE 4.2. THE PRIMARY TYPES OF BODILY ENGAGEMENT REQUIRED TO VIEW THE IMAGES ON A SAMPLE OF DIFFERENT ROCK AND ROCK PANELS IN THE NORRKÖPING AREA.

Carving locality/ panel	Passive or distanced	Direct participation	Linear movement	Staccato movement
Borg 51 (Herrebro)	+	+	+	
Borg 54 (Herrebro)	+			
Borg 53 (Herrebro)	+	+		
Borg 52 (Herrebro)		+		
Borg 31 (Skälv)		+		
St Johannes 14 (Egna Hem)	+			
Ö Eneby 45 (Karlsberget)	+			
Ö Eneby 44		+		
Ö Eneby 27 (Leonardsberg)			+	
Ö Eneby 23 (Ekenberg 1)		+	+	
Ö Eneby 23 (Ekenberg 7)		+		
Ö Eneby 8 (Fiskeby)		+		
Ö Eneby 1 (Himmelstadlund)				
Rock 1A		+	+	+
Rock 1E			+	
Rock 2B			+	
Rock 4	+	+	+	

Just as the character of the image fields on the rocks mediate or determine certain types of bodily movement and interaction with them, so too may individual images or closely associated sets of images. Here we can distinguish nine different basic relationships:

1. *Orientation*: Images that appear upside down or wrong way up from one position directly encourage movement to another position in order to gain the correct perspective. These are exclusively the boat, animal, human, and occasional tree designs. None of the other images—such as swords or axes, circles or spirals, or shoe-soles—ever appear upside down but can be satisfactorily viewed from almost any angle or position on or off the rocks.

2. *Directionality*: There is an obvious directionality to certain designs seen in profile. For example, boats with clear prow designs may face, or seem to move, to the left or the right or up and down the rock. The same is true for animals and human figures. Similarly, swords, spears, or axes may point in one direction or another. But this sense of directionality is largely 'internal' to the image and does not of itself provide any clues as to how an observer might move from one set of images or one panel to another across the rocks. By contrast, the bear footprints on Himmelstadlund rock 4 provide a very clear sense of directional movement and invite one to follow the track. Sometimes the directionality of shoe-soles, either paired or single, seems also to provide a direct sense of how or where to move, as discussed above, even though by contrast with the track of bear footprints, they appear peculiarly static. In these cases the images themselves very powerfully mediate bodily movement, not just because they point a way forwards, up and down, or across the rocks, but also because they themselves are directly related to and intimately connected with the human body at rest and in motion.

3. *Dominance*: Other types of interaction are related to the manner in which the images exert visual dominance over the viewer, attracting attention. Particularly large individual images, such as the massive boats on Himmelstadlund rock 4, the horse and mantle design at Egna Hem, or the swords at Ekenberg, have this effect.

4. *Complexity*: Intricate images—such as some of the frame/net designs with elaborate internal subdivisions, boats with decorated hulls, or spirals—draw in the eye and hold the spectator enthralled by their inherent power and complexity. These are 'sticky images', from which the eye finds it difficult to move. They captivate and seduce.

5. *Transformation*: Situations in which one motif changes into a completely different form also attract attention. Some such motifs suggest an action, such as the bear footprints at Himmelstadlund rock 4 or the ambiguous circle cross images that also resemble shoe-soles, occurring on Himmelstadlund rock 4 and elsewhere. Others suggest transformation by depicting related human figures in different body sizes, shapes, or postures.

6. *Narratives*: Sets of images that appear coordinated so as to convey a narrative, such as a hunting or herding scene, attract and draw in the eye in a way that seemingly unrelated images do not.

7. *Symmetry*: Sets of images arranged in an obvious symmetrical or structured oppositional pattern may be designed to deliberately attract the eye and invoke attention.

8. *Packing*: The sheer massing of images of the same kind, such as flotillas of boats or herds of animals or groups, is an obvious way to attract attention and inspire fascination and awe. Visual fields with only a few scattered designs simply do not have the same power to impress and thrill.

9. *Confrontation*: Images that appear to directly face or confront an observer exert power. Confrontational images are exclusive to some human depictions. All the boat and animal designs are depicted in profile, and the animal heads are never turned. They are seen from the side, as if from a distance, implying detachment rather than engagement.

Participation

Table 4.3 lists these types of visual relationships in regards to the rocks discussed above. On some, only a few or none occur. Other rocks or panels, such as those at Ekenberg or rocks 1A and 4 at Himmelstadlund, have far more varied and complex visual effects on an observer. Each of the rocks is similar to, or differentiated from, others in relation to its own *effects* and where on the rock surface the images occur. None of the aforementioned types of bodily and visual interaction with the rock carving panels or with individual images rely on what the images may mean or connote. Denotative meaning is sufficient for them to influence the body and exert visual power: this is a boat, this is a boar, and so on. What is being stressed here, however, is the manner in which the carved panels and the individual images physically affect an observer and the manner in which one's perception of them is mediated through the human body itself, either at rest or in movement. The images clearly perform work: they exert an agency through the body that must move, turn, look down, look up, move among them, or view them at a distance, walk to the right or to the left, and so on. They may also, to various degrees, exert a visual fascination and power by drawing in and transfixing vision. Moving around, between, and over the rocks always involves an encounter with image fields of different densities and intensities: those that hold attention and those that require only a glance, those that make you stand still and those that demand changes of position and posture. There is thus a theatrical and performative element to the power of these images in terms of the degree of attention they hold and the experience of encounter they offer. For the images to have dramatic impact, it was clearly necessary for them to be scaled in relation to the rock surface, so the long, narrow grooves require small linear sequences which can be quite striking within the context of the groove. The same designs would lose much of their visual power if carved on wide expanses of sloping

Carving locality/panel	Orientation	Directionality (Shoe-soles)	Dominance	Complexity	Transformation	Narrative	Symmetry	Confrontation	Packing
Borg 51 (Herrebro)		+		+	+	+		+	
Borg 54 (Herrebro)							+		
Borg 53 (Herrebro)	+			+			+		
Borg 52 (Herrebro)	+								
Borg 31 (Skälv)								+	+
St Johannes 14 (Egna Hem)	+		+						
Ö Eneby 45 (Karlsberget)									
Ö Eneby 44									
Ö Eneby 27 (Leonardsberg)						+	+		
Ö Eneby 23 (Ekenberg 1)			+	+	+	+	+	+	+
Ö Eneby 23 (Ekenberg 7)	+			+	+	+		+	
Ö Eneby 8 (Fiskeby)	+		+	+	+		+	+	+
Ö Eneby 1 (Himmelstadlund)				+	+	+	+		+
Rock 1A	+	+	+				+		+
Rock 1E	+	+							
Rock 2B			+	+			+		+
Rock 4	+	+	+	+	+	+	+		+

Note: For explanation of categories, see text pp. 246–247.

or flat rock pavement. These areas require larger images that spread out and occupy the space. The spacing of motifs on particularly large pavement areas, such as at Himmelstadlund rock 4, is orchestrated in a carefully considered way, with collections of images set apart by areas of the rock unoccupied by carvings. Busy areas of the rock surface packed with images are set apart by the calm frames of uncarved rock surrounding them.

While the power of these images relates, on the one hand, to physical and bodily interaction with them, on the other hand it relates to the properties of the rock surfaces themselves on which they are carved—smooth or rough, steep or flat or sloping, grooved or not, the presence of quartz or other mineral inclusions, colour, texture, and so on, as discussed above—and also how they are carved—deep or shallow, bold or slight. These images were not just meant to be seen, they were probably intended to be felt as well.

ROCKS, IMAGES, AND MEANING

Our contention is that what these images mean is bound up with the landscape settings and particular qualities of the rock surfaces on which they occur, forms of bodily interaction and encounter, as well as their own particular properties and forms and relationships with other images. Consequently, the same images—a boat or a spiral, for example—are likely to have had very different receptions, from the point of view of an observer, according to the landscape setting of a rock and how it was encountered, the particular physical properties of that rock (such as the sensuous qualities of the stone), and their mode of bodily reception. This is to argue that meaning was not somehow internal to the specific image or panel of images, but was dialectically related to the rock itself, to landscape and the body. We have been primarily concerned to analyse, up to this point, the power of the images: *how* they come to have bodily and visual effects. We have also discussed, in relation to the individual rocks analysed, what the images might mean: the traditional focus of all rock art research. These two types of questions, *how* the images have effects and *what* they mean, are intimately related. Having considered the images on specific rocks and panels in some detail, we now return to a consideration of the latter question in more general terms.

Quite obviously, knowing what the images mean profoundly increases their reception and effects on either a contemporary or a Bronze Age observer. There is a fundamental distinction between panels that appear simply to be variously structured collections of individual elements or motifs versus others that represent specific iconographic or narrative scenes, such as pig hunting, processions, boats being pulled by horses, herding, or movements of a bear (see Table 4.4). Where the latter images imply motion, by contrast, the others appear strikingly static. The significance of the narrative scenes involves recognition of the specific iconography and its meaning, so they have a dual power: as representations of myth and life and as images perceived in specific ways through different modes of bodily encounter and posture in relation to the significance of the rocks themselves prior to the addition of carvings.

TABLE 4.4. NARRATIVE SCENES ON THE ROCKS DEPICTING HUMAN BEINGS IN
THE NORRKÖPING AREA, WITH ILLUSTRATION NUMBERS FROM THE
DOCUMENTATION OF NORDÉN (1925) AND BURENHULT (1973).

Carving locality/ Panel	Narrative Scene Depicted	Nordén 1925	Burenhult 1973
Borg 51 (Herrebro)	Human transformation	—	Herebro 7D
Borg 54 (Herrebro)	Chariot scene	HB3	—
Borg 24 (Skälv)	Dancers and animals	—	Skälv 11C
Ö Eneby 27 (Leonardsberg)	Processions and boat-carriers	LB1	Leonardsberg 1
Ö Eneby 23 (panel 1) (Ekenberg)	Horses and people dragging boat	FE1	Ekenberg 1
	Human transformations	FE1	Ekenberg 1
Ö Eneby 23 (panel 7)	Human and animal transformations	FE10	Ekenberg 7
	Hunting	FE10	Ekenberg 7
Ö Eneby 8 (Fiskeby)	Spear bearers, processions, fighting	FM18	—
Ö Eneby 31 (Leonardsberg)	Hunting	LT44	—
Ö Eneby 24 (Leonardsberg)	Fighting and dominance	LB13	Leonardsberg 4
Ö Eneby 84 (Leonardsberg)	Super human ship bearer	LB27	Leonardsberg 2
Ö Eneby 1 (Himmelstadlund)			
Rock 1A	Pig and animal herding (three scenes)	H50	Himmelstadlund 1A
	Boat lifting	H50	Himmelstadlund 1A
	Frame/net carriers	H50	Himmelstadlund 1A
Rock 4	Animal herding	H2	Himmelstadlund 4
	Boar hunting	—	—
	Bear/human transformation	H29	Himmelstadlund 4
	Hunting	H31	Himmelstadlund 8A
Rock 3	Multiple spear-bearers	H25	Himmelstadlund 3
	Boat dragging	H23	Himmelstadlund 3

Grooves, Water, and Narratives

During the Bronze Age the grooves on the rocks may have been interpreted or understood as the creations of ancestral beings as they moved across the landscape. The grooves themselves, linear in form, narrow or wide, symmetrical or asymmetrical in profile, suggest in the most general way routes or paths of movement, lines, or channels to be followed, and these lines are followed and further emphasized by the linear fields of images. The grooves create an image field that transcends a distinction between a two-dimensional plane and three-dimensional form, being somewhere in between. This in itself again gives the imagery part of its bodily significance and power. If carving images along these grooves was an embellishment of a form already created by ancestral beings in the past, then people in the act of carving made a direct connection between past and present, between themselves and ancestral forces and powers. Part of the significance of the carvings may have been the stories they told about ancestral origins and the continuity of local groups in relationship to the land, thus enabling them to lay claim to it and the resources—material and non-material—it provided. There are strong grooves and weak grooves, by implication strong and weak ancestral marks, lines, or paths. Controlling the most significant rocks and the strong grooves that run across them thus sustained relationships of social power. The rocks north of the river generally have more and better developed grooves than those south of the river, and there too the images are more frequent, diversified, and elaborate. Similarly, north of the river the most dramatic of these grooves occur at Himmelstadlund, which is also the largest and most complex carving locale.

The linear directionality of these grooves is from the northwest to the southeast, and they are always more prominent and well defined at the northwest end of individual rocks, being successively broken up and fading away towards the southeast. We know that virtually all the Bronze Age houses at the Pryssgården settlement were also orientated northwest to southeast. In other words, the long axis of these houses repeats that of the grooves, in a relation of mimesis. Furthermore, the most important ritual end of these houses, where offerings took place, was at the northwest end, which again is precisely where the grooves are most prominent on the rocks. The houses, following the lines of the grooves, were orientated in the same propitious ancestral direction. The grooves do not crisscross or run into each other. Similarly, the foundations of the houses on the Pryssgården settlement, built at different dates, do not overlap each other. They rather run parallel to each other in an analogous fashion to the grooves.

The directionality of the grooves and the houses is further represented in the movement of the boats, animals, and human figures along them. Narrative scenes with human figures occur almost exclusively along the lines of the grooves. There are only a few cases, such as at Fiskeby, where such scenes occur on flat or sloping areas of rock where grooves are absent. Yet if the grooves were so significant, we clearly need to explain why it is that the most monumental of these, occurring on the rock island to the southwest of Leonardsberg, were not carved. Because of the density of carved rocks in the area, and the association of the images with the lines of the grooves, one expects carvings to be found here, making their absence particularly remarkable. It may be that the grooves here were so monumental and powerful that they 'demanded' not to be carved. Perhaps they neither needed nor required any kind of embellishment with images. The grooves on this rock may have been regarded as the supreme work of the ancestors, repeated elsewhere in the landscape but on a smaller and lesser scale. This relatively isolated rock island, located next to the flow of the Motala River as it disgorged out of Lake Glan, could well have been a sacred and taboo place in the Bronze Age landscape, a place where the ancestors themselves were thought to have had their residence or origins.

We have already noted that the grooves run parallel with the flow of the Motala River to its north but at right angles to it to the south, and that they are more dramatic to the north. We can suggest that the parallelism between the lines of the grooves and the flow of the river water gave them an added power and significance to the north of the river, associating them with freshwater and its flow to the sea and metaphorically with the flow of life interconnecting everything. We have seen that it is only to the north of the river that there is direct visual contact between some of the carved rocks and the river, notably where it flows out of Lake Glan and at Himmelstadlund. The carved rocks at Fiskeby were probably also in sight of the river in the past (a large paper factory is now sited there), and the roar of the rapids would definitely have been audible.

The bands of carved rocks, with the exception of those at Himmelstadlund, effectively end, both to the north and south of the river, at the Fiskeby rapids. The narrative or iconographic scenes on the rocks depict journeys: journeys of people through life, animal movements, the movements of boats, and so on (Table 4.4). The directionality of the grooves predetermines the directionality of the designs and the manner in which the body must move in order to experience them. The animals, boats, and people depicted on the rocks north of the river are shown travelling in both directions along the grooves: inland and seawards. Those to the south of the river move either towards or away from the river. The most general theme here is one of journeying and transformation: flows, movement, connections, and links. North of the river these flows appear to be primarily directed outwards towards the sea rather than inwards. On the major carved rocks at Himmelstadlund, Ekenberg, Fiskeby, and Leonardsberg, twice as many of the striking sword and dagger motifs point downstream rather than upstream. Similarly, the majority of the boats, animals, and humans face or 'move' downstream rather than upstream. As Hauptman Wahlgren has argued, the rapids at Fiskeby, and those that formed later downstream, may symbolise thresholds or doorways to another world in rites of passage (Hauptman Wahlgren 2002: 208).

As discussed above, land uplift throughout the Bronze Age radically altered the character of the river. In the Early Bronze Age, Himmelstadlund, situated below the last rapids before the sea, became cut off from it as the lower rapids formed. Navigation of the river became more and more difficult. It would require dragging boats out of the river and across the land. The theme of dragging boats over land, around rapids and different parts of the river system, would have had a particularly powerful resonance in the Bronze Age at a time when the land was rising and parts of the river system previously navigable became impassable. Myths almost always explain origins and connect past to present. What were the origins of the grooves? One possibility is that they might have been taken to represent places where the ancestors dragged boats across the land, permanently marking the rocks in the process. Here it should be noted that some of the grooves are strikingly similar in form and profile to long canoes. This theme of dragging boats across the land or carrying them finds direct iconographic expression at a number of rock carving localities, all to the north of the river. At Ekenberg panel E:1, a boat is depicted being dragged by horses. At Leonardsberg, people appear to be carrying boats. Similar scenes occur on another rock at Leonardsberg and on two panels at Himmelstadlund (Table 4.4).

CONCLUSIONS: THE BRONZING OF THE ROCKS

There is little doubt that the depiction of swords and axes signifies an obsession with bronze, a prestigious metal, and a desire to obtain it, which we know was largely unsuccessful. The art depicted what was desired, as Malmer and Larsson have argued. The sword depictions almost always occur in the bottoms of the grooves and are deeply carved, thus emphasizing connections with ancestral powers and forces. The enormous amount of time and energy expended on producing these and other carvings was clearly intended to impress and dazzle. Someone being led to the carved rocks would be able to see this display of material wealth and what it signified: the prestige and importance of the local group. Interestingly, unlike spears, swords are never shown being used offensively. Carved in careful detail and at unusual scale, they exist as symbolic objects. Now, because of the character of the mineral inclusions in the mica-schist, discussed above, the rocks themselves had metallic qualities. So carving images of swords, daggers, axes, and spearheads into this particular rock would have had a particularly powerful symbolic resonance, calling forth the desired bronze. The images, when freshly carved—or as Hauptman Wahlgren suggests, on occasion recarved—would be seen to give forth a metallic sheen and light: wealth of bronze was a metaphorical property of the rocks themselves, shining in the sunlight and in the moonlight, and glistening in the rain.

The significant differences between the carved rocks north versus south of the river, and the peculiar relative isolation of both from Himmelstadlund, may suggest significant social differences between groups living to the south and north of the river, which acted as an economic and social boundary. Those groups south of the river do not appear to have been concerned to put on a show of their apparent wealth and prestige. The sword symbolism, and all that it implies, is virtually absent. Boats are significantly larger and much more impressive to the north of the river. Of 37 boats greater than 1 m in length, 28 (76%) occur north of the river, and a few of these, 2 to 3 m long, occur only at Himmelstadlund and Ekenberg. Boats with very elaborate hull decoration, with internal subdivisions decorated with rows of cupmarks and occasionally spirals, occur only north of the river. Similarly, large boars are conspicuously absent south of the river, as are hunting or herding scenes. There are only three obvious narrative scenes with human figures south of the river, on rocks at Herrebro and Skälv: a scene depicting a chariot with animals, the row of contrasting human figures running along the prominent groove on rock 51, and a scene depicting dancers and animals at Skälv (Table 4.4). North of the river, by contrast, at least nineteen obvious narrative scenes can be identified, involving humans in various acts of a very different kind (see Table 4.4). The iconography on the rocks at Himmelstadlund depicts some unique themes not found elsewhere on rocks either to the north or south of the river, such as boar hunting and pig herding. Motifs unevenly distributed elsewhere on rocks north and south of the river are frequent here. For example, the frame/net/trap designs are more common on the rocks south of the river but are well represented at Himmelstadlund where, indeed, the largest and most impressive examples occur. The rocks here may well have been a central place for ceremonies and exchange for groups both to the south and north of the river, which would account for its size and complexity and its relative isolation from both.

The sheer density and complexity of the carved rocks in the Norrköping area are, in a sense, quite outrageous. Who were these rocks being carved for: insiders or outsiders? It is clear that on some of the rock surfaces, the sheer size, density, and complexity of the images and the technological skill required to carve them were designed to dazzle and overwhelm. The scenario being created was of a powerful and affluent world: how the world might, or should, be rather than the reality of how it really was, which was probably in striking contrast to that being depicted in the wealth of bronzes, the huge wild boars, the massive boats, and so on. Such a display would not fool anyone living in the vicinity of the rocks. It may well be that much of this world of images was created to impress people from the outside, people who would be taken to and shown the rocks and participate in the feasting and ceremonies that no doubt took place in relation to them. These rocks are likely to have been those at Himmelstadlund, Fiskeby, Ekenberg, and Leonardsberg, all to the north of the river.

Designed to bewitch and beguile, seduce and deceive, the images empowered those who created them in a world of competitive exchange obsessed by bronze, the supreme symbol of prestige and power. These would be the images of this society that would stick in the mind of an outsider and were intended to have a powerful bodily and emotive effect as people moved around and between them: outsiders would convey the fame of this part of Östergötland to the wider world. Indeed, the images still have precisely this effect today, for both specialists and tourists. People come and see and admire and remember. The images on the rocks to the south of the river are far more modest in scale, and most are rather ordinary and prosaic in character. A sense of scale and drama is largely missing. Likewise, patterns of bodily movement and visual relationships between observers and images are generally far simpler. It may well be that here the people were carving the rocks solely for themselves. They were representing themselves for themselves rather than for outsiders. In such a social and ceremonial context, elaborate imagery was not required. There was no need to bronze the rocks.

CHAPTER FIVE

CONCLUSIONS

THE EMPOWERMENT OF

IMAGERY AND THE

PHENOMENOLOGICAL WALK

EMPOWERED IMAGES

S pecific interpretations of the images in each of the three landscapes have been undertaken in Chapters 2–4 in relation to bodily kinaesthetics and sensory dimensions of the landscape. Rather than repeating these observations, the intention of this concluding chapter is to focus on more general interpretive and methodological issues informing the individual discussions, together with some comparative notes.

The very different rock art images in the areas considered in Chapters 2–4 all require different forms of performative bodily posture and movement in order to experience them. The central argument being made here is that the rock art images were not just *expressive of* cognitive thought but constituted a major element in the *formation of* those cognitive thoughts—by virtue of their kinaesthetic experience. The imagery provided a specific cultural form through which bodies were manipulated and structured in space-time. From Foucault's (1977) essential insight that power is directed through the body, we can understand the images as technologies for reproducing power through the kinaesthetics of the body. Power here is meant as both positive empowerment and as a medium through which meanings and knowledge become channelled, directed, and controlled through encounters with the images themselves. Experiencing the images entailed various embodied actions

255

and performative forms of bodily movement. Movement through these landscapes of images simultaneously constituted an orientation to the landscape itself and established different forms of social identification with it. The carvings in each of the different areas made possible certain kinds of bodily performances rather than others and articulated different kinds of corporeal relationships. In other words, the images acted as technologies for the cultural production of bodies moving in relation to them, both providing performative affordances and acting as 'disciplinary' arenas, restricting thought and action in the context of their very different landscapes and 'sensescapes' mediated through the body.

Thus, at Vingen, it has been argued, movement is directed from the west to the east, and then east to west around the fjord. It entails very different kinaesthetic acts at different moments in this sequence: weaving between the decorated rocks on Vingeneset, climbing sheer rock faces at Elva (requiring ropes), then climbing again to reach the flattish pavement with carvings at Nedste Laegda, and then entering into and becoming a participant within the image fields. The experience of the carvings at Urane requires negotiating a way through a huge and hazardous boulder field, moving up and down, around, and through the stones. The carvings at Brattebakken, Hardbakken, and Vehammaren require observers to move from east to west along steeply sloping rock faces, looking up and across at the images. Here bodily movement is highly structured and constrained in character, contrasting with the greater freedom to choose one's movement implied by the locations of the images on the rocks of Bak Vehammaren. The surfaces across which the body is required to move are fundamentally different in character—from those that are smoothly sloping to broken surfaces with numerous obstacles, chasms, and fissures through which one might fall. In this manner, the kinaesthetics of the body are produced in and through the landscape of rock carvings, and the relationship between person and place has a quality of an embodied and embedded identity, both divisible in terms of different qualities of the rocks and linked together in the sequences in which they are encountered.

The kinaesthetic experience of the imagery in relation to the characteristics of the rocks themselves in the Norrköping area is far less extreme and variable, and the images themselves differ significantly to the north and south of the Motala River. The presence of grooves in the rock and the distribution of the mica-schist outcrops here were critical factors for the presence of the imagery, the manner in which it was structured in relation to the rocks, and even for the size of the images. Overall movement in this landscape may have been from the southwest to the northeast south of the Motala River, and from the northwest to the southeast, following the orientation of the grooves themselves, to the north of the river, with movement culminating in the ceremonial arena of the great rock pavements of Himmelstadlund, on which the most complex and differentiated bodily movements and postures were required as one entered into and became a participant within the great image fields themselves, moving back and forth and across the grooves.

At both Vingen and in the Norrköping area, some of the image fields have to be seen from off the rocks; others require moving along the rocks in a linear fashion, yet others demand more complex sequences of movement in and among the image fields. All the nine relationships listed in Chapter 4 (pp. 246–57 and Table 4.2) between an observer and individual image forms in the Norrköping area also occur in relation to the Vingen rock carvings but differ between individual rocks and carving surfaces. However, at Vingen there are only a few huge deer images, compared with many large boat and sword images in the Norrköping area. The visual complexity of the internal body differentiation found in many of the Vingen deer is only matched by that found in the relatively few net/frame motifs in the Norrköping area and in the internal decorations found on the larger boat images. The animals on the Norrköping rocks are depicted in a much simpler fashion. None have internal body differentiation, and most appear static rather than in vigorous movement. It is the cultural artefacts and symbols here that have primary significance, as opposed to the deer at Vingen. As one might expect, whereas at Vingen it is animal–human relationships that are being stressed in some 'narrative scenes' (as on Brattebakken with the deer riders and at Leitet), in the Norrköping area it is relationships between people and boats and weapons that are being emphasized. The carvings at Vingen seem to stress the social and metaphoric interconnections between human and animal domains. In the Norrköping area where hunting and herding scenes do occur, the emphasis seems to be on the separation of animals from people and the exploitation of the former by the latter. At Vingen there is an emphasis on states of bodily transformation from life to death, from skeletal to fully fleshed forms. In the Norrköping area there is little emphasis on the human body itself. Instead, the humans are all depicted doing things: engaging in heroic acts such as boat lifting, taking part in processions and ceremonies, or in boar hunting, wielding huge spears, and so on. If the narrative on the Vingen rocks appears to be primarily about the relationship between people and animals and states of human bodily transformation, in the Norrköping area it has to do with social relationships among people and between people and artefacts. People are never depicted holding the hook and scythe motifs at Vingen precisely because, as argued in Chapter 2, these may not depict tools or ceremonial regalia at all, but instead might be primary landscape signifiers representing scythe- and hook-formed fjords, movement, and journeying.

The Vingen and Norrköping imagery contrasts greatly with the graphic imagery encountered inside and outside the Irish passage graves. Here, because of the virtual absence of iconic designs, the orientation of individual images in relation to an observer is not really an issue: none appear upside down and there is no indication of directionality in relation to the images themselves. They are not obviously moving or going anywhere and appear static. Most are rather small, and only those on some of the kerbstones outside Knowth might be described as visually dominant, contrasting with the huge deer depicted on a few of the rocks at Vingen and many boats and swords found among the Norrköping carvings. In Ireland there is an absence of narrative scenes or stones with clear image transformations. Here complex, intricate images occur on some of the stones, such as the three-spiral motif in the Newgrange chamber, and there is an emphasis on symmetrical relationships and the packing of images on some stones.

The structuring of bodily movement in relation to the images inside and outside the Irish temples is far more predictable and less variable than at either Vingen or in the Norrköping area. It has been argued that the Irish temples required circular movement to the right outside the temples, in accordance with the passage of the sun across the heavens. This contrasts significantly with the constricted and linear movements imposed by moving up and down the narrow passages to the internal chambers, when bodily movement and posture became far more variable and differentiated according to the particular architectural characteristics of these spaces.

At various points in each of the landscapes being considered, experience of the images either had to be individual or permitted collective experience. In an obvious sense, experience of the images in the Irish temple passages had to be individualised. Only one person could physically experience them at any one time, given the physical constrictions of the space; and even in the chambers, collective experience would only have been possible for a few. At Himmelstadlund and Ekenberg in the Norrköping rock carving landscape, the huge rock pavements leant themselves to collective forms of experience taking place on the same rocks. Elsewhere images on the smaller rocks were such that they could only be simultaneously experienced by individuals or a few persons at most. In the Urane boulder field and in many other areas at Vingen, it was only possible for individuals to experience a large number of the images, such was their size and locational context. Thus, in all three landscapes we can refer to different images and different image fields as being related to either individual or collective experience—carving panels that bring people together or serve to separate them. Only the young and physically fit could have ever reached some of the carvings at Elva on Vingen, perched as they are on an almost sheer rock face.

Distance and Intimacy

A very different kind of relationship exists between observers and the images where one must walk over and across the carved rocks and actually enter into the image fields, as in many locales at Vingen and in the Norrköping rock carving area. In these cases, the images are below the body or under the feet. Inside the Irish temples the situation is completely different. One passes through a space in which the images may simultaneously be to the left, right, or above the body. One may reach out to touch such images but may never walk over, in between, or on them. The experience itself occurs in the process of moving through and within a kind of stone body. The images remain, relatively speaking, both intimate and distant, surrounding the body yet still apart. Some high up in the chamber roofs could never even be touched without clambering up to them on some form of scaffolding or support. The imagery of the Irish temples always occurs on a vertical plane in relation to the body, whereas in Norway and Sweden imagery placement is far more varied, occurring on a horizontal plane, a vertical plane, and all gradations in between.

Hiding Images

At Vingen, only a small number of the images, which appear to have been of minor importance, were deliberately hidden under natural rockshelters or under boulders. However, many others were in fugitive locations by virtue of their placement in the vast scree and boulder fields. None of the imagery at Norrköping appears to have been deliberately hidden in either a direct or indirect manner, although much of it in more peripheral areas of the landscape or on the carved panels may effectively have become hidden or lost over time. In Ireland, some of the stones in the kerb at Newgrange, and in the temple interior, are like playing cards, their outward surfaces hiding more than they reveal. At the Irish temples we witness imagery related primarily to a cult of the dead. Much of the imagery inside Newgrange and the other temples discussed in Chapter 3 were probably never intended for general public display and consumption. Much of it at Newgrange and Dowth, even on the external kerbstones, was hidden or not visually striking. The whole point about the architecture of the Irish temples, essentially solid cairns but with tiny internal passages and chamber spaces, seems to be about symbolically containing the spirits of the dead and preventing them from getting out. Sensory experience inside the temples may have been primarily tactile and auditory rather than visual. It simply did not matter whether or not the graphic imagery could be seen, for this imagery belonged primarily to the dead, who could 'see' and experience it from inside the temple. Unlike the living, the ancestral dead could still benefit from the experience of that which was hidden away, seeing the unseen, knowing the unknown. The important thing was that their remains be buried in the context of the magical power of decorated stones. Newgrange and other Irish temples may be understood as architectural snares for the spiritual forces associated with the ancestral dead. The emphasis is on containing ancestral forces within the monument and preventing them from escaping outside into the world of the living. By contrast, at Vingen and in the Norrköping landscape, the visual experience of the images was of essential significance, because these images were connected with cults for the living rather than for the ancestral dead. The iconic power of these images, in looking like what they represented, was an essential part of their meaning. Some of the animal and human images at Vingen clearly possess an animated corporeality, as do the bear footprints at Himmelstadlund and the 'narrative scenes' in the Norrköping area discussed in Chapter 4. Animals might be controlled through their mimetic imitation. In Sweden the great displays of bronzes north of the Motala River represented prestige for the local group in the absence of actual bronze. If Vingen was a display of images that had significance for insiders (local foraging groups), some of those in the Norrköping area seem to have been specifically created to impress outsiders in the context of a radically different social and economic system in which exchanges of raw materials and alliances were far more important.

Marking the Landscape with Images

The carvings areas themselves in all the three locales considered convey an almost palpable sense of the carver's presence; and specific motifs, such as the footprints on the Norrköping rocks and the human imagery there and at Vingen, further communicate this presence. The performative act of creating the carvings not only embodied in stone the actions of those who carved the images, but was a symbolic act drawing together localised and more distant landscapes quite literally through the action of stone on stone. The images carved on and in the Irish temples were produced by pecking, with either flint or, more probably, quartz from the Wicklow Mountains to the south (Figure 5.1). Those at Vingen were made using diabase quarried from a striking dyke at Stakaneset running up to the top of a mountain towards the end of a peninsula 50 km to the south (Figure. 5.2). Those in the Norrköping area may have been produced using flint tools whose closest source was Skåne in southern Sweden or Denmark to the south. Interestingly, in all three cases these were magical stones derived from distant and powerful places to the south.

All three rock carving areas considered in Chapters 2–4 might be described as transitional places in the landscape. In every case they occur where freshwater mingles with seawater: along the Boyne and Motala Rivers, and at Vingen where the waterfalls plunge down the mountains into the fjord. The presence of the rapids on the Motala River and the freshwater pond along the Vingen terrace in particular appear to have been especially significant in relation to the meanings of the images.

Figure 5.1. View along a glacial valley in the Wicklow Mountains, source of the quartz found at the temples in the bend of the Boyne.

Figure 5.2. The bottom of the Stakaneset diabase dyke running vertically up the mountain from the fjord. Above the modern wall it is entirely quarried away, creating a dramatic fissure through the rocks.

The rock carvings in the Vingen and Norrköping landscapes are like sequins sewn onto a cloth. Together they form a larger network in an embedded matrix consisting of the landscape itself. The contrast with the Irish imagery could not be greater. There the images, rather than being located with reference to preexisting significant places (rocks) in the landscape, are found on stones that were gathered together from local and more distant places to construct the temples and create new places of cultural significance in that landscape, defined by the presence of the temple architecture. In Ireland, stones walked or were made to walk.

At Vingen, the mountains around the fjord frame the carving area in a very obvious way. In Ireland, the bend of the river Boyne frames the locations of the major temples with images there. By contrast, the Norrköping carvings lack any such obvious frame. It is primarily the presence of the grooved mica-schist rocks and their contrast with the surrounding granite rock outcrops that attract and collect the carvings there.

The Pursuit and Husbandry of Images

In all these very different rock carving landscapes, experiencing the images pushed bodies to do unusual things, go to peripheral spaces, place themselves in unusual situations, sometimes exert themselves in exceptional ways, stimulating a concatenation of sensory experiences beyond the normal. These diverse performativities folded these landscapes and the places within them in and through the body, which thus became *of the place*. They produced different kinds of people and social relations and were at the same time the product of these people and their relationships. Knowing how to go on, how to experience the rock carvings in the Norrköping landscape, would provide no guide with regard to Vingen or Ireland or vice versa. That which is predictable in any one of these landscapes cannot be generalised to another. The sensations of movement registered in the joints, muscles, and tendons, the performative bodily acts, their sequencing and timing, and the character of interactions with others, were completely different. The experience of the images in the Irish temples was of a highly structured character. Intimately associated with the monuments themselves, their locations in the landscape were known and associated with calendrical rites, the agrarian cycle, and husbandry. In Ireland the stones were gathered together and the images experienced at the focal points of the temples, marking, changing, and presenting the surrounding landscape. At Vingen and in the Norrköping area, the stones were not moved to specific places but were encountered by moving through and around the landscape itself. Appropriately, at Vingen, experiencing some of the images required one to actively stalk them, just as the Vingen hunter-fisher-gatherers of necessity stalked their prey. If one was not highly attentive to reading the signs, both the prey and the images would remain forever lost in a landscape that was only seasonally occupied and exploited. In the Norrköping landscape, some image fields were in well-known and significant locations in the landscape, natural monuments, huge stone pavements, closely associated with permanent dwellings and the collective husbandry and appropriation of domesticated resources. Others required a much more active process of stalking and seeking in order to encounter them at all in the context of an economy in which hunting, fishing, and gathering remained of considerable significance. What is being suggested here and in Chapters 2–4 is that the structuring, form, and experience of these images in these three landscapes was, in general terms but not in any deterministic sense, intimately related to the use of their wider landscapes as 'taskscapes' (Ingold 1993), to hunting, fishing, and gathering in Norway, to farming in Ireland, and to both in Sweden. This occurs in the manner in which the images are structured in relation to the rocks themselves as well as in their form and content, as discussed above.

Sensory Shifts

Part of the embodied kinaesthetic meanings of these images is conveyed through sensory shifts in their encounter in the landscape, in their changing relationships to water and the land, to rivers and the sea, to sound and silence, darkness and light, sun and shade, the odours of these places, to fire and food, touch and taste. The images in the three case studies differ not only in their form and content, but also in relation to the wider sensory worlds of which they are a part. In relation to the

Irish temples, it has been argued that the sensory experiences of touch and sound became intensified within them in a manner that contrasted with their experience from the outside. The rock carvings at Vingen were located in a place that was a huge amplifier of the sound of running water, of wind, and of thunder. The presence of the constant roar of the rapids on the Motala River constituted an important part of the auditory experience of the carving locales in their vicinity. By comparison, other carved rocks were situated in a quiet landscape. It rapidly becomes apparent, however, that every rock in each of the three landscapes has its own particular sensory mix in terms both of its material presence and the sensory skills and values required to create the images and subsequently experience and encounter them. The images are sensed, and the senses are part and parcel of the significance and meaning of the images.

The differing colours of the stones and their other manifold sensory qualities are co-presences in the social construction of the significance of the place. The literal and symbolic weight of these stones in the landscape makes each place heavy with meaning. The stark whiteness of the quartz façade at Newgrange and its distant origin constitute part of the power and force of this monument in this landscape. This captivating power, on the southern side, was directed towards the river and the bend of the Boyne, entirely apt for a water temple. The muticoloured and textured façade of Knowth was altogether different, and here the contrasts between the kerbstones and their images were fundamental. The colour as much as the architecture itself structured place and created its own topographical relationships. The transformation of the exterior of Newgrange from dull to brilliant underlines the power of this temple as a sensory technology of power and containment in relation to ancestral rituals. Similarly in the Norrköping area, the presence of the bronzed areas of the grooved mica-schist was of essential significance in relation to the depictions of bronzes on the rocks themselves, while the orientation of the grooves across the rocks became duplicated in the orientations of the long houses in contemporary settlements.

The images considered in this book make a new kind of landscape come into being, one in which the invisible, the cosmogenic world, instituted in space-time, always itself hidden from perception (one cannot perceive space-time except through its material objectification or mode of being), becomes visible through the mediation of the images. They draw out the hidden powers of the rocks on which they are inscribed and draw attention to them through the body. They create a new tactile domain on the rock surface itself across which the body moves, commingling with the specific auditory and olfactory experiences of being in and of the place.

Temporality

Knowing where the images were to be found and on which kinds of rocks they belonged was no doubt part and parcel of the constitution of both an individual body image and an image of the social body. Different kinds of bodily motion and posture were required on different rocks at different places and at different times and seasons. Thus, the rock art imagery and bodily dispositions were linked to cyclical patterns of seasonal temporality, the movements of the sun, the moon, and the stars, and conceptualisations of the cosmos. These images were obviously not created all at once but were added to over time. The addition of new images altered the experience of those who had visited previously and possibly required different bodily motions to see them. One might have had to walk farther through the landscape, visit different rocks, move in different ways between, over, and on them. Thus, the structuring of the imagery and its bodily effects would be subject to constant change over time. Some images might have been collectively experienced by everyone, in the social context of rituals and ceremonies, others by only a few persons with restrictions related to status, age, and gender. Those images entirely hidden away became part of individual and social memory, their locations and forms known only to a few or a matter of ancestral rather than living memory. The manner in which the images were experienced in the landscape would alter their power and efficacy. Some of their effects on bodily kinaesthetics had intended consequences; others, particularly when new rocks were carved or new images added to existing ones, might have had unintended effects on bodily movements and routines. After many years and seasons, the experience of the images might have been engrained as part of bodily habitus and tradition. A regular or frequent observer would know how to move and encounter various images without consciously seeking them out and would know the right way to move from rock to rock and across the rocks themselves. By contrast, for the novice or stranger (like the anthropologist today), unless being led by someone 'in the know', the process would be very different, requiring constant attention, seeking, learning, trying to work out how and why one must walk or move. It is, of course, this very process that I have tried to reconstruct, by attempting to learn something about the traces of the past through embodied experience in the present. This is not a matter of personal empathy, but a process in which the human body itself (that of the researcher, of you or I) becomes a primary methodological tool in the landscape, allowing oneself to be open to its agency and its effects. Of course, this is a contemporary experience—but then so are all experiences of the past. We inhabit the present, of which the past is a part. The individual images discussed in this book are by and large impossible to date with any certainty. We simply do not know which rock or rocks were carved first or which was the first image. What we experience today is the end of a long series of events in which temporal sequences become collapsed into space. The internal temporality of the images related to their patterns of inscription is lost to us, and we see the final result, the end of this process. But in moving through the landscape and engaging with the images, they temporally inscribe themselves in another way, through their sequences and bodily encounter. So the time of these images is no longer a matter of abstract chronological time, a matter of dates, but plays itself out in relation to our bodies and the weather and the seasons. In other words, the time of the images becomes human and humanised time, part of our contemporary experience linking together past, present, and future. Abstract linear and measurable time is the time of modernity, the time of the clock, of capital and wage labour, the time of wealth and poverty, the time-space compression of global flows of money and information, goods and services. Human, cyclical, and seasonal time is the time of the past and the time of embodied experiences, past or present. This is the time of the rock art imagery, and it is the same time in which we encounter these images today through their bodily encounter. So to experience these images phenomenologically is to relinquish the time of the present, forever the same, and reconnect ourselves to a human and humanised time of the past. It is to appreciate that the landscapes of rock art possess their own spaces and times and that these times constitute a fourth dimension of the images, experienced through the sequence of their bodily encounter. The time of the image is the time of the body at rest or in motion in relation to seasonal time. The seasonal time of the rock art imagery encountered in the Norrköping area of eastern Sweden was during the summer and autumn months, after the final April melt of the snow that had filled up and concealed the images during the dark winter period. The growth and regeneration of the land and the crops and the spring births of the animals within it would be linked with the reappearance of the carvings. Vingen is also likely to have been seasonally visited by hunter-fisher-gatherers during the summer, when the carvings would first be illuminated by the sunlight absent for much of the year. It is clear that the significance of the Irish imagery was intimately linked to calendrical rites marked by the cycles of the rising and falling of the sun and the moon in the sky, to the shortest and longest days of the year and the equinoxes. Light was integral to the kind of light, or intellectual illumination of the cosmos, provided by the images themselves. Thus, the changing seasonal colours and illumination of the landscape were intimately linked with the agency of the images.

WALKING THE PAST IN THE PRESENT

This book is a study grounded in movement, movement shaped in space-time in relation to landscapes of images. Walking the three landscapes discussed in Chapters 2–4 has been developed as an art of knowing, that is to say, thinking in and through the walk. Walking is an experience of the lived body, and the various studies have attempted to develop a technique of walking in relation to a phenomenology of the lived body. The attempt has been to gain experience of these landscapes of images from the 'inside', and theories with regard to the structure and meaning of the images are based upon such a viewpoint. Walking the landscape is an attempt to understand the landscape at a human scale. The limits of this knowledge are thus essentially the limits of the body and the manner in which this body both limits and facilitates perception. The objective is to gain an insider's knowledge of place and landscape, as opposed to a knowledge acquired by mediated representations which can only provide an outsider's perspective.

The vast majority of landscape research is thoroughly mediated by various representations and abstracted technologies. By the former I mean the representations provided by texts, photographs, paintings, sketches, maps, or, in other words, the entire discursive panoply by which we normally inform ourselves about places and landscapes. This is, in effect, all about perceiving the landscape through the minds and eyes of other people. Such representations are inevitably selective, framed (often quite literally in the borders of the painting, photograph, or map), and ideological. We encounter the landscape through its always partial representation, and such an encounter encourages us to build new texts and representations on the basis of old ones in an endless series of repetitions of the same. This is never a lived landscape but is forever fixed in the words or the images, something that becomes dead, silent, and inert, devoid of love and life. By abstracted technologies, I refer to statistical analyses of landscape involving measurement and quantification, computer simulations and the creation of virtual landscapes one might walk around in with cursor and computer screen, and the use of various forms of geographical information system technologies for landscape analysis which, like all new technologies, are popular largely for their newness rather than for the kind of information they are actually capable of providing.

The two problems I have with all such mediated approaches to the landscape are that, first, they obviously constrain and limit my possibilities for perception in that I need not leave my desk in order to learn, and, second, textual and visual representations tend to encourage the highly suspect view that landscape and landscape research are just about representation. This view recognizes that landscapes are being represented in a particular manner within a particular cultural or historical context but that these are only representations and so might always be different. Such representations are therefore essentially arbitrary and ideological, and we set about investigating this. Ultimately, in a Foucauldian sense we end up talking about the discursive construction of power, landscapes of power. The landscape itself becomes inert, a blank slate upon which culture is writ large. Such a relativist and 'postmodern' view makes perfect sense when we study the landscape through mediated forms in which stone and wood, grass and trees, the sun, the moon, and the stars, the heat of the day, or the coolness of the evening become words and images. The literary turn in anthropology in which ethnographies become just forms of writing has undoubtedly encouraged an involuted style of thinking which, rather than encouraging a meaningful encounter with landscapes, has operated as a means of escape from them. This has frequently been combined with an ocularocentric view of landscape as image.

The approach that I have undertaken demands, by contrast, that I take my own body into the landscape and allow *it*, rather than texts or images or diagrams, to mediate my encounter so that I can re-present it in a fresh way. When I feel the sun or the rain on my face, landscape becomes anything but representation; it becomes part and parcel of my lived sensual experience, of my carnal being. And it is this experience that this book has attempted to express (although the irony here is that inevitably the text produced cannot itself avoid being a representation). The sensuous character of this human experience is absolutely primary, and the form this takes in the research conducted here is the walk. There are three bases for this: (1) the material character of the walking; (2) walking as an act of gathering; and (3) the temporality of walking. I shall consider each of these in turn.

Walking and Materiality

Walking involves embodied experience, and by this term I also subsume other modes of movement such as crawling, climbing, jumping, stumbling, and so on. The character of the walk is such that it is mediated through the effects of the weather and the qualities of the light on perception. The landscape varies according to the time of the day, the day of the week, or the months and seasons of the year, whether the rain falls, the sun shines, or the wind howls, whether it is misty or clear. All these affect how I sense and relate to the qualities of the landscape. To walk is to adopt different bodily postures, sometimes upright, sometimes bent, sometimes looking up, sometimes looking down. This is, in turn, related to the surfaces on which I walk and their characteristics: hard or soft, dry or slippery, even or stony, flat or rising or falling, firm or boggy. In a stony landscape I must look down most of the time or I will fall over and bump into things; in a bog I must test every step; on a flat pavement I can move less tentatively and look straight ahead. My calf and leg muscles sense and register various degrees of energy and strain. These direct sensory relations engage my body as part of the landscape. I may feel that it has been very easy to reach this place and very difficult to reach that one. This directly affects the manner in which I think about places, landscapes, relationships. Sometimes on the walk I may find myself high up on a hilltop with a panoramic view of the world with a circular horizon. I can see a great deal of the sky. I am exposed to the wind and the elements. At other times I might be in a sheltered valley. My lateral vision is restricted by the valley sides, as is my view of the sky; my senses of sight and sound and smell reach out before and behind me to a farther horizon line. The power of the wind and rain may be broken. I feel that I am in a different world.

Perceptive experience as mediated by the body in this manner is understood as always changing and processual in character. It inevitably has profound effects not only on what I can perceive but on what I am able to think and emotionally feel. My body becomes the measure of all things in relation to me and the possibilities, or affordances, and constraints that the landscape provides. I am a part of that which I seek to describe and understand. I rapidly learn that in order to inhabit a landscape, I need to know how to walk in it, and that certain practices of walking are appropriate in particular places at particular times and seasons. After a while they become routinised and embodied; the landscape becomes part of me in a way that is never possible if I encounter it from a car or a train or an aeroplane, where my experience is more or less limited to the visual appreciation of something shut away and distanced from my physical being.

Gathering

Walking is always a gathering together of places encountered along the way and the sequences in which they are encountered and the effects these have on my body. A walk is thus a material journey and a temporal narrative. A walk gathers together the landscape in relation to my body. A walk gathers together visionscapes and smell-scapes and touchscapes and soundscapes and tastescapes in relation to my body, always in various degrees of association and intimacy: it has synaesthetic effects.

A walk not only gathers together and mediates places and their material proper-ties, including the weather, along its path but also events, things that take place, social encounters with people and plants and animals. It was Bergson's fundamental insight, discussed in Chapter 1, that there is no perception that is not replete with memories. Such memories are almost always place-bound; everything is always somewhere, in some place with its thresholds, boundaries, and transitions to other places. The changing human and non-human horizons of the walk continually alter my under-standing, so much so that one walk will provide a whole series of expectations about what may be encountered on another. My expectations may be fulfilled or continu-ally dashed or perhaps exceeded. Thus, to walk is to fuse past with present with future. Walking thus gathers known past histories, practices, and traditions; follow-ing a path (for the most part), I am walking where others have walked, in the foot-steps of previous generations and the ancestors. The paths I take may, in this sense, be weak or strong, well-trodden and known, or new and fragile. Walking a landscape is thus to gather together through my body its weathers, its topographies, its people, histories, traditions, and identities. The walk gathers itself through my own body to create my own identity. In this sense, the sum of my embodied being is the sum of the walks I have taken and what and whom I have encountered along the way.

The Past in the Present

Until very recently in modern industrialised societies, everybody walked and for most of the time. Walking was life. To live was to walk, to be a socialised being was to walk and work, usually involving particular practices of walking, whether hunting or gath-ering or fishing and farming, in the landscape. Being in that landscape, being part of that landscape, inevitably resulted in the kind of intimate knowledge of it that is large-ly lost today. Walking the past in the present is an attempt to regain at least some of that intimacy and lost experience. It is simply to walk the landscape as earlier peoples would have done and to familiarise oneself through the process of walking in it. The contemporary skin of the land has itself more often than not been irrevocably altered, but its bones—the hills and the valleys, springs, river courses and coasts, high and low-lying areas, rocky and steep or flat places—are often the same.

The walk unites the walker and the landscape in a lived dialectic of being and becoming, acting and being acted upon. In the process of walking we communicate with the landscape that surrounds us, not with words but through our bodies. To experience the walk is to experience our own carnal bodies. My walk involves embodied immersion in a landscape. By contrast, I am not embodied in the same sense in any image or artefact I might produce. It is always externalized, out there, apart from my body. I walk my sentient embodied existence in a lived metaphysic. Walking is in and of the body; it cannot take place outside of the body. It is a wholly lived and participatory corporeal practice. The body cannot be reduced to the status of an object because it is always a minded and mindful body, and the relation is internal. The mind is not external to the body controlling it, as it were, from the outside, but part of it. Thus, thought is of, through, and in the body. The body is lived through its actions, and movement is both the medium and outcome of embodied knowledge. Walking the past in the present thus involves a material experience and a mode of gathering together of this experience in a temporal mode of narrative understanding.

A new walk may jog one's memory of a previous walk, encounter, or understanding. It is a process of linking different kinds of experiences. While the walk is obviously in one sense a personal experience, it is directed to a broader, more generalised understanding in relation to characteristics and qualities of the walk that stand out not only for oneself but for others. Only when approaching a landscape from a certain specific direction, for example, does one see that distant hill for the first time, or notice that the rocks look far more jagged from this vantage point than from that, or hear that this place in the landscape echoes, whereas another does not, and so on. Thus, the art of walking the landscape is one in which experience of the particular leads to considerations of the general and the gradual building up of a holistic interpretive account through comparing and contrasting and reflecting on these experiences.

The Phenomenological Walk

The kind of walk described throughout this book is what I will term the 'phenomenological walk'. This is the walk of the walk, a walk that may be undertaken either in relation to a study of the present or of the past. It is an attempt to walk from the inside, a participatory understanding produced by taking one's own body into places and landscapes and an opening up of one's perceptual sensibilities and experience. Such a walk always needs to start from a bracketing off of mediated representations of landscapes and places. It is an attempt to learn by describing perceptual experiences as precisely as possible as they unfold during the course of the walk. As such, it unfolds in the form of a story or a narrative that needs to be written as one walks. Walking and writing become synonymous acts, as language and knowing are synonymous. This is simply because the act of writing slows experience down and focuses attention. To write is always to write about something. To be able to write, one must look, listen, smell, and feel that which is in reach. Filming the walk while walking it (except afterwards on another walk) as an alternative, or equivalent, is entirely problematic because one cannot film before one knows how to look and how to hear, and it can only frame and encase visual and auditory perception. So one walks in order to be able to write; one writes in order to be able to walk. Different landscapes provide affordances and constraints for different forms of motion and perception. Walking the landscape allows that landscape to exert its own agency in relation to my body. There are the shifting and changing horizons beyond which I cannot see, the hills and valleys that come into sight and disappear, the specific places where monuments and settlements were built, places for the living and places of burial and death, the streams and rivers I must cross or navigate. My perception and understanding are intimately related to these material presences and absences and gradually develop as a structure of feeling and an awareness of the material character of place and landscape. Walking the landscape takes time, and in principle, the more time and care one takes in this art of walking, the more that is likely to be understood. As I walk the landscape, this very landscape becomes embodied in my being, unfolds itself, and I can begin to build up a comparative understanding of places in that landscape and their relationships: similarities and differences. How similar is that river valley to this? How does the location of the imagery on this rock or temple compare with that one? What influence might that hill or that river have on places deemed suitable for inscribing images in the landscape?

It is only after walking in a landscape that I can learn how to see, and more broadly, sense that landscape through my body, for the act of walking is sensing that landscape at a human pace. The encounter is radically different from those kinds of speeded-up and essentially visual experiences available from a vehicle. I can stop, turn, pause, change direction. I do not need to keep to the road. The process of walking is one in which the landscape teaches me, and it opens up my experience to this landscape. I am always surprised at first and cannot predict what I will find. After I have walked the landscape, places and their relationships become much more predictable. I know how to find my way, the kinds of relationships to expect, and those that will not occur.

The phenomenological walk involves a gathering together of synaesthetic and material and social sensory experiences as they unfold in the sequence and duration of the walk. It shows what is there from the perspective of the flesh, from embodied experiences. Such a walk is utterly different from a real walk in space-time, since it involves temporal expansion. Attempting to write such a walk involves pause, looking around, sensing place from different perspectives along the route, going back as well as moving forward. There is always sensory overload, and decisions have to be made with regard to what appears to be significant. Such a walk takes time and is far from spontaneous. It is an analytical walk that selects from experiences often gathered at different times to create the narrative. The process of walking is one in which one perceives in order to be able to know. To know is to know how to perceive, and bodily perception is a form of cultural knowledge. As well as describing some perceptual experiences, it must inevitably filter out or ignore others. The words never capture experience. They can only evoke, and in the final result, the phenomenological text is inevitably another mediated representation, for all representations are, of course, mediated.

The present is where we meet the past in and through the medium of our carnal bodies. We meet then, *here*, in a place and in a landscape, in stasis and in movement, through the medium of the walk. The phenomenological walk is a performative kinaesthetic walk connecting past to present, here to then and now. It involves a distillation of perceptive experience, of embodied memories that sit in the body rather than in the mind. Through movement in it, the landscape effectively writes itself in me by virtue of my participatory experience in it. The images discussed here have been described in terms of the perception of the landscape as experienced through the body, but the account is not personal in intent. The writing is propelled by a generalising imperative to try to describe what is fundamental to the imagery, being considered from a bodily point of view. This involves not only an attempt to describe what is there, but also conceptual reflection in relation to that experience. The descriptions undertaken are inevitably based upon personal experience, but the experiences being described are those that can be held in common with others—in other words, shared and generalised beyond the autobiographical self, in the form of what I have termed the phenomenological walk.

Landscape is a set of placial relationships in which the experience of one place, landmark, carved rock, or monument depends on its relationship with another and its mode or directionality of encounter. The phenomenological walk attempts to annotate and record these experiences such as the main direction taken, intermediate directions, going up or going down, moving to the left or right, the manner in which horizon lines increase or recede with reference to other places in the landscape, the different forms of bodily motion required, the sounds and smells and tactile experiences encountered along the way. For such a walk to be successful, the landscape needs to be as familiar as it would be to a hunter. Just as hunters need an intimate knowledge of their game and their movements, a phenomenologist needs to hunt out the forms and characteristics of the landscape and the places and paths within it that constitute it. This is a move from naïve to informed experience. One ideally tries to understand a place from the point of view of moving towards it or away from it, from another place at different times, days, seasons, directions, orientations, sensory points of view. Such a practice of walking encourages an account stressing a progressional or syntagmatic ordering of reality in which sequence and succession become primary in the account rather than an abstracted categorical ordering of landscape in terms of geology, topographic features, settlement patterns, and the like.

Walking is thus fundamentally linked with orientation. Having a sense of orientation, knowing where to go, is dependent on familiar and place-bound memories. To be orientated in a landscape is to know it through these embodied experiences. Being a walk of the walk, a walk informed by previous walks, the phenomenological walk is always a composite walk, a synthesis of temporarily sequenced perceptions that must be imaginatively understood. Thus, it has an inherently ambiguous character in relation to a single real walk, insofar as it records much more than could ever be perceived or remembered and far less as regards various embodied sensory experiences. It thus has a simultaneous character of excess and indeterminance. It attempts to embrace an aura of the real by being surreal, through writing the kinaesthetic experiences of the body in motion, in being, and becoming.

References

Almgren, O. (1927). *Hällristningar och Kultbruk*. Stockholm.

Bäckman, L., and Hultkrantz, Å. (1978). *Studies in Lapp Shamanism*. Stockholm: Almqvist and Wiksell.

Bakka, E. (1973). 'Om aldern på veideristningane'. *Viking* 37: 151–87.

— (1975). 'Geologically dated Arctic rock carvings at Hammer near Steinkjer in Nørd-Trondelag. *Arkeologiske Skrifter* 2: 7–48. Historisk Museum, Universitet i Bergen.

— (1979). 'On shoreline dating of Arctic rock carvings in Vingen, western Norway'. *Norwegian Archaeological Review* 12 (2): 115–22.

Bergson, H. (1991). *Matter and Memory*. New York: Zone Books.

Bergström, R., and Kornfält, K-A. (1973). *Beskrivning till Geologiska Kartbladet Norrköping NW*. Stockholm.

Bergsvik, K. (2002). *Arkeologiske Undersøkelser ved Skatestraumen I*. Arkeologiske avhandingar og rapporter fra Universitet i Bergen 7. Bergen.

Bermudez, J-L., A. Marcel, and N. Eilan (eds.) (1995). *The Body and the Self*. Cambridge, Massachusetts: MIT Press.

Bertilsson, U. (1987). *The Rock Carvings of Northern Bohuslän: Spatial Structures and Social Symbols*. Studies in Archaeology 7. Stockholm: University of Stockholm.

Bing, K. (1912). 'Helleristningsfund ved gaarden Vingen i Rugsund, Ytre Nordjord'. *Oldtiden, Tidskrift for Norsk forhistorie* II: 25–39.

Boas, F. (1955). *Primitive Art*. New York: Dover.

Bøe, J. (1932). *Felszeichnungen im westliche Norwegen I. Vingen und Henøya*. Bergens Museums Skrifter 15. Bergen.

Borna-Ahlkvist, H. (2002). *Hällristarnas Hem*. Skrifter 42. Stockholm: Riksantikvarieämbetets Förlag.

Borna-Ahlkvist, H., L. Lindgren-Hertz, and U. Stålblom (1998). *Pryssgården. Från Stenålder till Medeltid*. Riksantikvarieämbetet Rapport 1998, no. 13. Linköping.

Broström, S-G., and K. Ihrestam (1993). Rapport över inventering och dokumentation av Hällristningar utefter väg E4:as nya sträckning förbi Norrköping sträckan Borgs kyrka—Åby. Unpublished report. Stockholm: Antikvarisk-Topografiska Arkivet.

Bourdieu, P. (1977). *Outline of a Theory of Practice*. Cambridge: Cambridge University Press.

Bradley, R. (1989a). 'Deaths and entrances: A contextual analysis of megalithic art'. *Current Anthropology* 30: 68–75.

— (1989b). 'Darkness and light in the design of megalithic tombs'. *Oxford Journal of Archaeology* 8: 251–59.

— (2000). *An Archaeology of Natural Places*. London: Routledge.

Brennan, M. (1983). *The Stars and the Stones. Ancient Art and Astronomy in Ireland*. London: Thames and Hudson.

Breuil, H. (1934). 'Presidential address for 1934'. *Proceedings of the Prehistoric Society* 7: 289–332.

Buczacki, S. (ed.) (2002). *Fauna Britannica*. London: Hamlyn.

Burenhult, G. (1973). *The Rock Carvings of Götaland*. Acta Archaeologica Lundensia. Series in 4Å number 8. Lund: Rudolf Habelt Verlag.

Burton, S. (1969). 'The wild red deer'. In S. Burton, *Exmoor*. London: Robert Hale.

Campbell, S. (2001). 'The captivating agency of art: Many ways of seeing'. In C. Pinney and N. Thomas (eds.), *Beyond Aesthetics. Art and the Technologies of Enchantment*, pp. 117–36. Oxford: Berg.

Carlsson, E-S. (1960). *En Östgötsk bronsåldersrakkniv*, Tor VI: 58–62.

Chapman, N. (1991). *Deer*. Guildford: Whittet Books.

Clutton-Brock, T., F. Guiness, and S. Albon (1982). *Red Deer*. Oxford: Oxford University Press.

Cochrane, A. (2005). 'A taste of the unexpected: Subverting mentalities through the motifs and settings of Irish passage tombs'. In D. Hoffman, J. Mills, and A. Cochrane (eds.), *Elements of Being: Mentalities, Identities and Movements*, pp. 5–19. Oxford: British Archaeological Reports International Series 1437.

Coffey, G. (1912 [1977]). *Newgrange and Other Incised Tumuli in Ireland*. Poole: Dolphin Press.

Cooney, G. (2000). *Landscapes of Neolithic Ireland*. London: Routledge.

Crawford, O. (1957). *The Eye Goddess*. London.

Devlet, E. (2001). 'Rock art and the material culture of Siberian and central Asian shamanism'. In N. Price (ed.), *The Archaeology of Shamanism*, pp. 43–55. London: Routledge.

Dronfield, J. (1995a). 'Subjective vision and the source of Irish megalithic art'. *Antiquity* (September): 539–49.

— (1995b). 'Migraine, light and hallucinogens: The neurocognitive basis of Irish megalithic art'. *Oxford Journal of Archaeology* 14: 261–75.

— (1996). 'Entering alternative realities: Cognition, art and architecture in Irish passage-tombs'. *Archaeological Review from Cambridge* 6(1): 37–72.

Edsman, C-M. (1965). 'The hunter, the games and the unseen powers. Lappish and Finnish bear rites'. In H. Hvarfner (ed.), *Hunting and Fishing.* Luleå: Norrbottens Museum.

Eilan, N., A. Marcel, and J-L. Bermudez (1995). 'Self-consciousness and the body: An interdisciplinary introduction'. In J-L Bermudez, A. Marcel, and N. Eilan (eds.), *The Body and the Self,* pp. 1–28. Cambridge, Massachusetts: MIT Press.

Eogan, G. (1984). *Excavations at Knowth 1.* Dublin: Royal Irish Academy.

— (1986). *Knowth.* London: Thames and Hudson.

— (1996). 'Pattern and place: A preliminary study of the decorated kerbstones at Site 1, Knowth, Co. Meath, and their comparative setting'. *Revue Archéologique de l'Ouest,* Supplément 8: 97–104.

— (1997). 'Overlays and underlays: Aspects of megalithic art succession at Brugh na Boinne, Ireland'. *Brigantium* 10: 217–34.

— (1998). 'Knowth before Knowth'. *Antiquity* 72: 162–72.

— (1999). 'Megalithic art and society'. *Proceeedings of the Prehistoric Society* 65: 415–446.

Eogan, G., and Aboud, J. (1990). 'Diffuse picking in megalithic art'. *Revue Archéologique de l'Ouest,* Supplément 2: 121–40.

Falk, P. (1995). 'Written in the flesh'. *Body and Society* 1(1): 95–105.

Faris, J. (1971). *Nuba Personal Art.* London: Duckworth.

Fett, P. (1941). 'Nye ristningar i Nordfjord. Vingelven og Fura'. *Bergens Museum Årsbok* 6:1–9. Bergen.

Forge, A. (1970). 'Learning to see in New Guinea'. In P. Mayer (ed.), *Socialisation: The View from Social Anthropology,* pp. 269–91. London: Tavistock.

— (1979). 'The problem of meaning in art'. In S. Mead (ed.), *Exploring the Visual Art of Oceania,* pp. 278–85. Honolulu: University of Hawaii Press.

Foster, H., R. Krauss, Y-A. Bois, and B. Buchloh (2004). *Art since 1900: Modernism, Antimodernism, Postmodernism.* London: Thames and Hudson.

Foucault, M. (1977). *Discipline and Punish.* New York: Vintage.

Fowler, C., and V. Cummings (2003). 'Places of transformation: Building monuments from water and stone in the Neolithic of the Irish Sea'. *Journal of the Royal Anthropological Institute* 9(1): 1–20.

Fraser, S. (1998). 'The public forum and the space between: The materiality of social strategy in the Irish Neolithic'. *Proceeedings of the Prehistoric Society* 64: 203–24.

Gell, A. (1985). 'Style and meaning in Umeda dance'. In P. Spencer (ed.), *Society and the Dance: The Social Anthropology of Process and Performance.* Cambridge: Cambridge University Press. (Reprinted in Gell 1999: 135–58.)

— (1992). 'The enchantment of technology and the technology of enchantment'. In J. Coote and A. Shelton (eds.), *Anthropology, Art and Aesthetics*, pp. 40–66. Oxford: Oxford University Press.

— (1995). 'The language of the forest: Landscape and phonological iconism in Umeda'. In E. Hirsch and M. O'Hanlon (eds.), *The Anthropology of Landscape*, pp. 232–54. Oxford: Oxford University Press.

— (1998). *Art and Agency: An Anthropological Theory*. Oxford: Oxford University Press.

— (1999). *The Art of Anthropology: Essays and Diagrams*. London: Athlone.

Gibbs, R. (1994). *The Poetics of Mind*. Cambridge: Cambridge University Press.

Gil, J. (1998). *Metamorphoses of the Body*. Minneapolis: University of Minnesota Press.

Gibson, J. (1968). *The Senses Considered as Perceptual Systems*. London: George Allen and Unwin.

— (1986). *The Ecological Approach to Visual Perception*. New Jersey: Lawrence Erlbaum Associates.

Gjessing, G. (1932). *Arktiske helleristninger i Nord-Norge*. Institutt for Sammenlignende Kulturforskning Serie B: 21. Oslo.

Goldhahn, J. (2002). 'Roaring rocks: An audiovisual perspective on hunter-gatherer engravings in northern Sweden and Scandinavia'. *Norwegian Archaeological Review* 35: 29–61.

Guest, A. (1997). *Dance Notation: The Process of Recording Movement on Paper*. London: Dance Books.

Hagen, A. (1969). *Studier i vestnorsk bergkunst. Ausevik i Flora*. Årsbok for Universitet i Bergen. Humanistisk Serie 3. Bergen.

— (1976). *Bergkunst*. Oslo: Cappelens.

Hanson, F. (1983). 'When the map is the territory: Art in Maori culture'. In D. Washburn (ed.), *Structure and Cognition in Art*, pp. 74–89. Cambridge: Cambridge University Press.

Hallström, G. (1938). *Monumental Art of Northern Europe from the Stone Age. The Norwegian Localities*. Stockholm: Almqvist and Wiksell.

— (1960). *Monumental Art of Northern Sweden from the Stone Age*. Stockholm: Almqvist and Wiksell.

Hauptman Wahlgren, K. (2000). 'The lonesome sailing ship. Reflections on the rock carvings in Sweden and their interpreters'. *Current Swedish Archaeology* 8: 67–96.

— (2002). *Bilder av Betydelse*. Stockholm Studies in Archaeology 23. Stockholm: Bricoleur Press

Helskog, K. (1987). 'Selective depictions: A study of 3,500 years of rock carvings from Arctic Norway and their relation to Saami drums'. In I. Hodder (ed.), *Archaeology as Long-Term History*, pp. 17–30. Cambridge: Cambridge University Press.

— (1999). 'The shore connection. Cognitive landscape and communication with rock carvings in northernmost Europe'. *Norwegian Archaeological Review* 32: 73–94.

Herity, M. (1974). *Irish Passage Graves*. Dublin: Irish University Press.

Ingold, T. (1993). 'The temporality of landscape'. *World Archaeology* 25(2): 152–74.

— (2004). 'Culture on the ground: The world perceived through the feet'. *Journal of Material Culture* 9(3): 315–40.

Jay, M. (1993). *Downcast Eyes: The Denigration of Vision in Twentieth-Century French Thought*. Berkeley: University of California Press.

Johnson, G. (ed.) (1993). *The Merleau-Ponty Aesthetics Reader: Philosophy and Painting*. Evanston: Northwestern University Press.

Jones, A. (2006). 'By way of illustration: Art, memory and materiality in the Irish Sea and beyond'. In V. Cummings and C. Fowler (eds.) *The Neolithic of the Irish Sea*, pp. 202–213. Oxford: Oxbow Books.

Jönsson, S. (1980). 'Återfynd och nyfynd av hällristningar i Norrköpingsområdet'. *Östergötland* 1980: 61–73.

Kaliff, A. (1995a). *Ringeby. En Kult—och Gravplats från Yngre Bronsåldern*. Riksantikvarieämbetet 1995, no. 51. Linköping.

— (1995b). 'Gravskick och eskatologi'. In M. Larsson and A. Toll (eds.), *Samhällsstruktur och Förändring Under Bronsåldern*. Norrköping: Norrköpings Stadsmuseum.

— (1999). *Arkeologi i Östergötland. Scener ur ett Lanskaps Förhistoria*. Occasional Papers in Archaeology 20. Uppsala: Uppsala Universitet.

Keane, W. (2003). 'Semiotics and the social analysis of material things'. *Language and Communication* 23: 409–25.

— (2005). 'Signs are not the garb of meaning: On the social analysis of material things'. In D. Miller (ed.), *Materiality*, pp. 182–205. London: Duke University Press.

Korn, S. (1978). 'The formal analysis of visual systems as exemplified by a study of *Abelam* (Papua New Guinea) painting'. In M. Greenhalgh and V. Megaw (eds.), *Art in Society*, pp. 163–74. London: Duckworth.

Kramrisch, S. (1976). *The Hindu Temple*. 2 vols. Delhi: Motilal Banarsidass.

Laban, R. (1950). *The Mastery of Movement*. London: MacDonald and Evans.

— (1966). *Choreutics*. London: MacDonald and Evans.

Lakoff, G., and M. Johnson (1980). *Metaphors We Live By*. Chicago: University of Chicago Press.

— (1999). *Philosophy in the Flesh*. New York: Basic Books.

Lakoff, G., and Turner, M. (1989). *More than Cool Reason: A Field Guide to Poetic Metaphor*. Chicago: University of Chicago Press.

Larsson, T. (1986). *The Bronze Age Metalwork in Southern Sweden*. Archaeology and Environment 6. Umeå.

— (1993). *Vistad: Kring en befäst gård i Östergötland och Östersjökontakter under yngre bronsåldern*. Studia Archaeologica Universitatis Umensis 4. Umeå.

— (1995). 'Maktstrukturer och allianssytem in Östgötsk bronsålder'. In M. Larsson and A. Toll (eds.), *Samhällsstruktur och Förändring Under Bronsåldern*. Norrköping: Norrköpings Stadsmuseum.

Layard, J. (1936). 'Maze dances and the ritual of the labyrinth in Malekula'. *Folklore* 47: 123–70.

Layton, R. (2003). 'Art and agency: A reassessment'. *Journal of the Royal Anthropological Institute* 9(3): 447–65.

Lévi-Strauss, C. (1966). *The Savage Mind*. London: Weidenfeld and Nicholson.

— (1969). *The Raw and the Cooked*. London: Jonathan Cape.

Lewis-Williams, D., and T. Dowson (1993). 'On vision and power in the Neolithic: Evidence from the decorated monuments'. *Current Anthropology* 34(1): 55–65.

Lewis-Williams, D., and D. Pearce (2005). *Inside the Neolithic Mind*. London: Thames and Hudson.

Lødøen, T. (2001). 'Contextualizing rock art in order to investigate Stone Age ideology. Results from an ongoing project'. In K. Helskog (ed.), *Theoretical Perspectives in Rock Art Research*. Oslo: Novus forlag.

Lindeblad, K., and A-L. Nielsen (1993). *Herrebro—hällristningar och marknad. Archaeologiska undersökningar av fornlämning 51 i Borgs socken, Östegötland*. Linköping: Riksantikvarieämbetet.

Lødøen, T. (2003). 'Late Mesolithic rock art and expressions of ideology'. In L. Larsson, H. Kindgren, K. Knutsson, D. Loeffler, and A. Åkerlund (eds.), *Mesolithic on the Move*. Oxford: Oxbow Books.

Lødøen, T., and G. Mandt (in prep.). *Et naturens kolossalmuseum for helleristninger.*

Lopez y Royo, A. (2005). 'Embodying a site: Choreographing Prambanan'. *Journal of Material Culture* 10(1): 31–48.

Losche, D. (1995). 'The Sepik gaze: Iconographic interpretation of Abelam form'. *Social Analysis* 38: 47–60.

Lundström, P. (1965). *Gravfälten vid Fiskeby i Norrköping I. Studier kring ett totalundersökt komplex*. Kungl. Vitterhets Historie och Antikvitets Akademien. Stockholm: Almqvist & Wiksell.

— (1970). *Gravfälten vid Fiskeby i Norrköping II. Studier kring ett totalundersökt komplex*. Kungl. Vitterhets Historie och Antikvitets Akademien. Stockholm: Almqvist & Wiksell.

Malmer, M. (1981). *A Chorological Study of North European Rock Art*. Antikvariska Serien 32. Stockholm: KVHAA,.

Mandt, G. (1991). *Vestnorske ristninger i tid og rom: Kronologiske, Korologiske og Kintekstuelle Studier 1-2*. Ph.D. dissertation, University of Bergen.

— (1995). 'Alternative analogies in rock art interpretation: The west Norwegian case'. In K. Helskog and B. Olsen (eds.), *Perceiving Rock Art: Social and Political Perspectives*, pp. 263–91. Oslo: Novus forlag.

— (1998). 'Vingen revisited: A gendered perspective on "hunters'" rock art'. In L. Larsson and B. Stjernquist (eds.), *The World-View of Prehistoric Man*. Kungl. Vitterhets Historie och Antikvitets Akademien 40. Stockholm.

— (1999). 'Tilbakeblikk på Vingen. Forskning—Forvaltning—Naering'. In A. Gustafsson and H. Karlsson (eds.), *Glyfer och arkeologiska rum—en vänbok till Jarl Nordbladh*. Gotarc Series A vol. 3. Göteborg: Department of Archaeology, Göteborg University.

— (2001). 'Women in disguise or male manipulation? Aspects of gender symbolism in rock art'. In K. Helskog (ed.), *Theoretical Perspectives in Rock Art Research*. Oslo: Novus forlag.

Mandt, G., and T. Lødøen (2005). 'Vingen i Bremanger "et naturens kolossalmusaeum for helleristninger!"'. In G. Mandt and T. Lødøen, *Bergkunst Helleristningar i Noreg*. Oslo: Det Norske Samlaget.

Massumi, B. (2002). *Parables for the Virtual: Movement, Affect, Sensation*. London: Duke University Press.

Mauss, M. (1979). 'Techniques of the body'. In M. Mauss, *Sociology and Psychology: Essays by Marcel Mauss*, pp. 95–123. Translated by Ben Brewster. London and Boston: Routledge and Kegan Paul. (First published in 1935.)

McMann, J. (1993). *Loughcrew: The Cairns. A Guide*. Oldecastle: After Hour Books.

— (1994). 'Forms of power: Dimensions of an Irish megalithic landscape'. *Antiquity* 68: 525–44.

Meigan, I, D. Simpson, and B. Hartwell (2002). 'Newgrange: Sourcing of its granitic cobbles'. *Archaeology Ireland* XVI: 32–35.

Merleau-Ponty, M. (1962a). (Untitled contribution to the Bergson centennial in Paris). In T. Hanna (ed.), *The Bergsonian Heritage*, pp. 133–49. New York: Columbia University Press.

— (1962b). *The Phenomenology of Perception*. London: Routledge.

— (1973). *The Visible and the Invisible*. Evanston: Northwestern University Press.

— (1993a). 'Cézanne's doubt'. In G. Johnson (ed.), *The Merleau-Ponty Aesthetics Reader: Philosophy and Painting*, pp. 59–75. Evanston: Northwestern University Press.

— (1993b). 'Eye and mind'. In G. Johnson (ed.), *The Merleau-Ponty Aesthetics Reader: Philosophy and Painting*, pp. 121–50. Evanston: Northwestern University Press.

— (1993c). 'Indirect language and the voices of silence'. In G. Johnson (ed.), *The Merleau-Ponty Aesthetics Reader: Philosophy and Painting*, pp. 76–120. Evanston: Northwestern University Press.

Mézec, B. (1989). 'A structural analysis of the late stone age petroglyphs at Vingen, Norway'. Unpublished M.A. dissertation, University College London.

Michael, M. (2000). 'These boots are made for walking . . . Mundane technology, the body and human-environment relations'. *Body and Society* 6 (3/4): 107–26.

Mitchell, F. (1992). 'Notes on some non-local cobbles at the entrances to the passage-graves at Newgrange and Knowth, county Meath'. *Journal of the Royal Society of Antiquaries of Ireland* 122: 128–45.

— (1995). 'Did the tide once flow as far as Newgrange?' *Living Heritage*, Vol. XII: 34.

Mitchell, J. (1996). 'What do pictures *really* want? *October* 77: 71–82.

Moroney, A-M. (1999). *Dowth: Winter Sunsets*. Drogheda: Flax Mill Publications.

Morphy, H. (1991). *Ancestral Connections*. Chicago: University of Chicago Press.

Munn, N. (1973). 'The spatial presentation of cosmic order in Walbiri iconography'. In A. Forge (ed.), *Primitive Art and Society*, pp. 193–220. Oxford: Oxford University Press.

— (1986). *The Fame of Gawa*. Cambridge: Cambridge University Press.

Nordbladh, J. (1980). *Glyfer och Rum: Kring Hällristningar i Kville*. Göteborg: Göteborgs Universitet.

Nordén, A. (1925). *Östergötlands Bronsålder*. Linköping: Henric Carlsson.

Nordenskjöld, C. (1870–1873; 1876). *Östergötlands minnesmärken*. Stockholm: Antikvarisk Topografiska Arkivetet.

Olsen, A., and S. Alsaker (1984). 'Greenstone and diabase utilization in the Stone Age of western Norway: Technological and socio-cultural aspects of axe and adze production and distribution'. *Norwegian Archaeological Review* 17(2): 71–103.

Ouzman, S. (2001). 'Seeing is deceiving: Rock art and the non-visual'. *World Archaeology* 33(2): 237–56.

O'Kelly, C. (1973). 'Passage-grave art in the Boyne valley'. *Proceedings of the Prehistoric Society* 39: 354–82.

— (1982). 'Corpus of Newgrange art'. In M. O'Kelly, *Newgrange*, pp. 146–85. London: Thames and Hudson.

O' Kelly, M. (1982). *Newgrange*. London: Thames and Hudson.

O'Kelly, M., and C. O'Kelly (1983). 'The tumulus of Dowth, co. Meath'. *Proceedings of the Royal Irish Academy* 113: 136–90.

O'Shaughnessy, B. (1995). 'Proprioception and the body image'. In J-L Bermudez, A. Marcel, and N. Eilan (eds.), *The Body and the Self*, pp. 175–203. Cambridge, Massachusetts: MIT Press.

O'Sullivan, M. (1986). 'Approaches to passage tomb art'. *Journal of the Royal Society of Antiquaries of Ireland* 116: 68–83.

— (1993). 'Recent investigations at Knockroe passage tomb'. *Journal of the Royal Society of Antiquaries of Ireland* 123: 5–18.

— (1996). 'Megalithic art in Ireland and Brittany: Divergence or convergence?' *Revue Archéologique de l'Ouest*, Supplément 8: 81–96.

— (1997). 'On the meaning of megalithic art'. *Brigantium* 10: 23–35.

— (1998). 'Retrieval and revision in the interpretation of megalithic art'. *Archaeological Review from Cambridge* 15(1): 37–48.

— (2002). 'The Boyne and beyond: A review of megalithic art in Ireland'. In R. Joussaume, L. Laporte, and C. Scarre (eds.), *Origine et Développement du mégalithisme de l'Ouest de L'Europe*, pp. 651–88. Bugon: Musée des Tumulus de Bougon.

— (2004). 'Little and large: Comparing Knockroe with Knowth'. In H. Roche, E. Grogan, J. Bradley, J. Coles, and B. Rafferty (eds.), *From Megaliths to Metals: Essays in Honour of George Eogan*, pp. 44–50. Oxford: Oxbow.

Pierce, C. (1955). *Philosophical Writings of Pierce*. Edited by J. Buchler. New York: Dover.

Pinney, C. (2004). *Images of the Gods. The Printed Image and Political Struggle in India*. London: Reaktion Books.

— (2006). 'Four types of visual culture'. In C. Tilley, W. Keane, S. Kuchler, M. Rowlands, and P. Spyer (eds.), *Handbook of Material Culture*, pp. 131–44. London: Sage.

Pinney, C., and N. Thomas (eds.) (2001). *Beyond Aesthetics: Art and the Technologies of Enchantment*. Oxford: Berg.

Prior, R. (1987). *Deer Watch*. Newton Abbot: David and Charles.

Selinge, K-G. (1985). 'Om dokumentation av hällristningar. Metodiska synpunkter med östgötsk exempel'. *Fornvännen* 80: 97–120.

— (1989). 'Östergötland'. In S. Janson, E. Lundberg, and U. Bertilsson (eds.), *Hällristningar och hällmålningar i Sverige*, pp. 147–65. Stockholm: Forum.

Shee Twohig, E. (1981). *The Megalithic Art of Western Europe*. Oxford: Clarendon Press.

— (1996). 'Context and content of Irish passage tomb art'. *Revue Archéologique de l'Ouest*, Supplément 8:67–80.

— (2000). 'Frameworks for the megalithic art of the Boyne valley'. In A. Desmond, G. Johnson, M. McCarthy, J. Sheehan, and E. Shee Twohig (eds.), *New Agendas in Irish Prehistory*, pp. 89–106. Bray: Wordwell.

Sheridan, A. (1986). 'Megaliths and megalomania: An account and interpretation of passage tombs in Ireland'. *Journal of Irish Archaeology* 3: 17–30.

Sheringham, C. (1973). *The Integrative Action of the Nervous System*. New York: Arno Press.

Stålblom, U. (1994). *Klinga—Ett gravfält. Slutundersökningar av ett gravfält och bebyggelselämningar från bronsålder och äldre järnålder.* Riksantikvarieämbetet 1994, no. 11. Linköping.

— (1998). 'Fynden från Pryssgården'. In Borna-Ahlkvist, H., L. Lindgren-Hertz, and U. Stålblom, *Pryssgården. Från Stenålder till Medeltid.* Riksantikvarieämbetet Rapport 1998, no. 13. Linköping.

Stewart, N. (1998). 'Re-languaging the body: Phenomenological description and the dance image'. *Performance Research* 3(2): 42–53.

Stout, G. (2002). *Newgrange and the Bend of the Boyne.* Cork: Cork University Press.

Strathern, M. (1990). 'Artefacts of history: Events and the interpretation of images'. In J. Siikala (ed.), *Culture and History in the Pacific.* Finnish Anthropological Society Transactions 27: 25–44. Helsinki.

Thomas, J. (1992). 'Monuments, movement, and the context of megalithic art'. In N. Sharples and A. Sheridan (eds.), *Vessels for the Ancestors*, pp. 143–55. Edinburgh: Edinburgh University Press.

Thomas, J., and C. Tilley (1993). 'The torso and the axe: Symbolic structures in the Neolithic of Brittany'. In C. Tilley (ed.), *Interpretative Archaeology*, pp. 225–326. Oxford: Berg.

Thorseth, I., T. Lødøen, T. Torsvik, and G. Mandt (eds.) (2001). *Sikring av Bergkunst. Forvitringsfaktorer og bevaringstiltak.* Bergen: Bergkunstrapporter fra Universitetet i Bergen 2.

Tilley, C. (1991). *Material Culture and Text: The Art of Ambiguity.* London: Routledge.

— (1994). *A Phenomenology of Landscape.* Oxford: Berg.

— (1996). *An Ethnography of the Neolithic.* Cambridge: Cambridge University Press.

— (1999). *Metaphor and Material Culture.* Oxford: Blackwell.

— (2004). *The Materiality of Stone: Explorations in Landscape Phenomenology 1.* Oxford: Berg.

— (2006). 'Objectification'. In C. Tilley, W. Keane, S. Kuchler, M. Rowlands, and P. Spyer (eds.), *Handbook of Material Culture*, pp. 60–73. London: Sage.

Tilley, C., W. Keane, S. Kuchler, M. Rowlands, and P. Spyer (eds.) (2006). *Handbook of Material Culture.* London: Sage.

Viste, S. (2003). Bildene Forteller. Sjamanistiske Element i Veideristningene fra Vingen og Ausevik? M.A. dissertation, University of Bergen.

Warnier, J-P. (2006). 'Inside and outside: Surfaces and containers'. In C. Tilley, W. Keane, S. Kuchler, M. Rowlands, and P. Spyer (eds.), *Handbook of Material Culture*, pp. 186–96. London: Sage.

Weiler, E. (1994). *Innovationsmiljöer i Bronsålderns samhälle och idévärld. Kring ny teknologi och begravningsritual i Västergötland.* Studia Archaeologica Universitatis Umensis 5. Umeå.

Wigren, S. (1987). *Sörmländsk bronsåldersbygd. En studie av tidiga centrumbildningar daterade med termoluminiscens.* Theses and Papers in North European Archaeology 16. Stockholm: Institute of Archaeology, University of Stockholm .

Yates, T. (1993). 'Frameworks for an archaeology of the body'. In C. Tilley (ed.), *Interpretative Archaeology*, pp. 31–72. Oxford: Berg.

INDEX

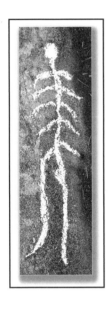

ABOUT THE AUTHOR

C hristopher Tilley is Professor of Material Culture in the Department of Anthropology, University College London. He has written and edited over twenty books on material culture and archaeology and is a founding editor of the *Journal of Material Culture*. He has conducted field research throughout much of Europe and in the South Pacific. He is currently co-director of the Stonehenge Riverside Project and director of the East Devon Pebblebeds Project. He is presently completing an ethnography of gardens and gardening in England and Sweden as well as conducting archaeological field research. Some recent books include *Metaphor and Material Culture* (1999), *The Materiality of Stone* (2004), *Handbook of Material Culture* (ed., 2006), and *Stone Worlds: Narrative and Reflexivity in Landscape Archaeology* (with B. Bender and S. Hamilton, 2007).